Broken Brains
or
Wounded Hearts

What Causes Mental Illness

OTHER BOOKS BY TY. C. COLBERT, Ph.D.

Why Do I Feel Guilty When I Have Done Nothing Wrong?

Depression and Mania: Friends or Foes?
(A non-drug approach to depression and mania)

For information about purchasing these books contact:

Kevco Publishing
2369 N. Grand Ave., Suite 265
Santa Ana, California 92705
(714) 569-0236

Broken Brains
or
Wounded Hearts

What Causes Mental Illness

Ty C. Colbert, Ph.D.

Kevco Publishing
Santa Ana, California

Grateful acknowledgment is made to the following for permission to reprint previously published material:

Alfred A. Knopf, Inc., for the use of excerpts from *An Unquiet Mind*, by Kay Jamison, 1995.

W. B. Saunders Company for use of excerpts from *Autobiography of a Schizophrenic Girl*, 1951.

Publisher's Cataloging in Publication Data

Colbert, Ty C.
  Broken Brains or Wounded Hearts/Ty C. Colbert

Includes bibliographical references and index

ISBN 0-9643635-4-2
Library of Congress Catalog No. 96-76762

1. Mental Illness 2. Psychology 3. Mental Health
I. Colbert, Ty   II. Title

Printed in the United States of America

DEDICATION

*I dedicate this book to my
ever faithful and encouraging mother
for her never-ending love.*

IMPORTANT INFORMATION

Stopping medication: This book emphases the destructive aspects of medications that are often used for emotional disorders. It is dangerous and can become life threatening to withdraw from these medications. Therefore, withdrawing from any psychiatric medication should be done under close medical and clinical supervision.

Seeking psychotherapy: This book is not to be used as the primary treatment resource for any emotional disorder. I strongly recommend that if anyone is suffering from any strong emotional discomfort or psychological disorder to seek professional help from a licensed psychotherapist. See Appendix A & B for further information.

Case studies: The case histories described in this book are actual cases, however some of the details have been changed to maintain confidentiality. In addition, the author takes full responsibility for the final editing of this material.

CONTENTS

ACKNOWLEDGMENTS

As with any book, this book could not be possible without the help and dedication of many individuals; in fact, so many of the following individuals were irreplaceable. Without their efforts, their dedication to truth, their honest sincerity in wanting to make our society a saner, less violating place, the resources necessary for this book would not have been available.

Leonard Roy Frank, now a close friend, lost his memory to shock treatment many years ago. To retrieve his memory and to try and understand what happened to him, he began to read about the history of psychiatry and consequently became an excellent historian in that area. He contributed many references to Chapter Two, as well as his spirit to this book.

Peter Breggin, M.D., and David Cohen, Ph.D., have made a valuable effort in their own professional lives to bring the truth about the evils of psychiatric medication to light and were willing to edit several chapters of this book. Virginia Carson, Ph.D., and Sherrol McDonough, Ph.D., were gracious enough to edit the chapter on the search for defective genes. Jack A. Braughan Jr., M.D., a retired neurologist who is spending much of his free time working to expose the inaccuracies of biopsychiatry, reviewed the chapter on brain imaging. Sheila Cooper and Rosa Harnetiaux spent considerable time helping to bring greater clarity to several of the chapters. Jeanne Hoffa, with her fighting spirit, helped light the fire inside me when needed.

There were many others that I called upon to review parts of this book and who gave me the necessary feedback to complete this book. These individuals included Don W. Brian, D. Ed., Mary Kay Pelias, Ph.D., Martin W. Hoffman, Ph.D., Kevin McCready, Ph.D., Thomas Greening, Ph.D., Lucy Joe Palladino, Ph.D., David Jacob, Ph.D., Father Joe Scerbo, and David E. Roy, Ph.D. Mickey Winberg did not help on this manuscript, but did add quite a bit to an earlier unpublished manuscript that eventually grew into this book.

A special appreciation goes out to Don Schrader, Ph.D., my dissertation chairperson, who supported me as I first struggled with the concepts in this book.

Such a book is also not possible without gifted and dedicated editors. Wendy Danbury took on the major task of doing all the original editing plus being responsible for the final editing. Joy Parker, with her many years of experience, helped tremendously to polish the document. Darlene Hoffa, a true friend, also helped edit some of the chapters. A special thanks to Nita Busby who was always immediately available to proofread the text helping to find those final little mistakes.

In its final stages, Viki Mason of Victoria Graphics performed with great precision in completing the typesetting as well as the diagrams. Ron Geisman was responsible for the outstanding cover and Bruce Bracken of Publishers Press helped to bring the book to completion on time as promised.

Of course this book would not be possible without the invaluable support of my wife Kathy, my close friends, and my family. A special thanks goes to my brother Gary and my mother for helping to finance this project.

A final thanks must go to all those who have suffered emotionally over the years and who, by their sharing and their courage, have become the real backbone and truth to the model presented in this book.

INTRODUCTION

As a part of the standard curriculum in any graduate school of psychology, students are asked to study the different theoretical positions concerning the origin of mental illness, or psychopathology. During my training, for example, we first studied Freud, then neo-Freudism, followed by behaviorism and other disciplines. The goal of this study was for us to eventually develop our own position on what causes mental illness and to find a label for our own brand of therapy. Even though I had been trained as a humanistic-existentialist, at the time I was less interested in choosing a particular philosophy than in simply finishing my training. I was anxious to begin my practice and start helping people; never did I stop to think that my theoretical view might ultimately determine the *destiny* of people's lives.

Once I was in private practice, and individuals with critical, difficult-to-understand cases began coming into my office, I soon found out why a proper understanding of the origin of emotional disorders is not just an intellectual-philosophical exercise but a process upon which people's very lives hang. Liz is one of the individuals who taught me this.

Refereed to me by a local minister, Liz was diagnosed as a paranoid schizophrenic by several psychiatrists. From the very beginning, it was clear to me that she was, indeed, an extremely paranoid person. For close to ten years she had periodically accused her husband, as well as her two grown children, of plotting against her and wanting to get rid of her. At the height of her paranoia, she would call the police and file divorce papers against her husband, as well as restraining orders against her children.

When I consulted with her former psychiatrist, he told me flat out that Liz had a biochemical problem, and that medical science had not progressed far enough to help her. He had tried giving her every type of medication possible with no success, and he did not want to see her again.

In spite of his pessimistic prognosis, I was not willing to give up on Liz. When I sat and listened to her paranoid conversations, I could see behind her strange behavior a person in deep pain. As I asked myself what this pain was about, I began to wonder if it might not simply be a case of "not feeling loved or worthy by her family." Could it be that Liz, for whatever reason, felt so unloved by everyone that she unconsciously feared that her husband or children would inevitably leave her? If this were the case, then it was possible that her subconscious mind was trying to find reasons to leave them first to spare herself the awful pain of abandonment.

As Liz's therapy continued, I discovered that my hunch was right. When she began making accusations, out of her helplessness, her family would start to avoid her. In her husband's case, he would spend more time away from her in his garage. For Liz, this distancing behavior from her family only confirmed that they were trying to get rid of her.

When I explained my thesis to her husband, who actually cared for her very much, I was able to give him some communication tools to help him stay better connected to Liz on an emotional level. I also encouraged Liz to speak openly to her family about her needs, and supported her in her efforts to communicate with them.

To my great surprise, all of her symptoms disappeared in a few sessions and did not return during the six years that I followed the case. Even though her cure seemed to be a miracle, because I did not get the chance to truly understand the origin of her behavior, I could not be sure that her paranoia would not someday resurface.

Nonetheless, Liz represented the first case where I witnessed firsthand how important a professional's perspective about the origin of his or her patient's problem is, and how this perspective can have a crucial and lasting effect on the patient's life. For over ten years, every psychiatrist whom Liz had gone to for help believed that her illness was caused by some kind of biological problem. What my time with Liz taught me was that even the most bizarre behavior, if understood properly, can be seen on the same continuum as anyone's behavior. When any one of us begins to mistrust someone, our unconscious minds have a tendency to defend us emotionally by building a case against that person, much of which is usually false. The difference between behaviors being perceived as "emotionally unstable" and "emotionally healthy" is often only a matter of degree.

When I looked at Liz, I saw, not someone who had a disease, but someone whose paranoia had been created by past hurt and broken trust, and the fear of being left alone. In essence, I saw her mind not as *dysfunctional*, but as functioning quite effectively as an attempt to protect her inner woundedness.

After my therapeutic breakthrough with Liz, and the understanding it gave me about the real causes of emotional illness, I started to experience success treating other "difficult" cases. Ironically at the same time, I began to notice that psychiatry was moving more toward a disease or biological-defect model, and that psychiatrists were consequently depending more and more upon medication as a possible "cure." At first, in spite of the success I was having treating the *emotional* problems of those often told that they suffered from a *biological* defect, I couldn't help wondering if perhaps I was wrong. Was a physiological defect involved in these cases? If so, was medication really the answer?

In spite of my initial doubts, in *every* case of so-called "mental illness" that I have ever become involved with, regardless of the symptoms, I found that if I looked hard enough into the patient's emotional state, and built sufficient trust with him or her, that behind the bizarre behavior existed an emotionally hurting person. Out of these experiences I began to develop what I call an "emotional pain model." This is the model you will find discussed in great detail in this book, and it is my hope that it will give readers a clearer understanding of what is behind the often strange behavior we see in those who are emotionally wounded.

As biopsychiatists kept increasing the number of so-called "mental disorders" on their list, and increasing the emphasis on medication, I began to realize the need for a clear understanding of what causes mental illness. On one hand, the field of biopsychiatry stresses that almost every emotional disorder, be it schizophrenia, depression, mania, compulsive behavior, anxiety, or hyperactivity, has its roots in some type of biological defect. On the other, I soon realized that I was not the only therapist to have success by directly addressing the inner woundedness, the inner innocence and pain of the person. As I began to read reports stating that as many as 81 percent of all women in mental institutions had been sexually or emotionally abused, and that the great majority of people in prison had also been abused as children, I began to wonder why medical science could still claim that these individuals' problems were caused by a biologically defective *mind*.

To develop an emotional pain model that could explain the origin of mental illness in clear and easy-to-understand terms, I first needed to understand the claims of the medical model. At first, the scientific literature I read that supported the biological-defect or chemical-imbalance model seemed quite convincing and difficult to find fault with. As I looked deeper into the actual research, however, listening to others who had challenged these studies, I began to see that the foundations that the claims of biopsychiatry stood upon were very weak indeed, and needed to be seriously challenged.

While it is true that some people appear to be helped by medication—and perhaps even by shock treatment and surgical lobotomy—this doesn't mean that these treatments, in any significant way, represent a cure. When I was younger, I could find almost instant relief from my anxiety about social situations through the use of alcohol. In spite of the chemical that I medicated myself with to make me able to handle these situations, my anxiety was not the result of a biochemical problem, nor did drinking to excess cure me, even though, for a short time, it would make my symptoms disappear. Ultimately, I knew that my anxiety was due to my feelings of inadequacy about myself and that those feelings were the issues that I needed to address.

As I continued my own search for answers to emotional illness, I saw more and more individuals becoming permanently dependent upon strong psychiatric medications and more children being introduced to these types of drugs at an earlier age. Witnessing the pain of these individuals, and the fact that this pain was being numbed, not addressed, I became firmly convinced that medication was not the answer to our culture's pain and stress. I began to realize that we, as individuals and as a society, could not progress without a firm understanding of what causes mental illness.

This book represents a fifteen-year journey in search of that truth, spanning the early days when I first began treating clients such as Liz, up to the present. It represents a desire to take the mystery out of mental illness and to provide a clear path for the future.

I do not claim that this book answers all of the questions concerning the origin of mental illness, but I hope it will, at the very least, start us on the right road. If by the end of this book, you have a much clearer view of what causes mental illness, and how to properly treat it, then I will have fulfilled my goal.

PART ONE

THE MEDICAL MODEL

CHAPTER ONE

Broken Brains or Wounded Hearts — What Causes Mental Illness?

Jack, at age eighteen, entered college and started showing signs of anxiety and depression. Encouraged to join a support group, he began expressing strong feelings of anger. At this point he was referred to the university health center and eventually was hospitalized.

After fifteen years, he finally left the hospital and board-and-care system to live on his own. For twenty years now, he has lived in an apartment by himself, staying as isolated as he can from the public. Diagnosed as a paranoid schizophrenic, Jack takes several different kinds of medication each day and faithfully waits for a cure to be found for his condition.

What happened to Jack has happened to hundreds of thousands of other individuals. Some are functioning at a higher capacity than Jack, others need even more assistance. Nevertheless, they are all destined to live the rest of their lives with their emotions and behavior highly controlled or monitored by the use of psychiatric medication.

Each year millions of adults begin to show symptoms of anxiety, depression—even schizophrenia—and fear that they too may end up in the same condition as Jack. Ken, a young man in his early twenties, entered therapy because he felt depressed and hopeless. He shared with me that he had felt a need to die since the age of twelve, and asked if his depression and desire to die could be the result of a chemical imbalance or genetic defect. He had heard about

1

the chemical imbalance/genetic defect model on TV and feared that something in his mind was defective and couldn't be fixed.

Betty, a client who is facing a possible divorce and the threat of being alone, has begun to hear voices that are not real and see objects move when they have not. She is scared and also wonders about the origin of the voices.

Nowadays, children as young as three are being given antidepressants and told that they may have a chemical imbalance. Their parents are understandably confused as to the source of their children's symptoms.

What has brought these individuals to this point; and what will happen to them? Is it possible that Ken, Betty, these children, and so many others are suffering from some defect in their biological system? Is the only solution to their emotional problems psychiatric medication?

THE GREAT MYSTERY

Most psychiatrists, psychologists and therapists today would answer yes to these questions. For them, it is pretty much an accepted fact that disorders such as depression, mania, schizophrenia, severe anxiety, addictions, and compulsions are due to defects in the biological system. Experts claim these defects may be due to genetic factors, a chemical imbalance, a virus, or any other of a number of possibilities.

Yet the truth is that researchers have never discovered a single defective gene or accurately identified any chemical imbalance that has caused an emotional disorder; nor have they ever proven that brain abnormalities are responsible for *even one* emotional disorder. In fact, the National Institute of Mental Health (NIMH), the United States agency in charge of funding research for the study of mental illnesses, openly admits that the causes of schizophrenia, depression, mania, anxiety, and hyperactivity are unknown. Furthermore, because researchers have not pinpointed anything truly defective within the brains of those who suffer from emotional disorders, a

2

growing number of individuals within the professional community openly oppose the position that brain disease is the root cause of these problems.

Ken Barney, a psychiatrist writing in *The Journal of Mind and Behavior*, states, "The idea that 'schizophrenia' is a hidden disease entity, with a soon-to-be discovered biogenetic 'cause' has been thoroughly debunked."[1] He follows his statement with no less than seventeen references supporting his point. Psychiatrist and author Peter Breggin says, "As yet there is no biology of depression."[2] David Cohen, a professor specializing in the study of schizophrenia and psychiatric drugs, states, "In France, Canada, and the United States, there have been unusually frank admissions by prominent bio-psychiatrists concerning major failures and the need for re-evaluations of the biomedical approach in psychiatry."[3]

Even psychiatrists who are prominent in their field are admitting to doubts. Susan Kemker, M.D., of the North Central Bronx Hospital in New York writes:

> The fact that I believed this dogma (biology is the science of psychiatry) made Pam's (1990) critique of biological psychiatry especially unsettling. When I read his work, I felt that my entire education as a psychiatrist was subject to question. Some of the studies being scrutinized were known to me as major contributions to the field. I was shocked to find not a single "landmark" study emerging as methodologically sound.[4]

Colin Ross, Clinical Associate Professor of Psychiatry at Southwest Medical Center in Dallas, Texas also writes:

> When I entered my psychiatric residency, I believed that research had demonstrated the genetic foundation of schizophrenia and had shown that schizophrenia is primarily a biomedical brain disease. This view was almost universally accepted at my medical school, and I never heard serious criticism of it while in training. It was by a gradual process that I began to become more and more aware of the cognitive errors pervading clinical psychiatry—unwittingly demonstrated to me by my residency supervisors.[5]

3

This awareness led Ross to also state that "Biological psychiatry has not made a single discovery of clinical relevance in the past ten years, despite hundreds of millions of dollars of research funding."[6]

WHAT ARE THESE PROFESSIONALS SAYING?

Many professionals in the area of psychiatry have openly challenged the claim that mental illness is caused by some biological defect. Even the NIMH, which believes that specific defects will some day be found, admits that currently we do not know the cause of a single disorder.

If a physiological cause for mental illness has not been found, and if many professionals believe that no actual biological defect exists, it could be that we are looking at these disorders incorrectly. In fact, I believe that even the most so called severe mental illnesses—schizophrenia, depression, and mania—are not biologically based, but a reflection of a person's emotional woundedness. These symptoms are defenses and strategies developed by a person to cope with emotional pain.

As we examine an *emotional pain* model as an alternative to the *medical/disease* model, you will see that, regardless of the person's behavior, the emotional pain model explains all of the symptoms of mental illness far better than the model that hypothesizes a physical cause for these disorders. From the time I began practicing as a psychotherapist fifteen years ago, some of my earliest clients convinced me that, behind even the most bizarre of behavior, there was not a defective brain but a hurting person. The next section will introduce you to one of these individuals.

BOB

Bob was referred to me through his parents, who attended a lecture I gave at their church. He was twenty-nine at the time and had been in and out of psychiatric hospitals since he was sixteen.

4

During his last hospital visit, he had been stabilized on medication and then sent back to his parents. After he had been home for a couple of months, when his symptoms began to increase in severity again, his parents contacted me.

Bob had been diagnosed as a catatonic schizophrenic. At times he entered a frozen state during which he sat nearly motionless for hours. At other times, he would stop in the middle of a room and stand motionless for a while. When he reached this degree of catatonia at home, he would be re-hospitalized. There, his doctors would prescribe different medications—along with electroconvulsive treatment (ECT), commonly known as shock therapy or shock treatment. When he emerged from his catatonic state enough to take care of himself (eat, bathe, etc.), he was again sent home. When his condition worsened, he was returned once more to the hospital.

At the start of our first session, Bob entered my room slowly and cautiously, sat on the couch, and said very little. At the end of the session, he got up, shuffled to the door, hesitated for a few moments, then slowly opened the door and left.

About a third of the way into our second meeting, Bob suddenly stood up. Without speaking, he walked over to the wall, positioned himself two inches from it, and stood there for the rest of the session.

I stayed in my chair and tried to carry on a conversation with him. He remained silent and continued to stare at the wall in a motionless state. When the session ended, it took me about thirty minutes to get him away from the wall and out the door to his parents. The third session continued much like the second.

During the fourth meeting, when Bob repeated this behavior, I thought, "Oh, what the heck," and joined him standing against the wall. For the next several weeks, we spent each entire session shoulder-to-shoulder, looking at the wall, and at times talking to one another.

During this time, Bob began to open up, giving me some clues to the mystery of his catatonic behavior. Bob had a couple of physical abnormalities that had led to some rejection from his father; and

5

these defects had also caused an almost continuous state of rejection and abuse by his peers. Even though his father's rejection was mild, and often took the form of jokes, the rejection Bob experienced from his peers was much crueler and more keenly felt. As a result of this lifelong abuse and shame, Bob had very little inner strength to fend off additional rejection.

Bob's explanation of his behavior was very enlightening. According to him, he sat on the couch during our first meeting and asked himself, "Did I open the door right? Did I say 'hi' to Dr. Colbert the right way? Did I sit where I was supposed to? Will he be angry at me if I didn't?"

He became so obsessed with these questions because of his inner need to be okay that he felt completely overloaded. He was unable to interact with me any further. At this point, he felt compelled to stand up against the wall where, by staring at it, he could block out any further input. This course of action gave him the time and the space to concentrate on the first few minutes of our interaction. Replaying our initial encounters over and over in his mind, he would first try to figure out if he had closed the door correctly. He had to get that figured out before he could go to point two in our encounter—whether or not he had said "hi" to me correctly.

As Bob shared this process, I began to see a whole different side of him. From the professional distance of my chair, Bob looked and acted "mentally ill;" sitting motionless or standing up against the wall, he appeared crazy. I could easily have concluded that his mind was "malfunctioning" because of some physical defect. Once he let me into his world, however, I realized that his mind was not sick; it was actually working *overtime* in an attempt to deal with the pain of my potential rejection.

The most important principle I learned while standing up against the wall with Bob was that his mind was not malfunctioning; indeed, it was working *no differently* than mine or any other person's. What made the difference was what Bob's mind was preoccupied with and the level to which it was focused.

As Bob continued to share the story of his life with me, I remembered times when I had acted much the same. Fearing that I had earned someone's disapproval, I recalled situations where I had also mentally rehashed events and conversations to see if I had made any mistakes. I was certainly more in control of my behavior and my mind than Bob was, but I saw that the differences between us were not based on a defect or a chemical imbalance, which is what doctors had told Bob and his parents. The contrast in our behavior was due only to the degree of our pain or inner woundedness, and our ability to handle emotional pain.

After a few more sessions, when Bob began to feel safer with me, he left the security of the wall and sat on the couch. As he began to allow himself to make better eye contact with me, feeling even safer, he gradually became more aware of the feelings behind his "mentally ill" behavior. He started to realize that he had felt so much hurt and loneliness from the day-to-day rejections of others, that he often went into his catatonic behavior to escape all chance of experiencing more pain. In fact, by standing up against the wall in his parent's house, by repeatedly needing to see if he locked the front door, he gave himself permission to avoid going outside as much as possible. Also as his mind was totally fixated on one particular thought or behavior, he was keeping his mind occupied and off the awareness of the deep pain inside of him. Again, his mind was not defective. His behavior was serving a very specific purpose.

A few months later, we started doing "buddy" activities, such as bowling and going to a show together. Since Bob's father had rarely done any of these things with him, and since Bob had never had a true friend, his newfound friendship with me at times had a greater therapeutic influence upon him than any of the professional techniques I had been taught. Just as important as the techniques, he needed to feel worthwhile in someone's life.

Unfortunately, his parents moved away before I was able to complete my work with Bob. Consequently, he did regress a bit, but not back to his extreme catatonic state. Luckily, both Bob and his parents now understood the reason and purpose behind his behavior.

7

This knowledge allowed Bob to play a more significant role in determining what he needed to continue his healing. His father also became more accepting of his son.

Broken Brains Or Wounded Hearts?

Even though researchers, psychiatrists, and psychotherapists have come up with thousands of different theories to explain the different emotional disorders, there have always been two dominant models. The first explanation, formally called the medical or disease model, claims that certain types of biological defects are responsible for the symptoms of mental illness. Just as insulin is given to a diabetic to correct his or her condition, so a drug is given to someone who has been diagnosed as depressed or schizophrenic in hopes of correcting some biological abnormality. The fundamental belief behind the medical model is that mental disorders are caused by physiological changes in the system and therefore require physical or biological remedies. The emotional pain model, on the other hand, simply states that, when confronted with an overload of emotional pain, the mind *purposely* creates the defenses necessary to deal with that pain. Thus, the disorders of schizophrenia, depression, and other so-called mental illnesses are seen as the person's own strategy for adapting to this pain.

Bob's case clearly illustrates the fallacy behind the medical model and the corresponding validity of the emotional pain model. Even though Bob's symptoms had an unproductive and debilitating side to them, they were his best strategy for taking care of himself. When the psychiatrists treating Bob interpreted these symptoms as indicators of a disease and attempted to medicate or shock them into submission, the best they could hope for was the "stabilization" of the client (suppression of the symptoms).

By taking the time to understand and explore the useful, purposeful side to his symptoms, Bob and I began to understand the nature of his pain. From this basis came a true healing, a growing

8

sense of inner congruency, and a transfer of empowerment back into Bob's life.

THREE-PHASE MODEL

Unfortunately, people like Bob, Jack, Ken, and Betty are not alone. Bob and Jack, especially, represent a tragedy in the mental health field that can and should be stopped.

As a result of my time with Bob, I have counseled and questioned several other individuals whose catatonic behavior was misinterpreted by the mental health profession. When I gave one client of mine Bob's story to read, she immediately identified with his emotional vulnerability and pain: "I felt so fragile that if I moved I might shatter and turn into powder on the floor." Another client who had been sexually abused by several members of her family as a child, *forced* herself into a catatonic state as a way of keeping her intense shame away from the direct awareness of her self or identity. In spite of the obvious emotional components to their problems, both of these women were told that they were mentally ill and would need to be on medication for the rest of their lives. Today neither is on medication and they are both living very responsible and productive lives.

The truth is that we all have felt so vulnerable at times that we felt our very essence might shatter and turn to powder. When subjected to the intense pain of a divorce, the loss of a loved one, or some violent act against us, there is a natural need to freeze our feelings. It is cases such as Bob's and Jack's that allow us to see the shortcomings of the medical model, begin to understand the emotional pain model, and understand how such cases can be handled in a different, more productive manner.

I do not mean to imply that solutions or a healing to such cases as the above come quickly and easily. But with an understanding of what causes emotional disorders and how they can be prevented, we can all begin to cooperate toward the goal of helping people achieve *real* recovery, not just a temporary alleviation of their more serious symptoms.

To help the reader properly understand what causes emotional disorders and how we can begin to minimize or prevent them, I will present and develop a three-phase emotional pain model. To solve the problem of emotional disorders, it is necessary to understand that we all go through the three phases in the development of emotional problems or disorders, regardless of the level of emotional abuse or pain in our lives. These three phases are illustrated in Figure 1.1.

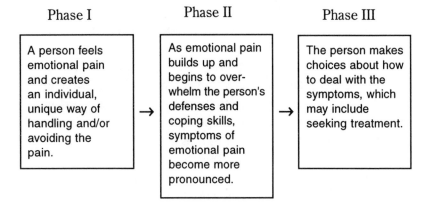

Phase I	Phase II	Phase III

| A person feels emotional pain and creates an individual, unique way of handling and/or avoiding the pain. | → | As emotional pain builds up and begins to over-whelm the person's defenses and coping skills, symptoms of emotional pain become more pronounced. | → | The person makes choices about how to deal with the symptoms, which may include seeking treatment. |

Figure 1.1: The Three-Phase Model

When we remove the mystery from all forms of emotional disorders and understand their true underlying causes, we move away from the medical model and toward the three phases described above. This is exactly what we did in the case of Bob. The emotional pain model begins from the position that every person is subjected to emotional pain as a child and, as a result, begins to create his or her own unique way of dealing with that pain. (Phase I)

These strategies often work quite well until we reach Phase II. At that point, our defenses are suddenly pushed to the limit and major problems begin to surface. These more pronounced symptoms or behaviors can include depression, anxiety, addictions, compulsions, a need to work excessively, extreme anger, religious fanaticism, extreme dependency upon others, the thirst for power or evil, and the classical symptoms of schizophrenia, which are severe indifference, withdrawal, delusions, and hallucinations.

Phase III represents the type and degree of help that is sought once the symptoms in Phase II begin to surface. In considering Phase III choices, we will compare the merits of the medical model with the emotional pain model. Denying the need for help or continuing to deny the behaviors that have surfaced in Phase II is also a type of Phase III choice.

Under the medical model for both the person or a caregiver, when Phase II behaviors begin to surface, the *biopsychiatrist* treating the case assumes there is a biological defect, and the person is then medicated. Sometimes this approach works in the short run, as the medication suppresses the behavior in the person. However, in many cases such as Bob's or Jack's, the person enters into a life-long state of disability.

From the perspective of the emotional pain model, the problem of emotional disorders is solved by developing the appropriate knowledge or program for all three phases. For example, if Bob and Jack had been taught as children how to understand their own individual emotional reactions to their pain (Phase I), and if they could have recognized their behavior as a response to that pain (Phase II), then the appropriate help (Phase III) would have been easy to implement. Their parents' understanding the true nature of the disorder enables them to be much more supportive and instrumental in the healing process. The three phases of the emotional pain model represent an important key to healing and preventing emotional disorders.

WHO IS TO BLAME?

While all abusive parents can and should be held responsible for the emotional distress in their children's lives, the emotional pain model does not automatically place the blame on the parents. For

11

example, Ken came from a good, caring home and was raised by dedicated parents. In spite of this, his parents could not have prevented the distressing incidents he experienced during his childhood. Since he tried to suppress these feelings from his own awareness, they were also helpless to discover his pain or to do anything to help him. Unfortunately, these experiences caused Ken to feel guilty and bad about himself. This "dark spot," as he called it, began to develop over time until he started feeling as if he wanted to die. His parents did not become aware of these feelings until, in his twenties, Ken became severely depressed.

Betty's home and parents were also warm and caring. From early childhood, Betty was able to excel in everything she tried, becoming the "ideal" daughter. As her achievements mounted, however, she began to develop a subconscious fear of failing, wondering if she would be acceptable if she were less than perfect. Since she was able to maintain a near perfect record, her parents never had the opportunity to affirm her at times when she fell below that mark.

When her marriage began to fall apart, Betty had little inner strength or experience to handle failure. Furthermore, even though her parents tried to support her, they could not hide their own disappointment in the failure of her marriage. As a result, Betty's mind began to distort reality and she began to display several symptoms of her inner turmoil.

Ultimately, the solution to Ken's and Betty's problems and their eventual healing came, not through blaming their parents or themselves, but through the understanding that their behaviors were really manifestations of their emotional pain—strategies they were using to protect themselves from further hurt. With this understanding, Ken and Betty were given the best chance to become responsible for their own emotional healing.

Although Ken's and Betty's parents are clearly not to blame for their children's problems, taking the blame off the parents by diagnosing Ken and Betty's behaviors as biological defects does not help either. This position just confuses the overall picture, taking more power away from the individual's ability to take care of him- or herself. Blaming such conditions on biological factors has resulted in disabling millions for life.

When Ken learned how he was strategically using his mind and emotions to intentionally deal with his pain (Phase I), he began to quickly make sense out of his behavior (Phase II). Once he and I understood his emotional survival strategy, we were then able to find the treatment that best fit him (Phase III). Although it took Ken about four months to get out of his depression, by then he understood how he had gotten into it in the first place. What's more, he now knew how to help himself avoid or cope with depression in the future. Many people who use medication to suppress their symptoms must rely on drugs for the rest of their lives. By understanding the *emotional* causes of his problem, Ken is in a good position to be in charge of his own destiny without ever using drugs again.

Because Betty was in the midst of a troubled marriage and had always used her drive for perfection to stay away from pain, she had a much rougher time. She had to learn to change her lifelong habits. Each time a Phase II symptom surfaced for Betty, we worked hard to understand the pain behind it. As time passed, however, she gradually was able to take charge of her emotional coping system in the midst of much external turmoil.

MOVING OUR SOCIETY FORWARD

The path to ultimately resolving the mystery behind emotional disorders, is to show that *we all* go through the same three phases when coping with our pain. The difference between us and a person who is severely emotionally troubled is only a matter of degree. We don't all end up being labeled as schizophrenic or clinically depressed, but we are all subjected to emotional pain during our lives and, as a result, we all develop certain behaviors.

When I chose to stand up against the wall to identify with Bob, I discovered the origin of his pain. I not only became available to help him, but I learned more about my own pain. Understanding and resolving the mystery of mental illness will not come about through the continued search for some mysterious biological defect, but through the understanding of one another's emotional pain.

As you progress through this book, these ideas will begin to make more and more sense to you, just as they have for Bob and my other clients. We can use the basic concepts of the emotional pain model to seek help when necessary, find the right kind of treatment for our loved ones, and begin to create proper solutions for our society in the future. Instead of blaming parents or searching for a hypothetical biological cause for emotional disorders, we can begin to find a set of common denominators that will move our society forward in an emotionally healthy way.

PSYCHIATRIC LABELING

When a person seeks help for emotional problems, the first thing that a psychiatric health professional does is try to come up with a diagnosis: a psychiatric label, based on the person's behavior and other symptoms. In Bob's case, his emotional pain, which had accumulated throughout his life, finally began to express itself in behaviors such as severe withdrawal, catatonic posturing, and the hearing of voices (hallucinations). We have seen how these "symptoms" were the strategies his mind used to try and deal with his emotional pain.

Bob's behaviors were categorized and given the label of catatonic schizophrenia. If we looked at Bob's records or spoke to his psychiatrist, his doctor might say, "Bob is a schizophrenic." Ken is another client who could have been labeled as a schizophrenic, or as someone suffering from a bi-polar disorder (mood swings of mania and depression).

These labels have become a very efficient way of categorizing individuals and giving substance to the medical model. If a person has been given the label of schizophrenia, it becomes easier to assume that he is "mentally ill," or at least that a disease of some sort is involved.

Although labeling might seem both helpful and harmless, it can become part of a very destructive process that often perpetuates a person's emotional condition. For example, as Bob, his doctors, and his parents began to focus on the label and what drugs worked for that particular label, no one searched for the truth behind his behavior.

The label of schizophrenia puts Bob at the mercy of his doctor and the rest of society, who now feel free to perceive him according to their label. Now that he has been "properly" diagnosed, it is easier to assume that he is someone who might be dangerous, an idiot, weird, or suffering from a brain defect.

In my clinical practice I try to stay away from the use of labels as much as possible. Unfortunately, we all have become accustomed to the use of labels in our society. At times, I will use such labels for the ease of communication. I apologize to those readers who have been hurt and crippled by the use of them. I also hope that, by the end of this book, you will have come to a better understanding of the inherent destructiveness of the psychiatric labeling process.

CHAPTER TWO

AN HISTORICAL OVERVIEW

Most of the general public, as well as the psychiatric community, continues to believe that the primary cause of mental illness is a biological defect of some kind. Yet, as we have seen, many credible professionals claim that no evidence exists for such a position, and the psychiatric community itself openly admits that no real biological cause for these disorders has ever been proven. Furthermore, there are thousands of individuals who, like Bob, were told that they were mentally ill due to some physiological defect, but became free of their illness as they came to understand that this was not the case.

If it is true that no biomedical theory has been proven, how has the medical model achieved such wide acceptance today? There are several complex answers, but I believe the primary reason is that people generally have a tendency to believe that there is something wrong with the mind of individuals diagnosed as mentally ill. We all have a tendency to say things like, "Has he lost his mind?" or "What is making her act so strangely?" when we see someone whose behavior or emotions seem to be out of control. When we observe someone like Bob acting a little crazy or weird and we don't understand why, it is all too easy to assume that there must be something defective about his mind.

This same natural tendency to conclude that something must be wrong with a person's mind is easily carried over into the formal study of emotional disorders. The result, which has been repeated throughout the history of psychiatry, has been the creation of a false set of *cause-and-effect* conclusions. If the mind is first assumed to be defective, and if some physical or biological treatment happens to reduce the symptoms or behavior, then the *cause* of the illness is assumed to be related to the *treatment*.

We saw this cause-and-effect logic in action when Bob was given medications to "cure" the symptoms of his illness. Since certain drugs appeared to reduce his symptoms, his doctors assumed that his symptoms must have a biochemical basis to them.

Unfortunately, the history of psychiatry is riddled with examples of faulty cause-and-effect relationships.

THE BEGINNINGS OF BIOLOGICALLY-BASED PSYCHIATRY

In classical times (400 B.C.), physical and mental diseases were often thought to result from imbalances in the four fluids found in the body: phlegm, blood, black bile, and yellow bile. According to the ancient theory an excess of phlegm rendered the person phlegmatic—that is, indifferent and sluggish. An excess of blood gave rise to rapid shifts of mood. Too much black bile made the individual melancholic, and too much yellow bile made him choleric— irritable and aggressive. However primitive such theories may seem, they foreshadowed, and in many ways made possible, today's physiological and biochemical research.

Doctors of that early era operated under the assumption that they could correct these imbalances by removing the excess fluid. Since blood was the most accessible fluid, bloodletting tended to be the most common practice. Obviously, after a significant loss of blood, certain symptoms such as excitability and irritability subsided. In fact, heavy blood loss may have even occasionally caused a state of amnesia or even brain damage in some individuals. In spite of the quieting result of bloodletting, the cause-and-effect logic underlying this "cure" was false.

Nearly a thousand years later, Jean Baptiste van Helmont (1577-

18

1644), a celebrated Dutch physician, had a different idea. He attempted to treat the mentally ill by suffocating the mad ideas of the insane. His subjects were stripped, bound to a bench, deeply submerged in water and then left there until he judged that their "upper parts were drowned."[1]

Even though many of his patients died, Jean Baptiste van Helmont felt his method was "reasonable" because "fools or distracted persons, by being bereft of their understanding, are of no use to the Commonwealth."[2] Of course, if his patients did not die and stopped acting insane (probably because of their fear of being drowned), then his cure had worked.

In retrospect, we can see that such methods were justified by those who used them because they believed that something was *physically* wrong with their patients. The cruelty inherent in these methods, and the cultural disregard for anyone who was troubled or different, is painfully obvious. If certain individuals could not conform to the behavioral norms of the day, they could be experimented on because, after all, in their present condition they were of no use to society.

Even today, the emotionally troubled are often seen as a nuisance, rather than as people of worth. This false assessment is the most important reason we must come to a true understanding of what causes these disorders.

Benjamin Rush (1745-1813), a signer of the Declaration of Independence and the designated father of American psychiatry, was another early theoretician with ideas about the causes and cures of mental illness. Rush writes the following about one of his favorite "scientific" methods, the tranquilizing chair, which is illustrated in Figure 2.1:

> I have contrived a chair and introduced it to our Hospital to assist in curing madness. It binds and confines every part of the body. By keeping the trunk erect, it lessens the impetus of blood toward the brain.... Its effects have been truly delightful to me. It acts as a sedative to the tongue and temper as well as to the blood vessels.

In twenty-four, twelve, six, and in some cases in four hours, the most refractory patients have been composed. I have called it a Tranquillizer.[3]

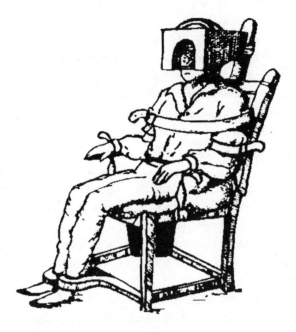

Figure 2.1: The "tranquilizing chair," used by Benjamin Rush as a means of treating mental disorders.

Rush believed that mental illness was due to the blood vessels in the brain becoming overloaded as the result of excitement. Besides using the "tranquilizer," he dropped patients suddenly into ice-cold baths and drained blood out of their bodies. When he tried to cure George Washington of a fever by draining blood out of his body, the process unfortunately resulted in the President's death. Hence the saying, "The father of American psychiatry killed the father of America."

As the history of psychiatry progressed, the same pattern was always present. Whatever medical treatment was used, if it

20

somehow appeared to reduce the patients' symptoms, then it was assumed to have something to do with the cause of the disorder.

One of the more outrageous medical approaches was used on women who wanted to divorce their (perhaps abusive) husbands. Dr. Isaac Baker Brown developed a popular procedure in which he surgically removed the clitoris of those women wishing to take advantage of England's new Divorce Act of 1857. According to Brown:

> After the operation, they humbly returned to their husbands and there was no recurrence of the *disease* after surgery.[4]

Brown concluded that wanting a divorce was a biologically based mental disease that was somehow correlated with having a defective clitoris. Once again, an assumed cause-and-effect relationship was used to justify the therapeutic method.

I don't want to leave you with the impression that all of these men were cruel and sadistic; most people who go into medicine and psychiatry are genuinely trying to help those who suffer. Doctors in the past often courageously took on the challenge of attempting to help the emotionally troubled, trying their hardest to synthesize the existing medical knowledge of the day into a compassionate, humanistic approach. Many of them were even quite progressive.

For example, even though Benjamin Rush advocated the use of drugs, bloodletting, and other physical methods of treatment for the so-called mentally ill, he also stressed the importance of gentleness and understanding. He was the first person to establish occupational therapy and to advocate regular employment for his patients. In addition, he strongly urged the hiring of better qualified asylum attendants—men and women who would be "a friend and companion" to the resident patients. Nevertheless, abuse, whether intentional or not, is a significant part of the history of psychiatry.

MODERN BIOLOGICAL PSYCHIATRY

Modern biological psychiatry had its beginnings in Munich in the early twentieth century, due mainly to the efforts of Emil Kraepelin (1856-1926). Kraepelin was a professor at several medical schools in Germany, and eventually became head of the Department of Psychiatry in Munich.

Kraepelin's main contribution to the medical field was to describe and identify specific types of major psychiatric disorders. Medicine's primary purpose is to define and diagnose specific illnesses, to properly treat them, and to make useful predictions. By categorizing the different symptoms of mental disorders, Kraepelin laid the foundations of biological psychiatry as we know it today. Because at that time, mental illness was viewed as a physical disease, individuals with different symptoms were considered to have different diseases. Consequently, in every country except perhaps the United States, Kraepelin is regarded as the founding father of modern psychiatry.

Even though Kraepelin is considered the father of *modern* psychiatry, some of the historical methods he studied and wrote about were certainly far from humane. Describing a nineteenth century technique, he writes:

> Tobacco smoke was administered in the form of an enema by a special machine in severe cases of imbecility and melancholia attonita.[5]

Kraepelin describes another technique that had formerly been used to calm patients:

> The patient was harnessed and tied in a standing position, and with arms outstretched for 8 to 10 hours. This was supposed to mitigate delirious outbursts, encourage fatigue and sleep, render the patient harmless and obedient, and awaken in him a feeling of respect for the doctor.[6]

22

Even though he may not have personally used the above methods, Kraepelin was fascinated with them and did quite a bit of experimentation on catatonic individuals, patients who exhibited the same kinds of symptoms as did Bob. To illustrate the bizarreness of their behavior or their seeming inability to respond to pain, Kraepelin would prick catatonic patients above the eyes with a needle or pierce their tongues all the way through. Quoting directly from Kraepelin:

> She does not generally react at all when spoken to or pricked with a needle, but resists violently if you try to take her hand or to pour water on her. She obeys no kind of orders.[7]

In 1933 Manfred Sakel introduced insulin coma treatment. Insulin was used to induce a comatose state lasting 15 to 60 minutes. His belief that *faulty brain cells* resulted in mental illness allowed him to correlate the use of insulin coma treatment and the subsiding of certain symptoms:

> With chronic schizophrenics, as with confirmed criminals, we can't hope for reform. Here the faulty pattern of functioning is irrevocably entrenched. Hence we must use more drastic measures to silence the dysfunctioning cells and so liberate the activity of the normal cells. This time we must *kill* the too vocal dysfunctioning cells. But can we do this without killing normal cells also? Can we select the cells we wish to destroy? I think we can.[8]

Of course, Sakel could not prove that he was killing only the diseased cells, but because he did see a change in patients' behavior, he was able to justify the use of his treatment.

Along with insulin-coma treatment came psychosurgery, or lobotomy, in 1935, and electroconvulsive (ECT, or shock) treatment in 1938. In the following quotes, notice the distorted line of reasoning arrived at by many leading psychiatrists of the day. Also notice that these statements were made in 1948, 1957 and 1962—relatively recent times:

We started by inducing two to four grand mal convulsions daily until the desired degree of regression was reached.... We considered a patient cured when he talked and acted like a child of four.... Sometimes the confusion passes rapidly and patients act as if they had awakened from dreaming; their minds seem like clean slates upon which we can write on. *(Cyril J. C. Kennedy and David Anchel, psychiatrists, 1948)*[9]

*   *   *   *   *

Genuine religious conversions are also seen after the new modified lobotomy operations. For the mind is freed from its old straitjacket and new religious beliefs and attitudes can now more easily take the place of the old. *(William Sargant, English psychiatrist, 1956)*[10]

*   *   *   *   *

Losses in intelligence, memory, and other measurable abilities are due to the psychosis, not to lobotomy. *(Walter Freeman, psychiatrist, 1962)*[11]

*   *   *   *   *

It is even more revealing, and tragic, to see how Ernest Hemingway, who suffered from extreme bouts of depression, wrote about the electric shock treatments he received, his "brilliant cure":

What these shock doctors don't know is about writers and such things as remorse and contrition and what they do to them. They should make all psychiatrists take a course in creative writing so they'd know about writers.... Well, what is the sense of ruining my head and erasing my memory, which is my capital, and putting me out of business? It was a brilliant cure but we lost the patient. It's a bum turn, Hotch, terrible.[12]

Hemingway was quite aware that the shock may have rid him of his symptoms of depression by erasing his memory, but it did not produce a permanent cure. What's worse, he found that his ability to write, the most important thing in his life, had been damaged. In

24

1961, a few days after being released following a second ECT series, he killed himself with a shotgun.

THE BIOLOGICAL REVOLUTION

It should be obvious by now that the history and development of modern psychiatry is firmly founded upon the belief that curing mental illness involves administering some kind of outward cure without looking too closely at the pain and woundedness *inside* the patient. In my own clinical work, from the perspective of the emotional pain model, I have seen time and time again that simply attempting to reduce symptoms can actually lead to more emotional woundedness—a concept that was not understood in the past.

In all fairness, I must point out that there have always been many caring psychiatrists who honestly believed that what they were doing for their patients was right. As the biopsychiatric revolution progressed, however, with its attendant modern-day technological and medical advances, it was accompanied by more patient abuse.

The belief that mental illness might be a neurological disorder perhaps had its real beginning in the discovery of the cause of Parkinson's disease. This neurological disorder was called the "shaking palsy" by James Parkinson, the man who first studied it in 1817. As the technology to study the brain was developed, researchers noted that victims of this disease suffered a loss of nerve cells in a small part of their brains called the *substantia negra.* Since the substantia negra helps govern body movement, a loss of cells in this area results in the out-of-control shaking movements of the victims.

As neurochemists became involved in the study of Parkinson's disease, they discovered that sufferers had a deficiency of a neurochemical called dopamine, which is usually found in the substantia negra. Based upon this research, neuropharmacologists suggested that a form of dopamine known as L-dopa might help to correct the chemical deficiency. The drug was successful, and patients experienced a marked decrease in their symptoms. Some individuals, once

25

nearly incapacitated, are now able to live nearly normal lives. Psychiatrists were encouraged by the *true* cause-and-effect relationship between administering L-dopa and the decrease in the symptoms of Parkinson's disease. From this research, however, many made the assumption that if certain drugs can reduce symptoms in a demonstrably damaged brain, other brain or mental disorders could also be helped by pharmaceutical treatments. With this in mind, they began to look for drugs that could help fight such disorders as depression, mania, and schizophrenia.

The first psychiatric drugs were discovered accidentally. In the 1940s surgeons were using antihistamines to attempt to prevent a serious drop in blood pressure during surgery. A French surgeon, Henri Laborit, noticed that the antihistamine phenothiazine did not affect blood pressure but did make patients sleepy and markedly less anxious.

Laborit's results triggered a search for new and better drugs that were created by slightly changing the drug's original chemical structure. When chlorine was added to the phenothiazine, the resulting drug, chlorpromazine, seemed to work well on animals, inducing an "artificial hibernation." Laborit wondered if this drug could be used in psychiatry.

The first psychiatric experiments with chlorpromazine (Thorazine) were done in Paris in 1952. This drug was given to patients with mania, depression, and schizophrenia. It soon became clear that chlorpromazine had powerful calming effects, especially in those diagnosed as schizophrenic. As these results were confirmed all over the world, this drug soon became the established treatment for people diagnosed as schizophrenic.

Because chlorpromazine had serious side effects, including tremors and shaking, and because only one company could obtain a patent on the drug, other companies became involved in the search for more effective drugs. In the process of trying to duplicate chlorpromazine, a Swiss pharmaceutical firm developed a new substance called imipramine. Roland Kuhn, a Swiss psychiatrist, found that this drug did not help much with delusions and hallucinations, but it did help relieve depressive conditions. Thus, a new class of drugs called antidepressants was created.

Also in the 1940s an Australian psychiatrist named John Cade who was testing lithium on guinea pigs noticed that they were sedated by it. By the 1960s lithium was in wide use for people suffering from mania.

As other drugs were developed, the current biological revolution in psychiatry was on its way.

THE CHEMICAL IMBALANCE MODEL

With the development of the microscope and other scientific advances that enabled researchers to look at very small processes, an understanding of how messages are sent from one neuron to the next began to unfold. A neuron is the information-processing and information-transmitting element of the nervous system. By the 1960s and early 1970s, laboratory techniques finally became sophisticated enough to map the locations of neurotransmitters within the brain. Neurotransmitters are the chemicals that flow from one neuron to the next, creating the potential for the next one to fire. Once a neuron fires, the electrical impulse is sent down to the end of the axon, resulting in neurochemicals being released into the synapse, which creates the potential for the message to be *transmitted* to the next neuron. Figure 2.2 illustrates how the basic neurotransmission system works.

In Figure 2.2, the nerve impulse in Neuron A reaches the presynaptic nerve end, where neurochemicals are released into the synapse. The neurochemicals then cross over and begin to attach themselves to the postsynaptic nerve surface, creating a potential for Neuron B to fire. When enough potential has developed, Neuron B fires, allowing the message to continue. The messages that are sent eventually affect all functions of the brain, including mental activity, respiration, motor impulses, speech, and so forth.

Excitatory neurotransmitters help the next neuron to fire, while inhibitory neurotransmitters reduce its firing potential. By study-

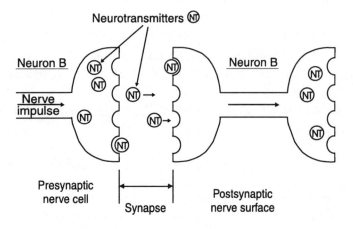

Figure 2.2: The basic neurotransmission system.

ing this interactive process, many neuroscientists have come to believe that mental illness is the result of a breakdown in the neurotransmitting system similar to the dopamine problem in Parkinson's disease.

It would certainly seem natural to assume that if emotional disorders were biologically-based diseases, then a chemical imbalance might be involved. In order to assume this cause-and-effect relationship, however, one must have actual hard proof that such a chemical imbalance exits.

OTHER MODELS AND FACTORS

To help substantiate the biological model, researchers started looking into other areas. One of these areas is genetic. For centuries people have noticed that mental illness runs in families, and, because of this, there is a tendency to believe that mental illness may be inherited—caused by genetic transmission. As we shall see, the verdict in this area of inquiry is far from decided upon.

In the last fifteen years, there has also been quite a bit of research done using brain-imaging equipment, technologies that give

ences in the structure or functional aspects of the brain of a so-called mentally ill person. The results of this research are also far from conclusive.

Thus, the modern biological model has as its primary foundation the following hypotheses:

* The *possibility* that drugs work by correcting a chemical im balance.
* The *possibility* that mental illness is inherited.
* The *possibility* that defective genes exist and can be found.
* The *possibility* that brain atrophy and other physiological markers show definite evidence of brain disease.

To date, however, not one proven biological cause for mental illness has been found. Even though biological psychiatry assumes a physiological cause for all major emotional disorders, there is still no proven cause-and-effect relationship between any specific disorder and any specific physical defect.

In addition, it has been well documented by researchers that medication and shock treatment can lead to permanent brain damage. In spite of these facts, more and more medication is being prescribed to our children at earlier and earlier ages, and there are still those who want to bring psychosurgery back for the more "hopeless" cases.[13]

In light of this evidence, we must honestly ask ourselves, "Is there any real theoretical difference between the present medical model and the models of the past?" Instead of draining someone's "bad blood" or using insulin shock therapy or psychosurgery, it would seem that biopsychiatry is just substituting drugs to achieve the same purpose. Are psychiatrists truly on track, correcting a physiological disease in the patient's brain, or are they simply giving drugs to a person based upon the same philosophy that has dominated the treatment of mental illness since classical times?

Summary

Many individuals such as Benjamin Rush were deeply concerned and brilliant physicians. They wanted to rid the so-called mentally ill of their pain. In their attempt to solve the mystery of these disorders, however, it became all too easy for them to experiment on patients. If some methods seemed to cure or reduce their clients' symptoms, it seemed only "logical" to draw what many modern mental health care professionals now feel are premature and inappropriate conclusions.

Of course, no one today believes in such methods as bloodletting, dropping patients into cold water, or witch hunting. Even though the present psychiatric methods of medication and shock treatment are accepted as more humane than the treatments of Rush's time, the justification for using these methods is still based on a medical model that as yet has no definitive proof. For this reason, as we attempt to move our knowledge of emotional disorders forward, we must first take an honest look at the evidence that is used to support the medical model. We will follow the development of the present-day medical model step by step as it evolved, starting with the claim that medication works because it corrects a chemical imbalance. Then we will examine the theory that mental illness is inherited and that someday defective genes will be found. Finally, we will look at one of the more recent theories, claiming that mental illness is caused by or associated with atrophy of the brain.

Much of our study will focus on the research for schizophrenia, but as we unravel the mystery behind this condition, it will lead us to a proper understanding of many other disorders.

CHAPTER THREE

THE TRUTH BEHIND PSYCHIATRIC MEDICATION

We have seen ample proof of how the mental health profession has historically operated under the following basic assumption: that if certain medical treatments change or alleviate the symptoms of emotionally troubled individuals, then a biological defect must be the culprit. Let's look now at how the effects of psychiatric medication are used to falsely justify the medical model.

Each month, Harvard Medical School publishes *The Harvard Mental Health Letter*. The major feature of the 1995 April and May newsletters was a two-part series on Attention Deficit Disorders (ADD), commonly known as hyperactivity. In the April issue the researchers who wrote these articles admitted that no one knows what causes ADD. They stated that "birth complications, head injuries, food additives, food allergies, sugar, vitamin deficiencies, radiation, lead and fluorescent lights"[1] are no longer acceptable as valid theories. They also imply that social circumstances and possibly traumatic stress may have an influence on the development of these disorders.

In spite of the list of physiological causes these researchers discount in their first article, due to lack of conclusive scientific data for any of them, they go on to propose in their second article that ADD *must* somehow be biologically based because Ritalin and other drugs often have a pronounced effect on the symptoms. "One reason for regarding ADD as a distinct disorder with a biological

origin is the immediate and striking relief from some of its symptoms provided by stimulant drugs."[2]

In the 1994 edition of *Review in Psychiatry*, the opening line in
a summary section reads "The first solid evidence that mental disorders are substantially determined by biological factors originated
from successful medication treatment trials."[3] Thus, modern researchers came to the same faulty conclusion as in the days *before*
drugs were used as treatment; if symptoms were reduced, a cause-
and-effect relationship was assumed.

Because so many emotionally troubled individuals in our culture have been told that they have a chemical imbalance and will
need to take drugs for the rest of their lives, it's important to discover the truth behind such claims. Alcohol, cigarettes, illegal street
drugs, and food can also reduce symptoms such as anxiety, depression, and hyperactivity. Many individuals who habitually use "energizing" drugs, such as cocaine, feel that they are more productive,
dynamic, and creative while "under the influence." In spite of this,
we would never tell a young person climbing the corporate ladder
to "medicate" herself with cocaine in order to secure a lifelong productive career. We would never tell an alcoholic, who uses alcohol
to numb his anxiety, that drinking helps him correct a chemical imbalance in his brain, and that he will need to drink for the rest of his
life.

To develop a clearer idea about the usefulness and misuse of
medication, we will look at the four different areas where psychiatric medications are primarily used. These areas are (1) psychotic
symptoms, for which neuroleptics such as Haldol, Prolixin,
Thorazine, Stelazine and Mellaril are prescribed; (2) depression, for
which Prozac and similar drugs are used; (3) mania, for which lithium
is prescribed; and (4) problems in hyperactivity or inattention, for
which doctors prescribe Ritalin.

We will start with the neuroleptics or antipsychotic medications
because they are widely used for many different disorders. Even
though the terms antipsychotic and neuroleptic are synonymous,
the term neuroleptic is often used. It means "seizes the nerves"

and was first used to indicate the toxic affect these drugs have on nerve cells.

NEUROLEPTICS OR ANTIPSYCHOTIC MEDICATION

Neuroleptics were first prescribed in the 1950s. Their principle use is in the treatment of schizophrenia, but because they are the most powerful of all psychiatric medications that control behavior, they are invariably employed to subdue people with non-schizophrenic behaviors when other classes of medications fail. For example, if lithium fails to calm someone who is manic, or Ritalin and other drugs fail to help the extremely hyperactive child, neuroleptics may be prescribed.

These drugs are known to produce a brain disease called tardive dyskinesia, especially after long-term high-dosage use. This disorder affects the basal ganglia and other centers of the brain, producing a wide variety of usually irreversible, uncontrollable movements, including spasms, twitches, and lip-smacking movements. Tardive dyskinesia should not be taken lightly. Approximately 50 to 60% of chronically institutionalized patients have the syndrome.[4] In 1980, an American Psychiatric Association official task force report on tardive dyskinesia found that, among elderly women treated with neuroleptics, 66% suffered from tardive dyskinesia.[5] Even though these rates vary from study to study, they all show that the prevalence of tardive dyskinesia is seriously high.

Neuroleptics are also used to treat retarded or delinquent children to help control their unwanted behaviors. In a study of retarded children who were treated with these drugs, Thomas Gualtieri and his colleagues found that 34% developed tardive dyskinesia.[6] How did such a potentially dangerous drug come to be so widely used?

As we saw in Chapter Two, whenever a new therapeutic method that seemed to alleviate psychiatric symptoms was discovered, those applying the therapy quickly assumed that the therapeutic approach was linked to the cause of the problem. In the 1950s the drug

33

chlorpromazine appeared to reduce certain symptoms of individuals diagnosed as schizophrenic. Adhering to the basic philosophy of the medical model, researchers began trying to discover how the drug reduced these symptoms. In the 1960s they found that chlorpromazine is a powerful receptor antagonist of the neurotransmitter dopamine.

As we have seen, when one neuron fires, an electrical impulse is sent down the neuron to its end, where neurochemicals are released into the synaptic gap between that neuron and the next one. These neurotransmitters move across the gap and become attached to the receptor sites of the next neuron, as shown in Figure 3.1. If enough neurotransmitters become attached, the next neuron fires, and the message progresses by electrical impulse.

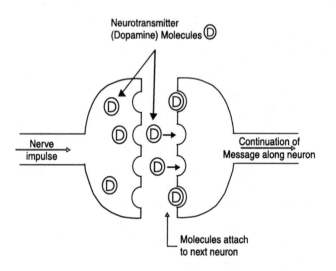

Figure 3.1: The neurochemical synapse

When chlorpromazine is added to the system, it attaches itself to the dopamine receptor sites, thus prohibiting the dopamine molecules from fitting into these "slots." An analogy would be someone trying to find a parking space in a lot where all the spaces are already filled. This process is illustrated in Figure 3.2.

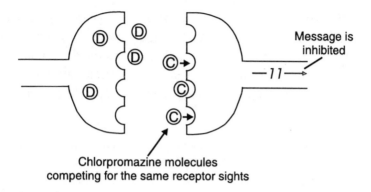

Chlorpromazine molecules
competing for the same receptor sights

Figure 3.2: Chlorpromazine acting as an antagonist to the dopamine
molecule

As the chlorpromazine molecules take over many of the dopamine sites, less dopamine becomes attached, thereby inhibiting the firing of the next neuron. When drugs that *inhibited* dopamine transfer seemed to reduce the symptoms of schizophrenia, researchers hypothesized that this disease might be caused by too much dopamine transmission within the system.

This theory certainly appeared to make sense, and researchers became quite excited about the possibility of discovering part of the mystery behind schizophrenia. Unfortunately, as scientists continued on this path, they began to run into problems with the model. For one thing, researchers discovered that most people with schizophrenia either have no evidence of increased dopamine activity, or actually have evidence of reduced activity.[7] Another study showed that the functioning of many individuals with schizophrenia actually improved when they were given drugs that *increased* dopamine activity.[8]

Instead of seriously questioning the dopamine model, however, the investigators kept modifying the model to fit each new discovery. As further research contradicted the existing information, the present theory was not discounted but simply modified, thus maintaining what seemed like a viable theory.

It is not important to go into the actual research or discuss how the theories have been changed along the way because the theories continue to change as new contradictory evidence is found. In fact, psychiatrist and researcher Colin Ross questions whether the dopamine hypothesis should even have been called a working theory. He writes that although the

> ...dopamine theory for schizophrenia is a "point of pride in biological psychiatry," it should not be called a theory because it was arrived at in reverse order. The theory concludes that dopamine is responsible for schizophrenia because chlorpromazine reduces the symptoms.[9]

He continues by stating that the "dopamine theory of schizophrenia is a political strategy" with the goal of obtaining additional research grants.

The dopamine theory has become accepted and popular not because of any unassailable scientific proof, but because the psychiatric community is deeply committed to the chemical imbalance model. There is a more valid explanation as to why neuroleptics often appear to reduce symptoms.

NEUROLEPTICS—CHEMICAL LOBOTOMIZERS

Although the vast majority of psychiatrists adhere to the "broken brain" hypothesis for people diagnosed with schizophrenia, many psychiatrists and biochemical researchers firmly believe that neuroleptics work by causing a *chemical lobotomy effect*, similar to a surgical lobotomy. What they are really saying is that neuroleptics work not by balancing out the dopamine transmission, but by blocking it, producing a chemically lobotomizing effect in the brain. According to psychiatrist Peter Breggin, "The neuroleptic drugs are chemical lobotomizing agents with no specific therapeutic effect on any symptoms or problems. Their main impact is to blunt and subdue the individual."[10] To better

36

understand the "lobotomy effect" of neuroleptics, let's first take a look at surgical lobotomy.

In the 1930s the Portuguese psychiatrist and neurologist Egas Moniz developed the technique of psychosurgery. He speculated that cutting prefrontal fiber tracts in the human brain might be useful in relieving the agitation of patients diagnosed with schizophrenia. Moniz later received the Nobel Prize for his work. Before the 1950s and the advent of antipsychotic medication, surgical lobotomy was used excessively, often primarily to control patients for the benefit of the hospital staff.

The frontal lobes that are severed from one another contain the seat of higher human functions, those that allow us to be human in the fullest degree. These functions include love, concern for others, empathy, self-insight, creativity, abstract reasoning, future planning, willpower, determination, and concentration.

How does surgical lobotomy affect the patient? Lobotomist P. Mac Donald Tow writes in his book *Personality Changes Following Frontal Leukotomy*: "Possibly the truest and most accurate way of describing the net effect on the total personality is to say that he is more simple; and being more simple he has rather less insight into his own performance."[11] Tow goes on to state that lobotomy performed on inmates in state mental hospitals causes them to become more dependent and more suitable for control in a structural institution.

Swedish psychosurgeon Gosta Rylander reports that patients who have been surgically lobotomized become less emotionally spontaneous, more shallow and relatively inert or blunted.[12] Obviously, surgical lobotomy does not heal someone of mental or emotional disorders. It simply cuts away, literally, much of the personality of the individual, who is then less capable of expressing emotional pain, and therefore, some conclude, he or she suffers less.

Surgical lobotomy is widely considered inhumane; yet the neuroleptic drugs, which attack the same centers of human mental functioning, are in continuous use worldwide. Neuroleptics, very toxic to brain functions, act as chemical lobotomizers. In 1952 Delay and Deniken described the effects of chlorpromazine given in relatively small doses:

> Sitting or lying, the patient is motionless in his bed, often pale and with eyelids lowered. He remains silent most of the time. If he is questioned, he answers slowly and deliberately in a monotonous and indifferent voice; he expresses himself in a few words and becomes silent.[13]

Patients who describe the effects of neuroleptics say that they experience a lobotomizing kind of effect. Janet Gotkin, an ex-patient testifying in 1977 before the Senate Subcommittee on the Abuse and Misuse of Controlled Drugs in Institutions, described her experience:

> People's voices came through filtered, strange. They could not penetrate my Thorazine fog; and I could not escape my drug prison.

Another ex-patient wrote:

> When they injected me with Prolixin I felt everything that was me—my ability to think, my ability to remember, and so forth—begin to dissolve.

According to another:

> It is very hard to describe the effect of this drug and others like it. That's why we use strange words like "zombie."

Wade Hudson, a survivor of psychiatric abuse, testified before a U.S. judiciary subcommittee in 1975:

> One injection of the long-acting neuroleptic Prolixin every week or two and you have a nation of zombies, easily controlled.

When describing the actual chemistry of neuroleptics, Breggin claims that these drugs do indeed produce a lobotomy effect. According to him, neuroleptics have an

> ...especially well-documented impact on the dopamine neurotransmission system. As any psychiatric textbook will confirm, dopamine neurotransmitters provide the major nerve pathways from the deeper brain to the frontal lobes and limbic system—the very same area struck by surgical lobotomy.[14]

Breggin continues by stating that psychosurgery cuts the nerve connections to and from the frontal lobes and limbic system, whereas neuroleptics interrupt the connections to the same region.

Peter Sterling, a researcher in the area of neurology, gives support to the drug's lobotomizing effect:

> The blunting of conscious motivation, and the inability to solve problems under the influence of chlorpromazine resembles nothing so much as the effects of frontal lobotomy.... Research has suggested that lobotomies and chemicals like chlorpromazine may cause their effects in the same way, by disrupting the activity of the neurochemical dopamine. At any rate, a psychiatrist would be hard-put to distinguish a lobotomized patient from one treated with chlorpromazine.[15]

So do these drugs correct a chemical imbalance in the schizophrenic, or do they simply cut off the areas most associated with human emotional pain and higher functioning?

Perhaps the most interesting aspect of neuroleptics and the chemical imbalance theory is that these drugs do not necessarily affect the symptoms (hallucinations and delusions) primarily associated with schizophrenia. Heinz Lehmann and his research team, writing about the effects of chlorpromazine in 1955, stated, "We have not observed a direct influence of the drug on delusional symptoms or hallucinatory phenomena." He then stated that in some cases "chlorpromazine may prove to be a pharmacological substitution for lobotomy."[16]

In 1970 Gerald Klerman published a study on how neuroleptics reduce specific psychiatric symptoms, claiming that his research confirmed an antipsychotic effect. A closer look at his results, however, shows something quite different. Klerman found that the most improved symptoms, in descending order, were (1st) combativeness, (2nd) hyperactivity, (3rd) tension, (4th) hostility and, finally, (5th) hallucinations and (6th) delusions.[17] In other words, it was not the symptoms most closely associated with schizophrenia (hallucinations and delusions) that were primarily affected by the drugs; it was the symptoms that tend to irritate staff personal.

These results have been confirmed time and time again by ex-psychiatric patients, who will tell you that the medications they took often had little effect on their delusions or hallucinations. Actually, these drugs had such terrible side effects that the patients quit telling the doctors about their symptoms for fear of being given increased dosages. Breggin describes his experience with one such individual:

> During her interview with me, she showed signs of brain damage from the drugs, such as inappropriate laughing, rambling, and difficulty focusing her attention; but she said nothing that sounded "crazy."... She had covered them [her schizophrenic symptoms] up with other doctors, not because the medication "helped" her, but because she wanted to keep from being drugged against her will.[18]

Alvin Pam, Ph.D, confirms this notion: "An agitated patient may be helped by a drug that renders him or her relatively lethargic; or, more precisely, the staff dealing with an agitated patient may be helped by a drug that renders the patient more manageable, with the patient benefiting secondarily."[19]

Psychiatrists can become incredibly blind or biased on this issue. In a debate with Breggin, a psychiatrist admitted to taking "one small dose of a neuroleptic and experiencing an overwhelming and unbearable sense of depression and disinterest." In spite of this, he still went on to claim that, "Because his clients had biochemical abnormalities they felt better taking the neuroleptics."[20]

I believe that neuroleptics have no specific therapeutic effect on people diagnosed as schizophrenic because schizophrenia is not a brain disease. Usually neuroleptics are used when it is deemed necessary to calm a person down or gain control over him. In many psychiatric wards neuroleptics are administered to 90 to 100% of the patients, regardless of their diagnosis. In addition, these drugs are given out in large numbers to elderly people in nursing homes, to prisoners, and to unmanageable children. Neuroleptics were used on political dissidents in the old Soviet Union. Although many U.S. psychiatrists were appalled and protested the use of neuroleptics in the former Soviet Union, neuroleptics are very much an instrument of social control in the U.S. today. How ironic that the drugs used to "treat" schizophrenia are the same drugs once used on those who protested Stalinism and Communism.

Although neuroleptics are used in veterinary medicine to calm animals, the veterinary literature limits the use of neuroleptics to short-term use only. These doctors consider neuroleptics too dangerous for animal consumption, except in emergencies.

In summary, the proponents of the disease model claim that schizophrenia is caused by an out-of-balance disruption in the flow of certain neurotransmitters. When the results do not substantiate the model, the current theory is modified and a new theory is developed, leading to more false hope for the public. In the meantime, the people who are given neuroleptics often find that their minds are being dismantled, whether or not they are schizophrenic.

When a child exhibits out-of-control behavior, he or she is often first given Ritalin. If Ritalin does not work, neuroleptics may be tried. In spite of the failure of Ritalin in many cases, biopsychiatry will continue to claim that the problem is primarily a biochemical one—that specific drugs correct specific imbalances for specific disorders. Due to the fact that neuroleptics

41

cause brain damage in large numbers of patients, this misinformation must not continue.

Let's now turn our attention to the drug Prozac and its chemical cousins.

PROZAC

No drug in the history of psychiatry has drawn more attention than Prozac. It has been hailed as a miracle drug for depression, and has been used by millions. Because researchers and doctors are convinced that it has the ability to "selectively" modify the serotonin neurotransmitter, Prozac has been one of the drugs used to support the disease model of mental illness. Researchers have theorized that serotonin has a lot to do with regulating the emotions. Like other drugs we have discussed, the theory behind the use of Prozac is the chemical imbalance model, which, in this case, goes as follows: Prozac is assumed to stimulate serotonin levels in the brain and is prescribed for depression. If a person taking it finds his depression lifted, it must follow that depression is caused by a serotonin deficiency. To understand what is really happening when someone takes Prozac, let's look closely at this "wonder drug" and its chemical cousins.

Prozac, Zoloft, Paxil, and Luvox are members of a new generation of antidepressants called "selective serotonin reuptake inhibitors" (SSRIs). Many researchers and doctors believe that clinical or severe forms of depression are the result of inadequate levels of serotonin in the system. Where chlorpromazine blocks the flow of the dopamine molecules, the SSRI drugs have an opposite effect on serotonin.

After a neuron has fired, many of the leftover serotonin molecules in the synapse are retrieved by the proceeding neuron: this is called reuptake. Figure 3.3 illustrates this process.

What the SSRI drugs do is prevent the reuptake, leaving more serotonin in the gap between the neurons, which raises the chance of the nerves firing. Theoretically, this model seems quite reason-

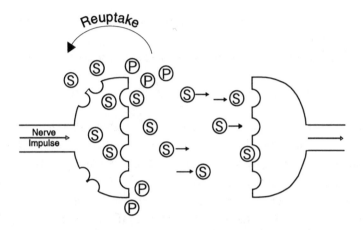

As Prozac blocks the reuptake of Serotonin, it causes more
Serotonin to remain in the synapse for a longer time.

Figure 3.3: The serotonin reuptake process

able. If we can stop the reuptake of serotonin, we can get the
nerves to fire more often, helping the person to *feel better*. Unfortunately, the brain does not work in such simple terms. First
of all, there are more than one hundred chemical substances that
control neurotransmitters, many of which are other neurotransmitters. Furthermore, the serotonin nerve system is the most
extensive neurotransmitting system in the brain. When an SSRI
drug such as Prozac changes the levels of serotonin, it eventually affects most of the brain.

When we understand how complex the brain is, and how many
different parts of the brain the serotonin nerve system interacts
with, we can see that it is sheer nonsense to think that we can
somehow take a pill and re-balance such a system—if indeed the
system were imbalanced to begin with. Even though many psychiatrists would quickly agree with this statement and follow by
stating that they would never make such a claim, it is precisely
this claim that is sold to the public. Thousands of people have
come to believe that SSRI medications, as well as many others,

help by balancing the brain's systems or need for a certain level of serotonin.

If SSRI drugs do not help balance the system, what do they do?

PROZAC AS A STIMULANT

Perhaps the most important fact to know about Prozac is that it works as a stimulant. It has been firmly established that Prozac's stimulant properties are very similar to the stimulant profile of amphetamines. FDA psychiatrist Richard Kapit, after collecting all the data on the adverse effects of Prozac, reported that, "Most frequently this new drug causes nausea, insomnia, and nervousness, which resemble the profile of a stimulant rather than a sedative drug." Kapit also warned that Prozac might actually worsen depression.[21]

Even though this stimulant property was kept off the Prozac label in this country, other countries were not quite so negligent. This issue is especially important in light of the fact that taking stimulants can result in both suicidal and violent reactions in certain individuals. The German equivalent of the FDA, in its list of guidelines for those prescribing the drug, included a warning that if a person is suicidal, he must be given sedatives along with Prozac. In France, the agency that regulates drugs requires that this warning be printed on the label when the drug is prescribed. In England, experts have also raised the issue of Prozac being a stimulant.[22]

There are several other facts about Prozac that are worth mentioning. In their report to the FDA, and as a result of their own testing, Prozac's manufacturer, Eli Lilly, listed depression as one of the common side effects of Prozac. For some unknown reason, however, this common side effect was edited out of the label by the FDA.[23] An outside testing consultant also informed the firm about Prozac's stimulant properties and suggested that these properties might agitate a person towards suicide.[24] Lilly's own data also confirmed that Prozac causes stimulant-type side effects such as agitation, irritability, excitement, nightmares, sweating, dry mouth, abnormal sensations, abnormal bodily movements, and palpitations.[25]

44

A woman comparing Prozac with other stimulants she had taken in the past said, "I remember the diet pill stimulation only lasted about thirty minutes to an hour—that feeling of being driven, of having to do things, and being euphoric. It was a short time. But on Prozac, there was constant stimulation. It didn't go away while you were on the drug."[26]

If Prozac acts as a stimulant similar to amphetamines, as confirmed by the FDA's own expert and Eli Lilly's own consultant, then we could expect people taking Prozac to have effects similar to those taking stimulants. We would foresee that some people would become "high" and feel good, while others would experience a "bad trip." Indeed, many people have reported such side effects while taking Prozac.[27]

There is another important feature of stimulant-type drugs that helps to explain why many claim Prozac has positive results. Research has shown that stimulants such as Prozac cause a compulsive narrowing-of-focus behavior. In animals, this behavior often involves purposeless, repetitive voluntary movements that are carried out for long periods of time at the expense of all other activities. Rats on stimulants have been observed spending unusual amounts of time licking, gnawing, or sniffing, while dogs and chimpanzees may compulsively run or walk around in a repetitive fashion.[28]

This drug-induced "narrowing of focus" is the exact state of mind sought by individuals who have to do boring or repetitive tasks. I have worked with many teenagers who take amphetamines when they must get their chores done at home or complete their school work. This same narrowing of focus may be why some people drink coffee, a much milder stimulant that Prozac. It may also be the reason the stimulant Ritalin seems to help children focus at school.

Thus if SSRI drugs help people to feel stimulated and also focus attention on getting through a routine task or a boring day, it is easy to see how these drugs would be popular in today's culture. These effects are achieved by adding an artificial stimulant to the person's brain; not by correcting a chemical imbalance.

It is unfortunate that, because of belief in the chemical imbalance model, Prozac is being advertised and sold as a solution to depression. In actuality, it is a stimulant and should be rarely prescribed and only with the same caution as any other stimulant.

Furthermore, because it does not correct an individual's underlying problems, Prozac may later result in increased depression, as illustrated by the research discussed above. Even psychiatrists are beginning to admit to this fact, as I found out while recently attending a "pro-drug" conference funded by a major drug company. One of the main speakers at the conference said that he and his colleagues were now starting to see clients on Prozac who "seem to have lost interest in life." In the end, we may have to conclude that Prozac is just a new kind of stimulant that will have the same eventual outcome as other stimulants previously in vogue, making the people taking it feel better for a while, but ultimately leaving them trapped in their pain.

LITHIUM

When researchers first discovered that the naturally occurring salt lithium could be used to calm highly agitated or manic individuals, bio-psychiatrists immediately claimed that this was, indeed, further evidence supporting the chemical imbalance model. Ronald Fieve, M.D., author of *Moodswing*, writes:

> The use of lithium constitutes a turning point in the mental-health field... A breakthrough has finally been achieved in the treatment and prevention of one of the world's major mental-health problems.[29]

> ...findings point to the fact that mania and mental depression must be due to biochemical causes handed down through the genes, since they are correctable so rapidly by chemical rather than talking therapy.[30]

Before the use of lithium and other modern methods such as shock treatment, some of the predominant methods used for "ex-

46

cited manic patients" were bloodletting, dunking in ice-cold water, and securing the patient in many different kinds of restraining devices. Of course, it would be reasonable to assume that such methods would calm down almost any agitated, hyper, or angry person.

The calming effects of lithium were first discovered, not through experiments with manic patients, but in animals. When Australian psychiatrist John Cade injected lithium into the bellies of guinea pigs, he noticed that they became sedated.

> A noteworthy result was that after a latent period of about two hours the animals, although fully conscious, became extremely lethargic and non-responsive to stimuli from one to two hours before once again becoming normally active and timid.[31]

Obviously the effects of lithium are not just specific to those individuals suffering from mania. Currently, this drug is being widely used in conjunction with neuroleptics for schizophrenia, as well as many other disorders, including alcoholism and aggression. In these cases lithium is prescribed not so much because it's effective in treating these disorders, or because schizophrenia is a disease caused by a lack of the lithium salt, but because it allows doctors to reduce the dosage of neuroleptics, which cause brain damage.

When researchers tested lithium on the general population, they discovered that it had the same dulling effect on every subject who took the drug. A study published in the *Archives of General Psychiatry* showed a "general dulling and blunting of various personality functions" and overall slowing of cognitive processes. The spouses and family members who were observing the volunteers reported "increased levels of drowsiness and lowered ability to work hard and to think clearly."[32] William Annitto and his research team state, "It is clear that conditions other than typical manic-depressive disorder respond to treatment with lithium."[33]

When comparing the use of lithium with neuroleptics for mania, R. F. Prien found that highly active patients responded less satisfactorily to lithium than did mildly active patients.[34] Other studies found that lithium was more effective in calming patients than the neuroleptics they were taking, but the dosages of the neuroleptics used in these cases were usually very small. In spite of this, today it is generally accepted that the more manic or out-of-control the individual is, the more neuroleptics, valued for their lobotomizing effects, become the drug of choice. According to Annitto:

> Most clinicians would now agree that neuroleptics should be used initially in the agitated, dangerously hyperactive patient as a means of gaining rapid motor control. Lithium would be the drug of choice for the more cooperative, less disruptive patient.[35]

Notice that Annitto is admitting that neuroleptics are used to *control behavior*, not to balance the chemistry responsible for psychotic behavior.

It is not uncommon for people who have suffered from mania for a long period of time to either be taking, or to have tried, many different combinations of medications. Because of this, we can't assume that lithium works to correct a chemical imbalance in people suffering from symptoms associated with mania.

If lithium doesn't correct a chemical imbalance, then how does it work? No one knows for sure, but Ron Leifer, M.D., has an interesting theory. He writes:

> Lithium is one up on the Mendeleev scale from sodium. And it's well known that sodium, the sodium pump, is what activates neural excitation, which is responsible for nerve transmission. So it's not out of bounds to speculate that lithium, which is a heavier molecule, replaces some of the sodium and simply slows down the nervous system, which is exactly the way a lot of people experience it.[36]

Based on the evidence we have, it seems fair to conclude that lithium is just another method used to control behavior by disabling the brain and reducing its functions. Without a doubt, this drug has subdued the behavior and emotions of many individuals; but the false notion that mania is a disease has also left thousands of individuals disabled and "hooked" on psychiatric drugs for the rest of their lives.

RITALIN

We now come to Ritalin—another drug that supposedly corrects a chemical imbalance in children and adults.

The theories behind the effectiveness of Ritalin in helping those who suffer from Attention Deficit Disorder (ADD) are similar to those used to support the other drugs discussed above. Proponents of the medical model believe that a neurological deficit or chemical imbalance must be present in those diagnosed with this disorder. However, none of the old theories about the causes of ADD, such as birth complications, food additions, food allergies, sugar, and so forth have withstood the test of time.

Opponents of the medical model see the behavior of the hyperactive child as a *natural*; an often positive aspect of his or her personality and/or environment. In her book *The Edison Trait*[37], psychologist Lucy Jo Palladino claims that many ADD children have quick and creative minds that make it difficult for them to learn at the slow linear pace set by most educators in public schools. These children have a tendency to take big leaps and bounds in logic and insight, often becoming passionate and interested in everything. Dr. Palladino has helped many children and adults come to believe in their "gifts"—their energy, originality, and capacity for innovative discoveries. She calls the ADD profile the "Edison trait" because she believes the brilliant inventor Thomas Edison, whose mind, talents, and imagination were indefatigable, could easily have been diagnosed with ADD when he was a child in school. Dr. Palladino states "It is my experience that drawing this distinction is liberating. It gives children (and adults) who have this profile a new self-concept that can be non-ADD and therefore sans impairment."[38]

In my own work, spanning fifteen years of counseling and research, I have discovered that some children become hyperactive or inattentive often because of specific emotional issues in their lives. Their parents might be fighting at home, a sibling might be in trouble, or a bully might be giving them a bad time at school. When these children attempt to concentrate on their work, the emotional pain of these issues begins to draw their minds away from the task at hand. In these cases, the mind is actually acting as a defense, purposely distracting the child from staying focused on his or her studies, which would cause him or her to become mentally quiet enough to begin experiencing his or her pain.

Whether the majority of ADD cases in this country are caused by natural aptitude or emotional crisis is not the issue. Each child becomes hyperactive or distractive for a different reason, just as each person who becomes catatonic has his own reason for developing this behavior. When the medical model claims that ADD children are physiologically defective and can be chemically "fixed" by a drug, this viewpoint is both incorrect and damaging. As with the other conditions described above, no evidence has ever been found that proves that ADD is biological in origin.

So how does Ritalin help? First, it is important to realize that Ritalin is a stimulant. In fact, the February 1996 issue of the *Harvard Mental Health Letter* showed that Ritalin and cocaine are very similar.[39] Both inhibit the reuptake of the neurotransmitter dopamine at receptor sites in the same regions of the brain. The feeling of pleasure after taking both drugs is about equal. The only real difference between the two seems to be the rate at which they are cleared from the brain. Whereas Ritalin maintains its peak effects for fifteen to twenty minutes, cocaine lasts from two to four minutes.

There is no doubt that Ritalin is a stimulant. Although it may seem contradictory, stimulants, when given in small doses, have a tendency to actually calm people down. Low dosages also help people to focus, as Freud noticed when he experimented with cocaine. Perhaps these small amounts stimulate the system just enough to enable us to block out certain feelings or thoughts that might be competing for our attention.

Often when I sit down to write, I notice that I have some low-level feelings such as anxiety, loneliness, fear of not getting a chapter done, or other emotions that might be associated with issues in my life. As I begin to drink some coffee (stimulant), these feelings are soon minimized, allowing me to focus my attention. It is interesting to notice that, before Ritalin was used, coffee was given to adults diagnosed with ADD.

I mentioned earlier that teenagers often use amphetamines to help them concentrate on their boring chores or homework. The 1992 *Oxford Textbook of Clinical Psychopharmacology and Drug Therapy* helps explain this strategy by suggesting that stimulants influence children in the same way they affect laboratory rats: "by inducing stereotyped behavior in animals."[40]

As with other drugs used for treatment of mental disorders, Ritalin has the same basic effect on anyone who takes it, regardless of whether he or she is "normal" or has been diagnosed as chemically unbalanced by a psychiatrist.[41] Furthermore, there is little or no evidence of long-term beneficial effects on children taking Ritalin.[42] The National Institute for Mental Health (NIMH) states that "The long-term effects of stimulants remain in doubt."[43] In fact the information sheet that the manufacturer of Ritalin (CIBA Pharmaceutical Company) includes with the prescription states "Sufficient data on safety and efficacy of long-term use of Ritalin in children are not yet available."

Recently, the news media has been reporting that Ritalin is becoming a popular and dangerous illegal street drug in the U.S. In Canada, Ritalin is first on their list of "dangerous drugs." In light of this, it is interesting to note that, all the way back in 1973, G.S. Omenn observed:

> Illicit traffic in Ritalin has increased among narcotic addicts.... Those on Methadone appreciate the "up" effect of Ritalin. Those on heroin can prolong the duration of action of a given dose of heroin by concomitantly taking Ritalin.... In Chicago's Cook County Prison, Ritalin is called "West Coast" by the heroin addicts.[44]

Fortunately, psychologists such as Dr. Palladino and other researchers are realizing that drugs are not the answer to our childrens' learning and behavioral problems. It is time that our whole society, including the medical profession, move away from the paradox of prescribing more and more medication to more and more of our children, while at the same time asking them to say "no" to illegal drugs.

SUMMARY

When we take a closer look at the drugs used for psychiatric purposes, we see that there is no great mystery about how they basically work on our emotional system. Their effects can be quickly summarized as follows:

Antipsychotics: Lobotomize, blunt, lessen responsiveness.
SSRI antidepressants: Cause slight prolonged stimulation.
Lithium: Numbs or deadens.
Ritalin: Provides strong stimulation to help focus.

The main point is that the use of medication for people suffering from emotional problems or for the control of individuals does not substantiate the chemical imbalance or medical model of mental illness. Clearly, prescribed medications are often being used for many of the same effects and purposes as illegal drugs, alcohol, coffee, and food.

CHAPTER FOUR

TWIN AND ADOPTIVE INHERITANCE STUDIES

Even professionals can get caught up in a false body of evidence, and this has happened in studies looking for genetic bases for mental illness, as well as those looking for imbalanced brain chemicals. Psychiatrist Colin Ross explains one reason that faulty theories are perpetuated as fact:

> It was not surprising that medical students accepted the dogma of biomedical reductionism in psychiatry uncritically: they had no time to read and analyze the original literature. What took me a while to understand, as I moved through my residency, was that psychiatrists rarely do the critical reading either. The dogma that the genetic foundation of schizophrenia has been scientifically established is by and large accepted without serious question in contemporary psychiatry.[1]

If psychiatrists in their residency do not read or question the basic research, and if the general public is not given a true picture, then it is very likely that we as a society, from the professional to the lay person, have a distorted view of the credibility of biological psychiatry. Keep this point in mind as we look at the evidence used to support one of the mainstays of the medical model of mental illness—the genetic inheritance research.

TWIN STUDIES

In attempting to substantiate the medical model, researchers often resort to indirect strategies to support their claims. One such strategy is the attempt to show that mental or emotional disorders run in families and develop, not because of some environmental factor such as abuse or neglect, but because of an individual's genetic predisposition. Therefore, such disorders as schizophrenia and manic depression are believed to be inherited. The most obvious tool for proving a genetic inheritance model is the use of twin studies.

By far the most common type of heritability study involves comparing two different types of twins: monozygotic (identical) and dizygotic (non-identical or fraternal). Identical twins result when a single ovum is fertilized by a single sperm. The zygote splits early in development, resulting in the birth of two *genetically identical* individuals. Fraternal twins occur when two separate ova are fertilized by two separate sperm. Fraternal twins, like all non-identical siblings, share about *50% of their genes*.

Because the genetic material of identical twins is exactly the same, it is reasonable to assume that genetically determined traits would show a higher correlation in identical twins than in fraternal ones. For example, we would expect the eye color of identical twins to be the same. On the other hand, the eye color of fraternal twins and other siblings could vary from a 25% to a 100% chance of being the same, based on the different genetic coding of the parents. Researchers express these genetic propensities mathematically by saying that, in the case of very high heritability traits such as eye color, the correlations between identical twins should approach 1.00 or 100%. For fraternal twins, the correlations between twins could vary from .25 to 1.00.

If we use studies of intelligence quotient (IQ) as an example, we can see that the typical correlations for identical twins range between 70% to 90%, as compared to a range of 50% to 70% correlations among same-sexed fraternals. Yet we can't con-

54

clude from these statistical differences *alone* that IQ is a strong hereditary trait. Physical traits such as eye color, height, and nose size cannot be equated with more abstract qualities such as intelligence or emotional disorders. We must be careful not to base our conclusions about factors such as intelligence or emotional makeup on statistics alone. The higher correlations between identical twins as opposed to fraternal twins might be the result of environment. For example, because of the nearly identical appearance of identical twins, parents, teachers, and friends could be more likely to treat them alike. This would not necessarily be the case with non-identical twins, whose differences in appearance would be more pronounced, making it easier to think of them as "two separate people." With identical twins, it is all too easy to think of them almost as one person: if one is affirmed as being bright (or slow), most likely the other will be thought of in the same way.

Studies have shown that identical twins tend to spend more time together, even more than same-sexed fraternal twins.[2] Identical twins are much less likely than fraternal twins to have spent a night apart from each other, and are more likely to dress in a similar manner, play together, and have the same friends. R. T. Smith reported that the identical twins did their homework together 40% of the time, while fraternals studied together only 15% of the time.[3] Such results led the authors of *Not In Your Genes* to conclude that "For all we know the heritability (of IQ) may be zero or 50%."[4]

I want to be clear that I'm not claiming that inheritance has no effect upon intelligence. Surely it does, but we cannot take twin studies *alone* and conclude that a trait is inherited, even if the studies strongly point in that direction. When trying to understand whether emotional illness is inherited, we cannot rule out environmental factors. With this disclaimer in mind, let's look at the twin research that is purported to support the genetic model for schizophrenia.

A LOOK AT SCHIZOPHRENIA

In their book *Schizophrenia and Manic-Depressive Disorder*, Torrey, Bowler, Tayor, and Gottesman tell us that the concordance rate between identical twins that is often quoted in textbooks of psychiatry is approximately 50%.[5] Translated into laymen's terms, this means that if one twin has been diagnosed as schizophrenic, there is a 50% likelihood that the other twin will be diagnosed as schizophrenic. This rate represents an averaging of all the latest studies.

Since concordance rates are used extensively in psychiatry to substantiate the medical model, we must examine them more closely. A few months ago I attended a one-day seminar mainly for psychiatrists. This seminar was funded by a pharmaceutical company and its focus was to bring together top researchers to discuss the newest therapeutic methods. The first speaker, a renowned research psychiatrist, started his talk by turning on his slide projector and flashing a table of concordance rates for schizophrenia onto a screen. At the top, marked clearly for everyone to see, was the figure of 50% for identical twins. After pointing out this figure, he then boldly said, "How can anyone believe that schizophrenia is not inherited?" There must have been nearly 400 psychiatrists in the audience nodding in agreement. The rest of his program was then devoted to the application of medication to all psychiatric disorders.

This concordance figure is one of the most highly distorted and misused figures in genetic studies today. In reality, the heritability factor between identical twins for schizophrenia is practically nonexistent. To understand how this figure has become distorted, let's take a closer look at the genetic studies upon which this assumption is based.

First of all, Torrey admits that when all the identical twin studies for schizophrenia are averaged together, the actual figure is really closer to 40%.[6] To achieve even 40%, however, the researchers used what is called a *proband statistical method* instead of the more conventional *pairwise method*. When the pairwise method is used, the average concordance rate drops to 28%.[7] Following is an example of the uses and differences between proband and pairwise methods.

Most twin studies were done in Scandinavian countries, where national twin registries are rigorously maintained. As the researchers went through the registries, if a diagnosed schizophrenic twin was found, he (or she) was counted as one proband. If the person's identical twin was found in the original search, he would also be counted as one proband. In other words, in the proband method a set of twins is often counted twice, because individual people are being counted, not sets of twins. In the pairwise method, individuals are not counted separately, but only as part as a pair.

It is interesting to note that the pairwise method used to be the research method of choice in twin studies, and was originally used in the study of schizophrenia. Some researchers started showing a preference for the proband method and by 1982 it was considered the standard and most appropriate approach.

Mary Boyle, author of *Schizophrenia—A Scientific Delusion?*, states that the probandwise data collection method almost always inflates concordance rates, more for identical twins than for fraternal ones.[8] Therefore, not only does the proband method create an inflated rate, it also creates a greater numerical difference between the concordance rates of identical and fraternal rates. In spite of this, Torrey uses figures about the inheritance correlations between identical and fraternal twins, derived from the proband method, to "confirm" that genetics play an important rate in the causation of schizophrenia.[9]

Just as there is a legitimate question about how much environment contributes to the formation of IQ, there is an even greater question involved in determining how much environment contributes to the development of schizophrenia. Part of the difficulty stems from obtaining accurate concordance rates between twins. The question of environmental influence can be partially answered by comparing the concordance rates between fraternal twins and their siblings. Since fraternal twins share a more similar environment than ordinary siblings, it would be logical to assume that the twins' concordance rates with one another would be higher, even though they are genetically no more alike than their other brothers and sisters. This assumption is correct. A number of studies *have* shown a higher concordance rate (two to three times higher) between fraternals than between them and their other siblings.[10] Therefore, since identical twins share a more common environment than fraternal twins, it would make sense that there would be a higher concordance rate between identical twins based, not only on possible inherited factors, but on their *environment* as well.

To help substantiate the influence that environment has upon twins, researchers have compared the concordance rates of same-sexed and opposite-sexed fraternals. In such a study, both types would share the same amount of common genetic material, but they would experience somewhat different environments because of the differences in socialization between the sexes. Again, studies show a higher environmental concordance rate for same-sexed twins, and most studies show results that are scientifically significant, meaning that it is highly unlikely that the results were by chance only.[11]

Not only do identicals most likely share a more common environment than other siblings, each identical twin can play a central part in the other's delusional system.[12] Therefore, if one identical twin tended to become delusional, the other would be similarly influenced, increasing the chance that both twins could be diagnosed with schizophrenia.

There are many other methodological problems associated with twin studies. In her book *Schizophrenia-A Scientific Delusion?*, Mary Boyle does an excellent analysis of the twin studies used to substantiate a genetic basis for schizophrenia.[13] This book, which also includes the critical analysis of other authors, brings out many methodological factors that might work to distort the concordance rates in favor of identical twins. For example, in the older twin studies, where the concordance differences were greater between identical and fraternal groups, hospital samples were used. First of all, if both twins are hospitalized, it is much more likely that both identical twins would be hospitalized than both fraternal twins. Also, once hospitalized, because of their striking similarities in appearance, these individuals would be more likely to be identified as twins. This identification would have a tendency to inflate the available research pool of identical subjects. In fact, E. Kringlen showed that the probability of being hospitalized and reported might be twice as great for identicals than fraternals, especially when researchers used small samples for their studies.[14]

Boyle also admits that it was often difficult to determine the zygosity of the twins. No studies of mental illness in twins used the standard procedures (blood and serological system testing) to determine whether *all* of the twins they were studying were actually identical or fraternal. Appearances alone cannot be used as "proof" in cases such as these. For example, if one identical twin became schizophrenic, was hospitalized for years, and was given medications, his appearance might have become quite different from his twin's. Under such a circumstance, it would be easy to regard him as a fraternal rather than an identical subject. This would add to the fraternal non-concordant pool instead of the identical non-concordant pool.

In many twin studies, other problems arose concerning whether twins were fraternal or identical. Often researchers interviewed the co-twin or other members of the family. If only one identical twin had been diagnosed as schizophrenic, there may have been a tendency for the other twin and family members to deny that the twins were identical, again taking away from the identical non-concordant pool.

Often, the collection of information about the twins was quite vague. For example, the *only* information made available about one subject was the following: "A friend of the family related that X was eccentric, living entirely alone in a small house, but no further details were known."[15] In another case, the subject hid upstairs while the investigators interviewed a relative.

According to Boyle, there were no twin studies in which those who collected the information were blind either to the twins' possible zygosity or to the diagnosis of their mental and emotional condition. Since there was a natural bias on the part of the researchers to assume that schizophrenia is inherited, the data collected could likely have been distorted toward that general direction. While Boyle claims that the calculation of actual concordance rates is relatively simple, she reports that the ways in which these rates are used and how the data is reported "serve to obscure the considerable methodological and conceptual problems presented by the twin studies."[16]

A HYPOTHETICAL CASE

To help the reader understand some of these variables and how they can be brought together, let's take a look at a hypothetical case in a twin study. While going through hospital records or the national twin registry, researchers find a subject named John who has symptoms that could indicate that he is schizophrenic.

The researchers' next step is to attempt to locate John and his twin. This can be problematic since John or the other twin might have been dead for some time. If John can be located, there is the additional difficulty of determining whether he is a fraternal or an identical twin, and whether his condition has been accurately diagnosed. When his co-twin is found, which may be some time later, the researcher might try to determine John and his twin's zygosity by means of appearance only. This might create another problem, since it is likely that a considerable period of time will have gone by since the investigator last saw John or had photographs taken of him. It is also likely that, since John has been hospitalized and is suffering from schizophrenia and/or the effects of institutional care and medication, his appearance may be quite different from his twin's, even if they are identical.

If the co-twin cannot be found or doesn't want to be interviewed, then relatives, records, or even neighbors are used to determine both the zygosity and the diagnosis. Since the investigators running the study are not blind to John's diagnosis, and because at the time of the collection of data, there were no precise scientific tests used to determine either John's zygosity or the accuracy of his diagnosis, there will be plenty of room for experimental error.

The scenario I have just described is not an exaggeration. If you were to read the twin studies yourself and see how the information was collected, you would realize that this hypothetical case represents a common situation.[17]

Summarizing Genetic Studies

As we have seen, one of the most popular tools that scientists, psychiatrists, and doctors use to back up the medical model of mental illness is the study of twins. For many years researchers have been trying to use these studies to prove that schizophrenia and other emotional disorders are inherited. In some of the earlier studies, however, concordance rates were quite inflated, to as high as 76%.

Since those earlier studies were loaded with methodological errors, it is not surprising that concordance rates dropped considerably in later, more widely accepted studies. Nevertheless, in their attempts to prove that schizophrenia is an inherited disease, researchers still have a tendency to highly distort their figures. The summary below demonstrates that, as we examine the errors involved in these studies, the concordance rate would have a tendency to drop in each situation.

Concordance rates for identical twins diagnosed as schizophrenic.

* 50% is the starting rate quoted in many text books.
* 40% is what Torrey says is a more accurate average of these studies.
* 39% is the average of the three studies considered the most accurate[18]
* 26% is the corresponding pairwise rate for the three most accurate studies.

The 26% figure represents the concordance rate for the three most accurate studies, and if this were a true biological factor that would still leave an environmental factor of 74%. Below is a summary of the other factors that would tend to lower the concordance rate even further.

* Shared environments will tend to lower the probability of any true genetic component.
* The fact that both individual twins were more apt to be hospitalized and/or identified as twins would tend to inflate the concordance rate.
* If only one identical twin was hospitalized, his appearance could be quite different from his twin, thus increasing the risk that he could be incorrectly counted as a fraternal twin.
* Family members interviewed might deny that twins are identical, raising the concordance rate in the identical twins pool.
* Vague information about twins would tend to distort the data in favor of an inheritance factor because of the difficulty in correctly identifying identical twins.
* Since those who collected the data were not blind to the possible zygosity and the diagnosis, there may have been an experimental bias involved.

After reviewing this data, I must ask, "How low is the actual concordance rate for identical twins?" If we start with a figure of 26% and then account for all the other factors that would tend to distort that rate, what would we have left?

It is incorrect to assume that the differences in concordance rates between identical and fraternal twins is proof of a genetic predisposition toward schizophrenia. Even if there were a slight genetic influence, it would still be wrong to conclude that a genetic defect was involved. Identical twins may certainly have similar personalities; for example, they might both be sensitive to the rejection of others. These similarities could account for the small element of heritability concluded in the researchers' studies. Twin studies can be misused in attempts to substantiate the medical model. The simple truth is that these studies, when analyzed correctly, firmly support an *environmental* model, not a genetic model. Let's now examine another major argument for the medical model, adoptive studies, and see what light they shed on our search for an answer.

ADOPTIVE STUDIES

Because there is a larger pool of subjects to draw from, and because it is possible to use control groups, adoptive studies have become another source of evidence in researchers' attempts to substantiate a genetic cause or predisposition toward emotional disorders.

The original adoptive research developed to support a genetic influence in schizophrenia is the series of studies conducted in Denmark under the supervision and funding of the National Institute for Mental Health (NIMH). Most of these studies were published between 1968 and 1974. The research was conducted in Denmark because their national health register allows cross-reference research on any adult in the population who has come under psychiatric attention. These studies were hailed as a great success, and Gothesman and Shields, two prominent researchers, refer to them as "the straw that broke the environmentalists' back."[19]

In a study conducted by a team led by Seymour Kety, a leader in psychiatric genetic research for Harvard Medical School, 33 adoptees who were diagnosed schizophrenic as adults were matched with a control group of 33 other adoptees never diagnosed as schizophrenic.[20] The researchers then began a search, eventually locating 150 blood relatives of the diagnosed schizophrenic adoptees and 156 blood relatives of the control group, including parents, siblings, and half-siblings. The search produced only *two* relatives who were diagnosed as schizophrenic: one in the index (schizophrenic) group and one in the control group.

The fact that only one schizophrenic relative was found in each group should have been conclusive proof that the study supported an environmental, not a genetic model. But because these results did not support their theories, the researchers tried again by pooling together a broader diagnostic category. This new "schizophrenic spectrum disorder" now included chronic and acute schizophrenics, borderline states, schizoid and inadequate personalities, and uncertain schizophrenic or borderline conditions.

Using this broader set of diagnostic criteria, nine biological families of index cases were found in which at least one spectrum diagnosis had been made, as compared to only two families among the controls. R. C. Lewontin, an evolutionary geneticist at Harvard, states that without including such vague diagnoses as "inadequate personality" and "uncertain borderline schizophrenic," the researchers would have found no significant data.[21]

This study was further weakened by many other factors, the most important being that a selective placement of the adoptees took place. Lewontin and his co-authors discovered that in 24% of the non-control group families, an adoptive parent had been in a mental hospital prior to adopting a child that was later used in the study. This was not true for any of the adoptive parents in the control group.[22] This statistically significant data strongly suggests that a child who later became schizophrenic may have been born into a dysfunctional family and then adopted into another dysfunctional family.

Perhaps most importantly, when the criteria of the study were expanded to include "spectrum diagnosis," there was still no increase in schizophrenia among the close biological relatives of the adoptees, including the mothers, fathers, full brothers and full sisters. The only increase was to be found in the *half-brothers and half-sisters on the fathers' side*.

In Peter Breggin's words, "We have a miracle gene that skips the biological mothers, fathers, brothers, and sisters—and even the biological half-brothers and sisters on the mothers's side—and strikes only the half—siblings on the father's side."[23]

There are more methodological problems that are worth investigating if the reader is further interested. Besides Mary Boyle's *Schizophrenia-A Scientific Delusion?*, Lewontin, Rose, and Kamin in their book *Not In Our Genes*[24] do an excellent analysis of the problems associated with this study.

The adoptive study analyzed above is the main one used to "prove" the genetic model. An in-depth look at this research gives the reader a little taste of how the information in any family study can be easily manipulated and then fed to the public as "conclusive evidence that schizophrenia or other disorders must be inherited."

The fact that the only people found who fit into the expanded diagnostic category were only half-siblings should be evidence enough that this study supports an environmental view. Breggin struggled considerably with the conclusions of this study. In an interview with psychiatrist Loren Mosher, director of the center devoted to research on schizophrenia at NIMH during the time the study was funded, Breggin asked him what the genetic studies really showed. Mosher declared that the studies "proved it's [the cause of mental illness] environmental and not genetic."[25] This is a strong statement coming from the NIMH official who sponsored the studies.

During a trip to Copenhagen, Breggin also challenged Fini Schulsinger, the Danish psychiatrist who was in charge of the research. When Breggin stated that the studies favored an environmental case for schizophrenia, Schulsinger agreed with him. Writing about this experience, Breggin expressed his astonishment: "Yet the whole genetics of schizophrenia rests on this house of cards. What hocus-pocus."[26]

In summary, 33 adopted diagnosed schizophrenic adults were matched with 33 non-schizophrenic adopted adults. The researchers found 150 relatives of the schizophrenic adoptees and 156 control relatives. Out of both groups, only two relatives had been diagnosed with schizophrenia, one from each group. In this study, virtually no schizophrenic parents produced schizophrenic children and virtually no schizophrenic children came from schizophrenic parents. It seems to me that this should have been the straw that broke the back of the genetic-biopsychiatrists.

Nevertheless, these studies were considered as landmark contributions to the medical model, and one professional after another came forward to praise them. In spite of the thin and inconclusive results, psychiatrist Paul Wender, one of the authors of the study, announced: "We failed to discover any environmental component."[27] Wender and Klein later went so far as to state that 8% of the general population are predisposed genetically to develop a disorder within their "diagnostic spectrum" in which only *medication* (my emphasis) could correct the underlying biochemical problems.[28]

As much as these studies have been criticized, they are still used today to help support a biological basis for schizophrenia. In their 1994 book titled *Understanding Schizophrenia*, Keefe and Harvey comment on the Danish-American research by stating "This study provides some of the strongest evidence available that genetic factors are important in determining who develops schizophrenia."[29]

As an interesting side point, these same Danish files were used to support evidence that alcoholism is a genetically transmitted disease. Questioning the methodology of these studies, Colin Ross and Alvin Pam pointed out that one or two subjects were switched without explanation from the control to the index group, and that the researchers admitted to adding four controls at the end of the study; nor were the interviewers blind to the diagnosis of these four additions. Quoting Ross and Pam directly, "This latter procedure is, of course, scientifically unacceptable," thus creating suspicion of investigator bias and statistical loading.[30]

SUMMARY

I hope that you are beginning to see a pattern in these studies. As researchers attempt to prove a genetic or biochemical basis for diseases such as schizophrenia, they end up with results that tend to favor an emotional pain or environmental model. Instead of admitting to such an obvious conclusion, however, it would appear that they often manipulate the data or the conclusions to favor what they hoped to find in the first place. Such inaccurate conclusions are then fed to professionals and the general public as unassailable scientific truths. In reference to the attempts to establish a genetic connection to the cause of schizophrenia, Harry Weiner, M.D., Director of Professional Information for a major pharmaceutical company states "The results of these 80 years of research are clear and indisputable: nothing has come of it to date except utter confusion."[31]

Unfortunately, if taken on face value only, the results of these studies can seem quite conclusive, fooling even the psychiatrists to whom Ross refers as having "no time to read and analyze the original literature."

CHAPTER FIVE

THE SEARCH FOR DEFECTIVE GENES

For decades, researchers have been trying to find defective genes for well established physiological disorders such as Huntington's disease, sickle-cell anemia, and Friedreich's ataxia. In 1983 a genetic marker was discovered for Huntington's disease using a new method called *genetic linkage analysis*, a technique that we will examine shortly. Even though the specific gene or genetic defect for Huntington's had not been found, the "marker" indicated the chromosome and general address where researchers might continue to search for that gene.

Ten years later, as the mapping of human genes progressed, the specific genetic defect for Huntington's disease was found. This discovery only increased the hope that genetic markers, and eventually defective genes, would be discovered for such disorders as schizophrenia, depression, hyperactivity, and the other psychiatric disorders.

In 1987 Janice Egeland, Ph.D., authored an article in *Nature* in which she claimed to have found a linkage between bipolar disease (manic depression) and a DNA marker on chromosome 11.[1] It was hoped that this marker would lead to the actual gene responsible for manic depression. In another article published in 1988, a team headed by Robin Sherrington announced that a genetic marker for schizophrenia had been found on chromosome 5.[2]

As the mapping of human genes continued, and as other genes were found for such disorders as sickle-cell anemia and Friedreich's ataxia, excitement grew over the possibility of locating the gene or genetic defect that would offer the first solid proof that psychiatric illnesses were biologically or genetically based.

Unfortunately, other studies failed to duplicate Egeland's 1987 research and, after new data from her own work failed to confirm her original results, the claim that a marker for bipolar disorder had been found on chromosome 11 had to be retracted. Eventually, for similar reasons, the claim for a genetic marker for schizophrenia on chromosome 5 was also withdrawn.

Other retractions followed these, and a pattern began to emerge. When biochemical or physiological diseases were studied—illness such as Huntington's disease or cystic fibrosis that show a definite physical and mental deterioration, often leading to death—researchers found genuine genetic markers that led to the actual gene and genetic defects behind each of these diseases. In fact, genetic tests are now available to determine who is carrying genes that cause some of these illnesses.

Just the opposite was taking place for psychiatric disorders, however. Biopsychiatrists tried to counterbalance these failures to find the genes behind mental illness by suggesting that many different genes might be involved or that different genes were responsible for different forms of the same disorder. This "new" multi-gene, multi-factor model is not valid; it's just another example of biopsychiatrists trying to hold onto a theory even as they discover evidence to the contrary.

If a marker for a true neurological disorder such as Huntington's disease eventually led to the gene responsible for the disorder, why have none of the markers for psychiatric illnesses led to the discovery of the genes that cause these disorders? Understanding the answer to this question will become increasingly important as biopsychiatry and molecular genetics continue to find a multitude of markers for psychiatric disorders in the future. The search is far from over, as can be seen in a recent issue of the *Advocate* (March/

70

April 1995), the newsletter for the National Alliance for the Mentally Ill. Two headlines in this issue read:

"Lab zeros in on mental illness gene."
"New gene linked to bipolar disorder."[3]

When we look at the actual story of the research behind such headlines, we discover that such claims are often misleading. To understand how scientists could find a "genetic marker," when further research indicates that no such gene exists, requires an explanation of the process of locating genetic markers.

GENETIC MARKERS/GENETIC LINKAGE ANALYSIS

Each human cell contains 23 pairs of chromosomes. A chromosome is a long, thin, rod-shaped chemical structure found in the nucleus or center of each cell. Each chromosome consists of DNA and carries thousands of genes along its length that are similar to the genes on the other chromosome of the pair.

A gene is a chemical piece of information that carries instructions on how to build part of an organism. Human genes contain instructions about every physical aspect of a person: what sex a baby will be, what color eyes and hair it will have and how tall it will grow. Since there are approximately one hundred thousand human genes, and since no one knows what a particular gene looks like, researchers have had a very difficult time locating the specific genes for specific traits or neurological disorders. Recent scientific advances, however, have made it possible to map particular chromosomes through a process called genetic linkage analysis.

In genetics, a linkage occurs when two genes or markers are located *measurably* close together on the same chromosome. What geneticists attempt to do in linkage studies is to find some *polymorphism*—a physical difference between individuals—such as sex, blood type, or different proteins manufactured by the body—that coincides with the occurrence of a disease.

71

For example, let's assume that a population of individuals have a sixth finger on their right hand. Suppose that within this population of six-fingered individuals, there exists a much higher incidence of a particular disease "ZZZ" than in the normal population. In such a situation, it would be logical to look for a correlation between the gene that causes the extra finger (the polymorphism or physical difference) and the "assumed" gene that causes disease ZZZ. If the correlation is high enough, researchers say they have found a linkage. Scientists can then reasonably conclude that the two genes exist in close proximity to one another on the same chromosome, as depicted in Figure 5.1.

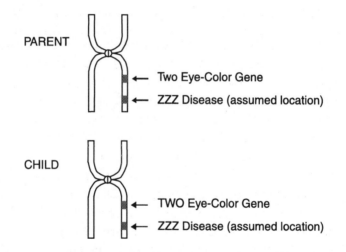

Figure 5.1: An illustration of the close proximity of a marker and genetic disease between generations.

It is perfectly logical to assume that if these two traits, sixth-finger and ZZZ disease, are passed down together from generation to generation, the genes governing these traits must be close to one another—"linked together." In the process of locating genes, scientists do not initially link defective genes directly with others, but with fragments of DNA polymorphisms created by *restriction enzymes.* Restriction enzymes are proteins that recognize a specific short sequence of DNA and biochemically clip any DNA sequence containing that exact combination of genetic material.

Geneticists use restriction enzymes as the molecular equivalent of scissors, to cut DNA into very small fragments. If a DNA fragment is found that is highly correlated with a particular disease, then scientists can safely assume that the gene for this disease is close to this DNA fragment or "marker," as shown in Figure 5.2.

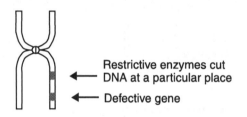

Figure 5.2:   Relationship between a restriction enzyme "marker" and a defective gene.

THE CROSSING-OVER PROCESS

Unfortunately, finding a marker that locates a *true* genetic defect is not as easy as finding an ant, then assuming that an ant colony is close by. The whole process is accomplished through a highly complicated statistical analysis. It is through this statistical process that hypothetical markers can found for psychiatric disorders, even though the actual gene may not exist. To understand why statistics are necessary when searching for markers, we must first understand the crossing-over process that results when one segment of a chromosome is exchanged for a segment of another chromosome.

There are two kinds of cell division: mitosis and meiosis. Mitosis is the ordinary somatic cell division by which the body grows, differentiates, and repairs itself. Meiosis occurs once in a lifetime in cells of the germline. It results in the formation of reproductive

73

cells: sperm and eggs.

In mitosis, two identical parts of the same chromosome split, forming two genetically identical cells. After the two new cells form, each chromosome duplicates itself, thus readying itself for the next cell division, illustrated in Figure 5.3.

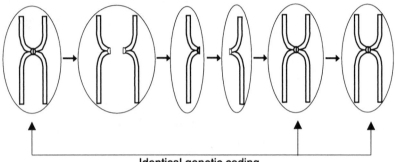

Identical genetic coding

Figure 5.3: Mitosis cell division.

In meiosis, two sets of chromosomes match up, then cross over to exchange segments of the different chromosome arms as shown by Figure 5.4.

Thus, as represented by the shaded areas, each of the two chromosomes has a new segment of genetic material from the other chromosome. As a result of this crossing-over phase, a new combination of genes or traits can be inherited from one generation to the next. It is also this crossover phase that allows scientists to find genetic markers through the help of statistics.

First of all, for a segment of DNA to be a marker, it must be located on the same chromosome as the gene. The farther the distance between the marker and the gene, however, the higher the probability that the marker will be separated from the gene during the crossover phase, as illustrated by Figure 5.5.

On the other hand, if the two genes are very close to each other, there is a tendency for them to stay together from one generation

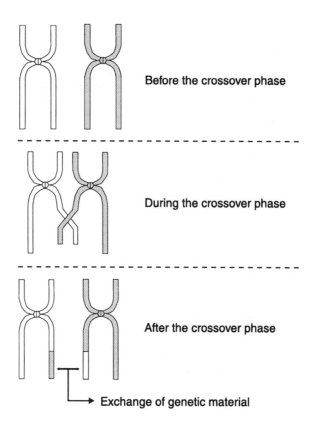

Before the crossover phase

During the crossover phase

After the crossover phase

Exchange of genetic material

Figure 5.4: Meiosis cell division illustrating the crossover phase.

to the next as shown in Figure 5.6. Thus, the closer the marker and the gene, the smaller the chance that the two will be separated during meiosis.

A common method for finding a marker and subsequent gene goes as follows: First the researchers find a multigenerational family (kindred) that has a high reoccurrence of a disease from one generation to the next. Then they begin to look for markers that are highly correlated with the individuals who have the disease.

This is where statistical analysis comes into play. If the correlation reaches a certain point, then statistically it is highly probable

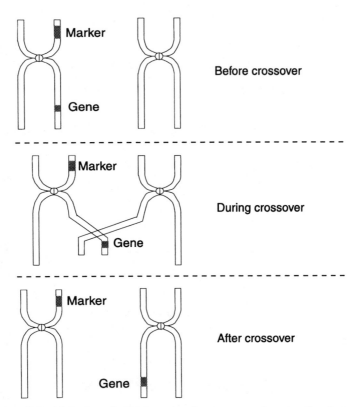

Figure 5.5: Meiosis cell division showing increased separation between a marker and a gene.

that the marker is close enough to have identified the approximate location of the gene. The actual search for the gene can now take place. With Huntington's disease, the marker was first found in 1983, but the gene itself was not located until ten years later.

When dealing with genetic linkage analysis, correlational figures are mathematically expressed in "logarithm of the odds" scores, or LOD. An LOD score of 2 is equal to 10^2, or odds of 1 in 100 that the gene has *not* been found. By convention, an LOD score of 3 or greater is considered strong evidence that a marker

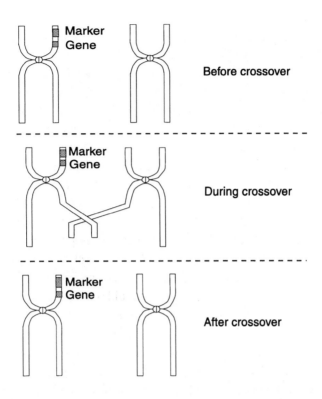

Figure 5.6: Meiosis cell division showing how a marker and gene remain "linked" together.

is linked to a gene. Let's look at how this process worked with a known genetic disorder.

FRIEDREICH'S ATAXIA

Friedreich's ataxia was first described by Nikolaus Friedreich in 1863. The symptoms usually emerge before puberty, when the child gradually begins to stagger or lurch while walking. Later on, his speech may slur and, due to muscular atrophy and weakness, his eyes may cross and his spine will probably begin to curve. Friedreich's ataxia is progressive and fatal, and, so far, no cure has been found.

The first step in locating the gene for this particular disease was to find an appropriate *kindred* to study, a very large group of family members with a clear propensity to develop a particular inherited disease. If a researcher can locate a kindred of several generations who exhibit a high incidence of the disease, this greatly increases the probability of finding markers that are close to the gene in most affected individuals. Studying a kindred can be a very difficult and tedious project. In the case of Friedreich's ataxia, it was Betty LeBlanc, a mother whose children were affected, who started the process by tracing her heritage back as many generations as possible. She started her search in the early 1980s, before the use of the DNA marker process was developed.

Because LeBlanc's heritage is Acadian, a close-knit clan of ancestors that emigrated from France to eastern Canada, and later to Louisiana, her job was easier than it would have been in the general population. Her search was complicated, however, by the fact that Friedreich's ataxia is a rare disease, difficult to diagnose, and that many individuals didn't want to discuss the disease because some people thought that the symptoms were due to syphilis.

After LeBlanc had completed her search, she turned her data over to researchers who worked on the second step, attempting to find a marker. They accomplished this by taking blood samples from the individuals in the study to help them look for a pattern. Their goal was to find a linkage between Friedreich's ataxia and ten different major blood types and twenty different proteins (polymorphisms) in blood samples whose genes had been identified. Unfortunately, they were not able to find a linkage.

One of the scientists, Susan Chamberlain, a British geneticist, had access to the newest research method, which used restriction enzymes. Instead of looking for variations in proteins, she was able to use the restriction enzyme technique to look for small variations in the DNA itself.

When Chamberlain began to test different fragments, she discovered that fragment MCT112 correlated highly with the inheritance of Friedreich's ataxia. A year after she reported her findings, another marker was found, conclusively pinning down the location of the gene for the disease. With both of these markers, statistical studies showed an LOD score of 50 (10^{50}-to-one odds) that the gene was close to the two markers.

As we have seen, once a marker is found, if it is a true genetic marker, then the search can begin for the gene that causes an illness. Once the gene has been found, a rational approach to a cure can be pursued.

Let's now take a look at the search for the gene that was hypothesized to cause bipolar disorder, also known as manic-depression.

THE SEARCH FOR A MANIC/DEPRESSIVE GENE

When Janice Egeland authored her ground-breaking article in the 1987 issue of *Nature*, she claimed to have found a linkage between bipolar disease (manic depression) and a DNA marker on chromosome 11. This claim was the result of a long and valiant effort, lasting for almost thirty years, to find the gene responsible for mania and depression.

Her search began in 1959 when, as a graduate student in medical anthropology and sociology at Johns Hopkins University, she traveled to the Old Order Amish area of Pennsylvania to do some field work. At the time, she was interested in why people chose alternative kinds of medicine.

A couple of years later, Egeland had become quite accepted by the Amish people. The bond was so close that when her father was diagnosed with leukemia, more than 500 Amish donated blood to help pay the debt left by the blood required for her father.

After noticing that some of her Amish friends suffered from emotional highs and lows, Egeland decided to write a grant proposal to study the genetics of psychopathology within this group. At first her proposal was rejected because of her lack of qualifications—she was a sociologist, not a geneticist or psychiatrist. But because of the uniqueness of the population, and because of her close ties to the Amish, the study was eventually approved by the National Institute of Mental Health (NIMH) and began in September 1976.

Her first step was to find the necessary kindred for the study. She tried to locate a few individuals who could be diagnosed as bipolar and who also might have close relatives with the same conditions. A lot of this information had to be gathered from hospital records, word of mouth, and listening to relatives talk about other relatives, especially when certain family members were no longer living. She often arrived at a house before dawn to get a chance to talk to the father before he left for work.

After four years of patient listening, Egeland located 102 individuals who showed signs of bipolar disorder. She sent the reports of her interviews, along with reports of non-bipolar individuals, to a panel of experts in diagnosing disorders to determine which ones they felt were bipolar. After she got these results, Egeland sat down with another group of consultants to determine which family had the most useful pattern to facilitate a study of potential genetic linkage. They chose one family, or pedigree, with 80 members, 19 of whom had been diagnosed as bipolar. Once Egeland had her pedigree family, she went back to the NIMH to request additional funding. Again, she was turned down at first, but later received her funding.

Grant in hand, Egeland went to work. First, she drew blood samples from her pedigree family and selected labs to search for the markers. Between 1979 and 1982 several researchers tested the Amish blood samples against 42 blood types and 17 immune system markers. They found no patterns.

Because more and more DNA fragment markers were being discovered for use in linkage studies—by 1985 over 1000 had been found—Egeland remained optimistic that one of those markers would eventually locate a gene for manic-depression. "We're closing in, and that's the exciting thing for everyone," she said, confidently.[4]

One lab, as part of the agreement to obtain access to the blood samples, had made a commitment to test for markers only on chromosome 11. After many months of searching for a marker on this chromosome, the computer gave out an LOD score of 1.7, which amounts to odds of about 50 to 1. The researchers trying to prove Egeland's theory became very excited. They were hopeful that they had discovered a possible marker, especially since a marker for Huntington's disease had just been located, with an LOD of 7. If they could find the marker, perhaps the discovery of the first gene causing a psychiatric disorder was just around the corner. Scientific reporters started showing up for interviews when they heard of the 1.7 score, but the researchers knew they needed an LOD score in excess of 3 before they could publish their results.

As a result of this encouraging score, Egeland made a decision to split the next set of samples between Yale and MIT. As the testing continued, the new samples pushed the LOD scores up toward an actual confirmation.

At this point, Egeland discovered that another member of the kindred in the study, a close friend of hers, had gone through a severe manic episode. This woman had not been previously diagnosed as bipolar. Adding this new member to the study pushed the LOD score almost to 4. When another marker was located, the LOD score now approached 5.

At this point, Egeland and her associates began to write up their results for publication. Their report, which appeared in *Nature*, was titled *Bipolar affective disorders linked to DNA markers on chromosome 11.*[5] Notice that the title implies that bipolar disorders *are* linked to a gene, even though the gene itself had yet to be found.

At this point, excitement in the scientific community was running extremely high, and Egeland and her team were making statements such as "We see this as a landmark study." "It is clear that DNA-based diagnostic procedures have a future in psychiatry," and "The next step for society will be to identify the particular gene or genes responsible."

Unfortunately, their enthusiasm was premature. In the same issue of *Nature*, two other research teams were using different populations to investigate possible linkages on chromosome 11. These teams reported that they had found no linkage between bipolar disease and this chromosome.[6] Two years later, there was still no confirmation of Egeland's study, and she and her team were no closer to finding the hoped-for gene.

In 1989 another research team was analyzing some of the Amish cell lines for another study, using some updated diagnostic information about the original pedigree. When two individuals in the control group were subsequently diagnosed as bipolar, this new information dropped Egeland's LOD score from 4.7 to 2. As Wingerson stated, "Where people had seen a gene for bipolar disorder on chromosome 11, it vanished."[7] It was at this point, with much disappointment, that Egeland's study had to be retracted. When Egeland realized how a change in the diagnosis of one or two subjects could have a major influence on LOD scores, she strongly recommended that subjects in such studies needed to be followed up indefinitely.

A similar sequence of events took place when researchers thought they had found a marker for schizophrenia on chromosome 5. In that study the LOD score ranged between 3 and 6, depending upon the conditions of the analysis. In the end, another research group was unable to confirm this study and it too was eventually retracted.

DO MENTAL ILLNESS GENES EXIST?

As you can see, it's possible for scientists to believe they have found a marker for a psychiatric disorder, even when such a "mental-illness" gene does not exist. The technique of genetic linkage analysis is currently so advanced that, if a gene for a disease actually exists, then chances are good that eventually it will be found. Yet, by the very nature of the process, it is just as easy to find markers that are later proven incorrect when statistical analysis is applied. Let's look at genetic linkage in more detail to see how this works.

As we have seen, if a gene for a particular illness exists, it will be transmitted from one generation to the next. Because there will be markers close to that gene, these markers will also be transmitted. Thus, it is only a matter of time before the right marker will be analyzed and a high LOD score will result.

This process works because markers are passed along regardless of whether or not there is a gene for a particular illness connected with them. Therefore, if a certain number of family members are diagnosed as manic-depressive, they will also inherit a similar set of markers since they all share the same basic genetic material. Just because these similar markers exist in each of the kindred and are passed along, however, does not mean that there is a gene for manic-depression.

Let's create an analogy using a trait that we are pretty sure is *not* genetically based: Republicanism. Although it's a political outlook, not a mental disorder, Republicanism can run in families. If we were to line up all the members of a kindred who have registered as Republicans, and begin looking for a marker that correlated with that characteristic, there is a good chance that we would find one. This would not necessarily be because all Republicans carry a particular gene, but because all the people in the study are related and have many genetic similarities. If the LOD score in such a study exceeds 3, then the study is publishable and everyone can start getting excited that a gene has been found for Republicanism. Right?

Actually, there could be some validity to the idea that such a gene exists. There could be a gene for a certain type of personality trait that would result in a higher percentage of individuals who carried it choosing to be Republican, just as a gene for extra emotional sensitivity could be associated with schizophrenia or depression. But that does not imply that the gene in question is defective, or that it results in a chemical imbalance that *forces* a person to choose to be a Republican.

In addition, just as one person who decides to switch from Republican to Democrat may invalidate that study, drastically dropping the LOD score, when one person in an emotionally healthy control group is suddenly diagnosed as manic-depressive, the same outcome may result.

Because markers are highly correlated among kindreds, it is always possible to find a marker for a gene that a researcher believes might exist.

In studies involving a known biological disease, however, finding a marker more often leads to a gene for that disease because there is no question that an actual physiological disease exists in the first place. We know the person is physically sick because he or she shows serious physical symptoms; and genetic diseases often lead to disability and death. With a condition such as major depression or schizophrenia, however, the symptoms can come and go. Almost everyone has experienced one or more bouts with depression, but most move out of it with time. No one moves in and out of Huntington's disease.

Remember, it was the false belief that drugs correct some defect and that mental illness seems to run in families that set up the assumption that twins and adoptive studies would show a genetic predisposition to emotional problems. When certain genetic studies were incorrectly interpreted, scientists assumed that defective genes would eventually be found.

When the public (and the professional community) sees headlines in major scientific publications that say, "Lab zeros in on mental illness gene," or "New gene linked to bipolar disorder," claiming that genes for mental illness exist, and that their discovery is only one easy step away, who can blame them for believing that such genes exist?

Remember this: just because a marker is found, it is no indication that a gene exists. Geneticists will continue to find such markers, and magazines and newspapers will continue to feature such headlines, even though there is no solid evidence that emotional disorders are genetically based. Such information is titillating and newsworthy. To date, however, there is absolutely no scientific evidence that the so-called psychiatric disorders of schizophrenia, depression, mania, ADD, obsessive/compulsive disorders, sociopathic behavior, or any others are inherited.

SEARCHING THE GLOBE

In their quest to prove that a genetic basis for emotional disorders exist, researchers have scoured the globe looking for the best populations with which to conduct studies. For example, in his book, *Genetic Prophecy*, Zsolt Harsanyi noted that scientists trying to establish a connection between genes and psychiatric diseases were in the "midst of a mad love affair with Denmark"—a small and relatively homogeneous population with a compulsive desire to keep records."[8]

When Victor McKusick set up his genetics program at Johns Hopkins University, he called the Amish families a "geneticist's dream"[9] because they were the product of the kind of inbreeding scientists produced in the laboratory when trying to analyze traits in animals and plants.

Yet after combing the world for the most ideal populations, researchers have found nothing to prove that mental illness is genetically inherited.

CHAPTER SIX

BRAIN IMAGING STUDIES

Because of the lack of any real progress in finding genetic markers and the inability to develop an adequate neurotransmitter
model, researchers searching for a biological basis for psychiatric diseases are relying increasingly on attempts to identify a
structural or functional brain abnormality. In *structural* studies,
the anatomy and physical dimensions of the brain are analyzed
and compared. The goal is to determine whether a "disease"
such as schizophrenia is characterized by a change, such as atrophy, in the structure of the brain.

In *functional* studies, on the other hand, scientists explore
how the brain works when it performs certain tasks. They accomplish this by studying the amount of blood flow through different regions of the brain and how the brain metabolizes glucose. Since glucose (sugar) is the fuel that provides brain cells
with nourishment to carry on their activities, it serves as a useful substance for identifying which parts of the brain are the most
active metabolically.

During a functional study, for example, a patient may be asked
to simply lie down and think about whatever he chooses. Researchers will then determine whether the brain of a diagnosed
mentally ill person processes glucose differently than that of a
"normal" person. Let's examine how each of these brain imaging methods work.

STRUCTURAL ABNORMALITIES

A large part of the increased enthusiasm in the field of brain imaging is due to the scientific advances of the technologies used. Current brain imaging instruments can obtain graphic representations of the living brain without having to wait for a post-mortem analysis.

The application of computerized tomography (CT) scans in 1974 and magnetic resonance imaging (MRI) scans ten years later created a massive revolution in brain structure research. Computerized tomography scans were invented by Hounsfield of Great Britain in the early 1970s. These scans work by sending an X-ray beam through the brain to a set of detectors on the other side. As the X-ray passes through the tissues of the brain, the beam is diminished (or attenuated) due to the differences in density between the different parts of the brain. A scanner reconstructs a computerized image of the brain while rotating around the brain, collecting information on its detectors.

Magnetic resonance imaging (MRI) devices produce images because cells rich in hydrogen, phosphorous, and other elements are sensitive to electromagnetic forces. The scanning is done by placing the patient inside a huge circular magnet. As the electromagnetic forces produced by the magnet cause the hydrogen atoms to move, different tissues will produce different signals, forming an image of the brain.

MRI scans have two major advantages over CT scans. MRI scans produce greater detail, and there is no risk incurred from the radiation that CT scans use to produce their images.

In *structural* studies, the area of the brain most often examined is the ventricular system. The brain contains a series of hollow, interconnecting chambers called ventricles, which are filled with cerebro-spinal fluid. Their function appears to be to help cushion the rest of the brain. The largest ventricles are the lateral ones. Because the ventricles show up vividly on imaging instruments, they serve as important structural landmarks. When parts of the brain have atrophied due to physical causes, the ventricles enlarge; therefore they serve as important indices of brain diseases.

In 1976 the first CT scan study in schizophrenia was performed by a research group led by E. C. Johnson. While examining a sample of thirteen chronically hospitalized schizophrenic patients, they found significantly larger lateral ventricles than those found in the eight normal volunteers used in the study.[1]

In the May 1995 issue of the *British Journal of Psychiatry*, S.E. Chua and P. S. McKenna reviewed and summarized the past and current research in this area. After examining all relevant studies, they stated that the most "consistently replicated brain abnormality in schizophrenia is structural, and takes the form of lateral ventricular enlargement."[2] In other words, when all the structural studies on schizophrenic brain imaging are analyzed collectively, differences are consistently found in the lateral ventricular area. When differences are found in the lateral ventricle area through the use of brain scans, the results look like those shown in Figure 6.1.

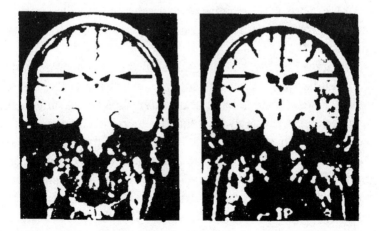

Figure 6.1: Increased lateral ventricular area in a diagnosed schizophrenic patient as illustrated by the image on the right side.

The pictures are MRI scans of identical twins. The twin on the right with the *larger* ventricle area, as pointed out by the arrows, has been diagnosed as schizophrenic. The other has not.

Judging only from the appearance of these two photos, it would be easy to conclude that something must be *wrong* with the brain on the right—the brain of the diagnosed schizophrenic person. In fact, many professionals have publicly made such a claim. In his book *Schizophrenia and Manic-Depressive Disorder*, psychiatrist E. Fuller Torrey states, "CT and MRI scans have proven conclusively that schizophrenia does change the structure of the brain."[3] Richard Keefe and Philip Harvey in their book *Understanding Schizophrenia* write, "These recent findings are exciting not only because they demonstrate that schizophrenia is a brain disease, but because they also begin to shed light on the complex way in which the brain may be diseased in someone with the illness."[4] The *Harvard Mental Health Letter* states that the clearest evidence that the size and shape of the brain associated with schizophrenia "comes from studies in which a healthy identical twin is compared with his or her schizophrenic co-twin."[5]

Yet, as with all other areas of research in mental illness, there is much controversy, with many conflicting results in the area of brain imaging.

As stated earlier, the first CT scan study of schizophrenia in 1976 did discover significant enlargement of the lateral ventricle area in subjects tested. Later scans often showed the same results, but it became increasingly clear that the degree of enlargement found in diagnosed schizophrenics was small. In fact, most of the patients had lateral ventricular dimensions within the range of the control group.[6] Furthermore, the degree of lateral ventricular enlargement in the early studies seemed to have lessened in later studies.[7,8]

Van Horn and McManus concluded that this trend could be at least partly attributed to methodological problems associated with the selection of controls.[9] For example, in 1986, when Smith and Iacono did an analysis of twenty-one studies, they made an interesting discovery. They observed that the control subjects used in studies claiming that schizophrenics had a significant amount of lateral ventricular enlargement actually had *smaller* ventricles than the controls used in the studies that *did not* find significant enlargements in the ventricles of schizophrenics. They concluded that the findings of lateral ventricular enlargement in schizophrenia had more to do with using controls who had smaller ventricles than with proving that schizophrenics had larger ones.[10]

Because the actual differences found in most of these studies are small, and because a large majority of schizophrenic patients have lateral ventricles that are within the normal size range, P. B. Jones and his research team have concluded that, at best, these findings are weak and represent a "risk factor" or "trait marker" rather than something that is of direct causal relevance.[11]

What else besides schizophrenia could cause an enlargement in the ventricles of the brain? Let's look closer. Torrey, whom I quoted earlier as believing that these studies have "proven conclusively that schizophrenia does change the structure of the brain," does leave the door open for other possibilities. In the conclusions of a study they co-authored, Torrey and his colleagues write:

> We cannot rule out the possibility that our findings may be due primarily not to the illness itself but to nonspecific aspects of schizophrenia or its treatment. For instance, affected twins differ from unaffected twins in their exposure to neuroleptic medications, history of hospitalizations, and possibly, nutritional status and level of stress.[12]

Thus the authors of the study admit that brain changes, if they exist, could be due to:

* The effects of neuroleptic medication
* Stress in the person's life
* Poor nutrition
* The effects of hospitalization

91

Breggin believes that one likely cause of the ventricular enlargements is the medication administered to people diagnosed with schizophrenia:

> The facts favor neuroleptic treatment.... All but two of the patients were receiving neuroleptics at the time of the study, and all of them had been given massive drug treatment, averaging a decade or more.[13]

Actually, Frederick Goodwin, one of the leading biopsychiatric researchers in the country, might have the most reasonable explanation for this slight shrinkage of the ventricles in some individuals. He believes this shrinkage is related to the improper functioning of the hypothalamic-adrenal-pituitary axis, resulting in the brain's inability to properly suppress cortisol.

Cortisol steroids affect water and electrolyte metabolism. In a talk on depression, Goodwin stated that elevated cortisol steroids (hypersecretion) is the most consistent biological finding in the brains of people suffering from depression.[14] In addition, individuals diagnosed as schizophrenic and manic have also demonstrated an inability to suppress cortisol.[15] In Goodwin's words, "If you have high cortisol floating around in your brain, it's likely to decrease the water content of the brain; that is, it's likely to cause the brain to shrink."[16]

Since the 1930s, researchers have known that the dysfunctioning of the hypothalamic-adrenal-pituitary axis is also associated with stress. Thus it is probable that the brain shrinkage is caused by or related to emotional stress. But the slight brain shrinkage that is sometimes found when groups of individuals are compared does not necessarily have a causal relationship to any emotional disorder. Just because someone's brain tissue has shrunk slightly due to a slight loss in the brain's ability to suppress cortisol, we can't conclude that the person's brain is malfunctioning.

The Real Problem

As with the other studies we have examined that sought to substantiate a biological cause for emotional disorders, the more researchers have tried to prove this conclusion through brain imaging, the more the evidence has pointed toward a non-biological model. This happens because, time and time again, they *start* with the assumption that schizophrenia and other disorders are brain diseases. If a study in a new area shows promising results, researchers draw the corresponding "disease" conclusion and pass this information along to the public. For example, when the study on identical twins led by Suddath seemed to support the disease model, the results were quickly publicized by the National Institute of Mental Health (NIMH). On March 22, 1990, the *New York Times* reported that this new study provided "irrefutable evidence that schizophrenia is a brain disorder."

It is not hard to imagine that some individuals, such as my client Bob, who have put stress on themselves in a consistent way over the years, and who may have had an improper diet, taken drugs on their own and/or been subjected to demeaning conditions in hospitals, might end up with a slightly different brain anatomy—one that, nevertheless, is still within the *normal* range.

In addition, a special 1992 report on mental illness published by the U. S. Congress stated that "the specificity of these findings for schizophrenia has been questioned because they also occur in normal aging and in a variety of other neurological and psychiatric conditions.[17]

In conclusion, simply finding slight ventricular enlargement does not indicate that such a difference has any effect whatsoever on the healthy functioning of the brain, or that it is linked to the symptoms of emotional disorders. Structural brain imaging studies use extremely sophisticated equipment, enabling researchers to discover minor differences in brain structure. If a researcher's goal is the discovery of evidence to support the medical model, it is only one small step to using these findings as proof of a biological cause behind mental illness.

FUNCTIONAL IMAGING STUDIES

The goal in functional imaging studies is to determine what areas in the brain are working the *hardest* and whether there are any differences in brain function between someone diagnosed as mentally ill and someone considered normal. This goal is accomplished by introducing glucose laced with a traceable radioactive substance into the brain to track how the brain uses the glucose for fuel.

Many different methods or instruments are used for these studies, including positron emission tomography (PET), regional cerebral blood flow (rCBF), single photon emission computed tomography (SPECT) and fast MRI. All these techniques are referred to as functional brain imaging, because they measure certain aspects of the brain as it is working.

PET is the most frequently used method. In PET scanning, radioisotopes and glucose are injected into a blood vessel and eventually taken up by the brain. When the most active parts of the brain begin absorbing the largest amounts of the isotopes, greater amounts of radiation will be emitted from those parts.

When an individual performs a task, an increase in the amount of glucose in a particular area should indicate the area being used. Similarly, an increase in blood flow, as measured by the rCBF method, will indicate, via the increased oxygen used to synthesize the neurotransmitters, which brain region is actively engaged.

In 1974, using a crude technique to measure cerebral blood flow, researchers D. H. Ingvar and G. Franzen published the first functional imaging studies on diagnosed schizophrenics. Even though differences in the blood flow rates between people diagnosed as schizophrenic and normals were not significant, there was evidence of a reversal in the normal pattern of flow in the brains of schizophrenics. This was accompanied by greater flow in the anterior regions than in the posterior ones. This pattern became know as hypofrontality. What it seemed to prove was that normal people tend to have the greatest brain activity in their frontal lobes—a "hyperfrontal" pattern—whereas people diagnosed as schizophrenic may have a "hypofrontal" pattern especially at rest.

Since then, over thirty functional imaging studies have been carried out on schizophrenic patients. When attempting to summarize the better designed studies, Chua and McKenna discovered that only four out of twenty of these studies found a statistically significant reduction in overall cerebral blood flow or metabolism in different regions of the brain.[18] They also noted that in most cases the differences between patients and controls were quite small—often in the range of only four to six percent.

In summarizing their results, they state:

> The rather surprising conclusion to be drawn from a considerable number of functional imaging studies is that a technique which is sensitive enough to register differences when the eyes are opened and closed, reveals no differences between schizophrenic patients and normal individuals. In particular, hypofrontality, or more precisely hypofrontality under resting conditions, does not seem to characterize schizophrenia as a disorder: positive findings are greatly outnumbered by negative ones and the two largest studies, one of them by a group including the staunchest advocates of hypofrontality over the years, seem if anything to point to the decidedly less interesting finding of hyperoccipitality.[19]

In spite of the researchers' doubts, however, they still leave the door open to some possible differences between the brains of diagnosed schizophrenics and normals. If there is any evidence at all for hypofrontality, this trait does seem to be associated with the negative symptoms of schizophrenia—withdrawal, extreme apathy, or catatonic behavior—versus the positive or more expressive symptoms of hallucinations and delusions.

In addition, the authors state that there may be evidence of hypofrontality when the "prefrontal cortex is challenged with a cognitive task."[20] Yet, studies by P. F. Liddle, C. D. Frith and co-workers, using the most sensitive functional imaging techniques and highly sophisticated methodology, tend to show no evidence of hypofrontality.[21,22]

Chua and McKenna finally concluded that schizophrenia may not be characterized by reductions in certain regional brain activity, but by "complex alterations in normal reciprocal patterns of activation between anatomically related areas of the cerebral cortex."[23]

If we use Bob as an example, we might see why the brain of a diagnosed schizophrenic might be working differently from that of a normal or showing some differences, if indeed these differences do exist. If we were to observe Bob from a distance, standing frozen against the wall or sitting in a catatonic stupor, we might assume that something is wrong with his brain. If we tested him, we might see that his brain is metabolizing glucose differently than the brains of so-called normals—especially since the symptoms he is displaying are characterized as the negative symptoms of schizophrenia.

Yet we know what Bob is thinking when he is in these states; we know that his mind is actually working overtime, stuck on the simplest cognitive task of figuring out whether he closed the door correctly, entered the door correctly, etc. Therefore, the extremely small differences that we have found in his brain don't necessarily indicate that his brain is "diseased," but could be explained by how Bob *chooses* to use his mind to take care of himself.

When I asked Fred A. Baughman Jr., M.D., a retired neurologist who is using his free time to stay up with the literature on brain imaging, to critique this chapter, he stated that it is important to remember that,

> Hypofrontality seen in a functional study is functional, not pathologic. It may be secondary to a brain disease—pathologic—but can be functional or physiologic due to how the brain is being used.[24]

He made this notation on the manuscript adjacent to the paragraph above, about Bob. In other words, any degree of hypofrontality that could be measured in someone like Bob can be the result of something pathological or simply "how the brain is being used." Not taking the time to understand Bob's behavior, biopsychiatry chooses the first assumption.

When you boil down all the brain imaging studies, here is what you have left. In structural studies, some studies have been able to show a slight enlargement in the ventricular areas of the brain. In functional studies, some individuals diagnosed as mentally ill might be using different parts of their brains in different ways than "normals." But none of these very slight differences, determined by highly sophisticated equipment, can actually prove that the brain is working in a defective way. All that these studies ultimately say is that people under emotional stress, who may be using highly potent drugs, on very inadequate diets, feeling very isolated from society, might have certain slight differences in their brains. In reality, what these instruments are most likely doing is simply measuring how the brain adjusts to internalized emotional stress.

SUMMARY OF THE MEDICAL MODEL

Even though billions of dollars have been spent on research, and even though there are hundreds of biochemical theories pertaining to what causes mental illness, we can now reduce the results of these studies down to very simple terms:

* Psychiatric medication does not correct a chemical imbalance; it works to disable the emotional-cognitive aspects of the human mind.
* Pedigree or family studies do not give evidence of a genetic inheritance and, in fact, when analyzed properly, point toward an environmental explanation.
* Genetic markers may continue to be found, but this is no proof that defective genes exist.

97

* Brain scans in schizophrenia have only shown consistent differences in the lateral ventricle area. Those *small* differences,
which often fall within the *normal* range of human brain
anatomy, could easily be due to stress, diet, drugs, or other
factors.

Remember, the conclusions stated above are not based on my
opinions, but on results and data that derive mainly from researchers who start from a position of believing in the medical model. In
their massive 20-page journal article titled "Schizophrenia-a Brain
Disease?" Chua and McKenna not only summarize all the brain
imaging studies, but also give us a great summary of the biological
model. In their opening paragraph, in reference to schizophrenia,
they state: "There has been no identification of any underlying causal
pathology."[25]

Even though they admit that *nothing has been found*, they go on
to state that the shift away from the environmental model to the
biological model can be traced to two basic findings:

1. The hereditary contribution.
2. The antipsychotic effect of neuroleptic drugs.

As summarized in this chapter, they report that the only "well-
established structural abnormality" is in the largest ventricle area.
Furthermore, because of the conflicting and overlapping results, it
is most "unlikely" that there is any causal relationship between ventricle enlargement and schizophrenia.

The Chua and McKenna article was published in 1995 in the
well-respected *British Journal of Psychiatry*. By Chua and
McKenna's own admission, biopsychiatrists have found *nothing* to
substantiate a physiological cause of mental illness, but
biopsychiatrists continue to believe in the medical model based on
an unproven heredity factor and an incorrect cause-and-effect relationship between the symptoms of mental illness and the effects of
drugs.

In a concluding statement, Dr. Baughman also stated that:

First, psychiatry, having failed to validate any of its "diseases" as diseases (organic, physical) nonetheless rushes to apply new physical technology to its studies. Now and then there are positive findings. The problem is, however, there is no certainty of physical similarities between subjects, none having been identified clinically, biochemically, or pathologically. This is why organic research goes on and on and on never proving anything, *weaving* illusions of disease and biology. This is also why the drug industry funds biological research overwhelmingly.[26]

For the sake of our society, our children, and our own emotional health, it is time to push the medical model aside and take an honest look at the emotional pain model.

CHAPTER SEVEN

PHILIPPE PINEL, PETER BREGGIN, AND SIGMUND FREUD

The best way to begin moving away from a biologically based model for emotional disorders and placing our attention where it should be, on the person's emotional pain, is to look at three prominent figures in psychiatry. The first two, Philippe Pinel and Peter Breggin, helped bring truth to a proper understanding of mental illness by reaching out in a courageous way to help the so-called mentally ill. We will look at Sigmund Freud because he also tried to reach out to help the emotionally troubled, but did not go far enough because he was swayed by his peers. In the end, he backed down from his core beliefs about the emotional foundations of mental illness and brought considerable confusion to its study.

PHILIPPE PINEL (1745-1826)

Philippe Pinel was the first person to make a significant impact on how the mentally ill were perceived and treated. During the Middle Ages there was a return to the belief in demonology as the cause of mental illness, and those suffering from these maladies were believed to be possessed. This belief led to the practice of witch hunting in the fifteenth century. Floods, pestilence, bad crops, miscarriages, and even lame horses were often blamed on whatever hapless individual in the village happened to be acting a little strange at the time. Since people who suffer from emotional disorders often feel overwhelmed with guilt, many were willing to confess to whatever crimes they were charged with. Others were tortured until they confessed their involvement with the "devil." It is conservatively estimated that from the middle of the fifteenth century to the end of the seventeenth, one hundred thousand people were executed as witches—many of them hanged and burned in town squares.[1]

In the eighteenth century, with the birth of rational science, witch hunting began to die out. During the Renaissance a number of hospitals for the mentally ill were founded in various cities. Unfortunately, the conditions within such "asylums" made the execution of witches seem almost merciful in comparison. Patients lay howling in chains while the curious public bought tickets to go in and watch them "perform." In addition, patients were caged, starved, preyed upon by rats, and left for years lying naked in their own excrement.

It was at this time in history that Philippe Pinel entered the scene. The chief physician at La Bicetre, a large asylum in Paris, Pinel held to a simple position: that the mentally ill were all ordinary human beings who had been deprived of their reason by severe personal problems; and that treating them like animals was not only inhumane but also obstructive to their recovery.

Pinel managed to convince the French government to unchain a group of patients, many of whom had not seen the light of day for forty years. With lame legs, their lungs unaccustomed to fresh air, their eyes dazzled by the sunlight, these patients hobbled out awestruck into a world that had all but forgotten them. Pinel's experiment with freeing these people succeeded far beyond his hopes. Not only did the patients become more manageable, but many recovered and were released. Instead of prescribing such treatments as bloodletting, Pinel spent long hours talking with them, listening to their problems and giving them comfort and advice.

During the same time, William Tuke, a Quaker, attempted similar reforms in northern England. Tuke began moving a group of mental patients to a peaceful rural estate where they could talk out their problems, work, pray, rest, and take walks.

Though vigorously resisted by their colleagues, Pinel's and

Tuke's techniques eventually became widespread under the name of *moral therapy*. This treatment was based upon the idea that the mentally ill were simply ordinary people with extraordinarily over-whelming problems. Most importantly, the aim of this therapy was to treat patients like human beings.

These two men were pioneers in showing that those diagnosed as mentally ill could be healed quite successfully through nonmedical means. This approach became highly successful, and at least 70% of those hospitalized for a year or less either improved or actually recovered.[2]

Let's take a look at a more recent figure.

PETER BREGGIN (1935-)

Psychiatrist Peter Breggin is an important modern figure because he is the most visible professional fighting the bio-psychiatric system today. His life is especially interesting because it parallels the lives of so many others who have come to understand the fallacy behind the medical model.

Breggin's pilgrimage started in 1954 when he was a freshman at Harvard. There a friend talked him into joining a volunteer group of Harvard and Radcliffe students who wanted to give some of their time to a local state mental hospital.

When they first entered the hospital (especially the back wards), these students were shocked. Breggin describes the patients as "undernourished, silent, stone-faced with sunken eyes. They would sit in corners or pace about. Some talked to themselves but absolutely no one socialized with anyone else. It was as if each was ashamed and afraid of the others."[3]

Breggin recounts that the volunteers spent the day trying to talk to the patients with little success. Then at the end of the day, as they were about to leave, some of the patients suddenly responded, begging the volunteers to stay. Some even said, "I don't belong here." Breggin remembers looking at the facility and saying to himself, "Nobody belongs at Metro State."[4]

As the volunteer program grew, Breggin soon became one of its leaders. One day, as he complained to the staff about the near-freezing conditions in the winter and the sweltering temperatures in the summer, he was told, "Schizophrenics aren't bothered by extremes of heat and cold the way normal people are."[5] Breggin says that, even thought he was just 18, such statements didn't make sense to him.

In fact, most of what he saw and was told by the doctors he spoke with and his psychiatric professors at Harvard didn't make sense. Breggin had begun his medical studies a year or two before the first neuroleptic drugs were tried, and vividly remembers the inhumane treatments that were then in vogue. He recalls the insulin coma room where rows of patients were purposely overdosed with insulin, causing a drop in their blood sugar until they fell into convulsions and a coma from starvation of the brain. In Breggin's words:

> As I watched them writhe about on mats, near death, it seemed like a scene from hell. I watched them being fed sugar and orange juice, to awaken into a state of fear and confusion. The once difficult and unruly inmates, with their brains now permanently damaged, became gratefully dependent on their keepers after being brought back from the edge of death.[6]

When he questioned the procedure, Breggin was told by staff psychiatrists that both electro-shock and insulin shock killed bad brain cells. He knew from his own personal reading in psychiatric text books that no physical defect or bad cells had ever been discovered to cause mental illness. This led him to honestly wonder why doctors would "make up stuff like that?" Breggin saw no mystery in what made these treatments work. They worked by damaging the brain.

Upset with asylum living conditions and with treatments such as insulin and shock therapy, the volunteers began to transform the hospital. Realizing that the more violent patients were most likely reacting to the violence done to them by the staff, Breggin and another volunteer stole the keys one day and took half of the women's violent ward for a trip into town. "We gave them money to buy trinkets in the local five-and-ten and returned them to the hospital without incident. They appreciated us and would do nothing to get us into trouble."[7]

The volunteers concentrated their efforts, painting and cleaning up the ward as much as possible. As a sophomore, Breggin approached the superintendent with a plan. He and a dozen or so others volunteers wanted to be assigned one patient each for a whole year to see what happened.

The superintendent became outraged, feeling insulted that freshmen and sophomores would think they could treat backward schizophrenics. With a little political maneuvering, Breggin got the superintendent's approval, but the president of the Boston Psychoanalytic Society protested, stating that without extensive training, these untrained students could harm and even ruin the patients. Eventually, however, fourteen volunteers were given some of the older, more chronic patients.

By the end of the year, eleven of the fourteen patients had been released from the hospital. By the end of two years, only three had returned. Breggin states that these were far better results than those later achieved by trained professionals working in conjunction with psychiatric drugs.

> We accomplished this "miracle" by showing our patients care and attention; by talking with them and taking them for walks, by helping them get properly fitted for eyeglasses, false teeth, or clothing, by reacquainting them with their forgotten families, or by connecting them with more humane supervised facilities outside the hospital.[8]

The program proved so successful that Breggin convinced The Department of Social Relations at Harvard to turn the volunteer project into an official undergraduate course.

It was at this very time (1955) that Breggin also saw drugs introduced into the hospital. He saw firsthand the contrast between the many patients who were "becoming alive" through the work of the volunteers and the "robotic indifference" and "less reachable" condition of those taking psychiatric medication.

As he left the volunteer program to concentrate more on his studies, he found himself wondering why his profession was so set on using drugs instead of humane solutions such as the efforts of volunteers. Though he had seen first-hand the healing effects of love and affirmation, Breggin said that "after I entered my medical and psychiatric training, I would never hear another word about the importance of love in helping people through their helplessness and despair." Instead, he was taught that people had diseases.

Once out of medical school, with the completion of his psychiatric residency behind him, Breggin had plans to settle into a nice private practice in an upper-middle class, professional area. He thought his advocacy days were behind him.

Then in the 1970s he came across an article in *Psychiatric News* saying that lobotomy and psychosurgery were coming back, and that a recent international conference had been held in Copenhagen. With some investigation, he found out that an international effort was going on to revive psychosurgery. He also discovered that two Harvard surgeons and a psychiatrist were receiving funds from the federal government to study this method, believing that psychosurgery might be the answer to ghetto rioting, which they assumed was due to brain disease in African-American rioters. These surgeons were not yet operating on any Black people, but Breggin did learn that other surgeons were operating on Black children in Mississippi to control aggression. With this information, support from several groups and support from the African-American community, Breggin helped stop the resurgence of psychosurgery in this country.

When the effects of tardive dyskinesia, the brain disease caused by neuroleptics, became known, Breggin and others got involved with a group of psychiatric survivors who were committed to political lobbying on this issue.

In 1987, Breggin's license came under attack as the result of his appearance on the "Oprah Winfrey Show." The show, which focused on institutional abuse, featured Breggin and three survivors of psychiatric abuse. The American Psychiatric Association (APA) and National Alliance for the Mentally Ill (NAMI) were angered by some of his remarks and tried to force Oprah into giving them their own rebuttal show. Oprah refused, asking them instead to have someone debate Breggin.

Breggin ended up debating Paul Fink, the head of the APA at the time. Fink also brought along one of his patients, who cursed Breggin for his position. Breggin brought along Judi Chamberlin, a psychiatric survivor, who is now on staff at Boston University. In Breggin's words, "We demolished them, and the result was that they got so angry that they brought charges against my medical license in the state of Maryland."[9]

NAMI brought the charges, claiming that Breggin had told patients on Oprah to stop taking drugs. He had only urged that people not start taking the drugs and instead find a therapist who loved and cared about them. Breggin was finally exonerated, and, in the end, the licensure committee apologized to him, actually thanking him for his contribution to mental health in Maryland.[10] Shortly after that, Breggin published his classic book *Toxic Psychiatry*.

Breggin, along with his wife, Ginger, and others, has recently formed an organization called Children First! Center for the Study of Psychiatry. This center is the only national program that focuses on the dangers of biopsychiatric interventions into the lives of children and youth, and supports and educates people about more caring alternatives.

Sigmund Freud (1856-1939)

Both Pinel and Breggin exercised great courage in bringing the truth of mental illness to light during their time. Pinel insisted that the mentally ill were simply ordinary individuals suffering from severe personal problems. Breggin believes much the same, and fights against the notion that people become emotionally troubled because of some unknown biological defect. Sigmund Freud was originally on the same path as Pinel and Breggin, but he bowed to intense pressure, ultimately denying and covering up his original findings.

Even through Freud originally believed that mental illness would eventually be explained from a neurological or biological basis, early in his career, he did come close to presenting a nearly *pure* violational or emotional pain model as the root cause. On April 21, 1896, he presented a paper entitled "The Aetiology of Hysteria" to his colleagues at the Society for Psychiatry and Neurology in Vienna. He started his talk with the provocative announcement "Gentlemen, Stones do speak. I have discovered the 'source of the Nile' of psychopathology. I have discovered the origin of human misery."[11] He then proceeded to reveal his findings: that the origin of neurosis was in early *sexual* traumas.

Freud based these claims squarely on what some of his patients were telling him. Many who exhibited the most severe symptoms had shared stories of childhood sexual abuse, often by their fathers. He called his idea the "seduction theory" because he believed that these early experiences were real, and that the damaging results had a lasting effect upon the lives of the children who suffered from them.

A year later, however, Freud had changed his position. He now believed that the traumas that his patients were reporting were fantasies of hysterical women who invented stories and told lies. As a result of this new position, he eventually developed his famous Oedipal complex and his insistence that sexual difficulties were the basis of all neurosis. He also claimed that these women patients had made up their stories because they envied the penises of their fathers. With this statement, Freud turned his back on the issue of sexual abuse, creating his psychoanalytic theories as a substitute for truth. Seeing how and why Freud made this switch will help us better understand the ongoing enthusiasm behind the medical model and the resistance to the development of an emotional pain model.

FREUD AND FLIESS

To properly understand Freud's developing psychoanalytic model and the choice he made to stop believing the accounts of his patients, it is necessary to understand his relationship with his colleague, Wilhelm Fliess, and their interaction with Freud's patient, Emma Eckstein.

When Freud first met Fliess in 1887, Fliess was a Berlin nose-and-throat specialist. Between 1894 and 1900 they became very close friends. During this period, the two men corresponded frequently and exchanged manuscripts, sharing their medical ideas and preliminary versions of forthcoming scientific publications.

Both men were also united by their common scientific interest in "abnormal" forms of sexuality, mainly masturbation and difficulties during menstruation. As Freud started to uncover his own psychological findings pertaining to his study of hysteria, he began depending upon Fliess to help him find and explain the *physiological* basis for such disorders. Because Freud was trained as a neurologist and believed that all psychiatric disorders would ultimately be explained from a biological basis, he sought Fliess's help, even as Freud was turning away from the biological model and developing his concept of the *unconscious*.

During this time Fliess was occupied with collecting "scientific evidence" to support his effort to create an "exact biology" of mental illness—a term he later used to describe his theories. His main thesis, which Freud urged him to publish, was based upon what he called "reflex neurosis," a set of complex clinical entities that flowed from the nose.

Fliess believed that symptoms such as pains in the head, shoulders, arms, and stomach originated from either organic disturbances within the nose itself, various infectious diseases, or from disturbances associated with the human reproductive system. He even claimed that there was a special physiological link between the nose and the genitalia localized in certain "genital" spots inside the nasal passages! Under his system, painful menstruation and painful childbirth were pathological conditions caused by the malfunction of these so-called genital spots. To provide clinical proof for this belief, Fliess cited such evidence as the visible swelling of the nose's turbinate bone during menstruation and the nosebleeds that often accompany menstruation and pregnancy.

Fliess' remedy involved a three-step approach. First, he attempted to relieve the symptoms by anesthetizing the patient with cocaine. Next, he attempted to cauterize the spots in the nose by means of a wire heated by a galvanic current. The last approach was to use surgery to drill out the turbinate bone, the area that swelled most during menstruation.

Even though Fliess was a very powerful and influential doctor in his time, in later generations his work was judged as a "well-developed form of pseudoscience." Professionals reflecting back on his work used such terms as "overvaluation of an idea," "psychopathological," "mystical," and "crackpottery" to describe Fliess and his theories.[12]

It is very likely that Freud was attracted to Fliess's ideas because, during that period, Freud was working with individuals suffering from hysteria and trying to build a bridge between psychological symptoms and physiology.

In the nineteenth century, the word *hysteria* came into vogue as a label for a wide variety of emotional disorders usually applied to women. The root word *hyster* is Greek for womb, hence the word hysterectomy. Individuals suffering from hysteria might show high emotional excitability, but it is the accompanying organic disorders such as blindness, deafness or paralysis that make the disorder so puzzling.

For example, I remember a case in which a woman with a growing desire to kill her abusive husband suffered from paralysis in her arm. Afraid that she might kill him, her subconscious mind came to her rescue and made her unable to move that appendage. Another example would be a person who witnesses a terrible crime and goes blind as a consequence of blocking out the memory.

Since hysteria had such obvious physical symptoms, and since psychiatry was just evolving out of neurology, many doctors felt the need to prove that there was a biological basis for hysteria.

Freud was caught right in the middle of this dilemma. He obviously wanted to hold onto a neurological/biological model, in spite of his discovery of the nature of the unconscious, and began to cling to Fliess for support. Writing about their relationship, Sulloway states:

> Freud's acceptance of Fliess's bizarre theories has thus been attributed to their strong personal friendship, which was not without an obvious neurotic side as well... both Freud's neurosis and his peculiar intellectual and emotional dependence upon Fliess in the 1890s have been rationalized as by-products of his pioneering efforts to explore the often "terrifying" depths of his own unconscious mind during this same period. His relationship to Fliess is therefore to be seen as a prototypic "transference relationship," in which Freud relived, in his attitude toward this convenient father substitute, the early dependence and latent hostility of his unconscious Oedipus complex.[13]

Eventually, all these elements came together to influence Freud's psychoanalytic model and his denial of child abuse.

THE OPERATION THAT CHANGED THE COURSE OF HISTORY

It was at this time that Freud began seeing Emma Eckstein. His work with this patient changed the course of history, in an unfortunate way.

When she was about 20, Emma entered analysis with Freud. Not much is known about her history, except that she suffered from stomach ailments, problems with menstruation, masturbation, and difficulties in walking. During Christmas of 1894, Fliess was visiting Freud and met Emma. When he suggested that surgery on her nose might help ease her symptoms, Freud agreed. Fliess believed that women who masturbate outside of marriage are generally dysmenorrheal (suffering from painful menstruation) and that the only cure was a nose operation to help them to "give up this bad practice."[14]

Much of the information that follows came from letters that were written between Freud and Fliess, most of them discovered by Jeffrey Masson when he was in charge of the Freud Archives. In 1984 Masson published his account of this period of Freud's life in his book *The Assault On Truth*.[15]

After Emma's operation, severe complications arose. Freud wrote Fliess a letter dated March 4, 1895, reporting that Emma was suffering from major swelling, pain, and hemorrhaging, and that he had removed two bowlfuls of pus from her nose. Freud also said that he had called in another doctor by the name of Robert Gersuny, who inserted a drainage tube into Emma's nose and threatened to break the bone open if the tube did not stay in. Freud ends his letter to Fliess with the words, "Please send me your authoritative advice. I am not looking forward to new surgery on this girl."[16]

A few days later Freud wrote Fliess again to give him an update and to warn him that what he was about to write might upset him. He writes that when Emma's "profuse bleeding" started again, he attempted to call in the doctor who had inserted the tube. When Gersuny was not available, Freud called in another doctor, an old friend named Ignaz Rosanes. As Rosanes was cleaning out Emma's nose, he ran across a thread that he began pulling on. Out came a half meter (twenty inches) of gauze that Fliess had left in, then a flood of blood. The next day Gersuny, who put the tube in, broke the bone and repacked Emma's nose. Freud shares in his letter to Fliess that he believed she was not "abnormal," strongly implying that she did not need the operation in the first place, and that they had done her an "injustice." If it had not been for the quick intervention of other doctors, Emma most likely would have died.

It is at this point that Freud begins to revise his own theories about mental illness, perhaps in an effort to protect his relationship with his friend, mentor, and father figure. In Freud's next few letters to Fliess, there are hints that he is already searching for a way to *blame* Emma for the hemorrhaging. Freud writes that she is almost well, but that he must now start treating her for her "nightly hysterical attacks." "It is now about time you forgave yourself the minimal oversight [of leaving in the cotton wadding],"[17] he tells Fliess comfortingly.

Quoting from another of Freud's letters, Masson writes:

The powerful tool that Freud was discovering, the psychological explanation of physical illness, was being pressed into service to exculpate his own dubious behavior and even more dubious behavior of his closest friend. Freud has begun to explain away his own bad conscience.[18]

A few days later Emma's situation worsens to the point that Freud believes she will die. Again she is operated on, this time leaving her face permanently disfigured. For a few days she seems to be doing better, then she regresses once more to a serious state. In his next letter to Fliess, Freud appears angry: "I am really very shaken that such a mishap could have arisen from the operation which was purported to be harmless."[19]

Later Freud once more backs down and begins to prepare the grounds for diagnosing Emma as hysterical. In another letter to Fliess, Freud refers to Emma as "my tormentor and yours." When he writes, "Eckstein once again is in pain; will she be bleeding next?"[20] he is clearly inferring that she is somehow intentionally causing the bleeding due to repressed wishes, not because of the mistakes of an unskilled surgeon.

Fliess' failed operation had painted Freud into a corner. If he admitted to himself that Emma's hysteria was actually based upon abuse in her early life, then the operation was unnecessary and the post-surgical complications and bleeding would have to be blamed on Fliess' medical incompetence. Freud's dilemma was further complicated by the fact that his own clinical work on hysteria and hypnosis was already forcing him to depart from Fliess' more "pure" biological model. If he were to affirm both these positions, that Emma was suffering from the effects of childhood abuse and that hysteria had emotional, not biological, causes, it would be necessary for him to reject Fliess, giving up his dependency on this mentor.

Masson believes that Freud's only solution to this painful personal quandary was to seek "the cause of the bleeding in Emma Eckstein herself."[21] To accomplish this, he would need to construct his theory of "hysterical lying, a theory whereby the external traumas suffered by the patient never happened, but are fantasies."[22] To get himself out of his corner, Freud decided that Emma's bleeding had nothing to do with the operation, but was the result of her hysterical imagination; and, he decided, if her imagination could generate physical symptoms such as post-operative bleeding, it was also probably generating fantasies and stories about her childhood. In this manner, Freud solved his dilemma by blaming the victim, Emma, for her own problems. He no longer had to take the blame for her recent suffering. In addition, he could let his friend Fliess off the hook.

On May 4 Freud explains more of his emerging theory in another letter.

> So far I know only that she bled out of *longing*. She has always been a bleeder... When she saw how affected I was by her first hemorrhage... she experienced this as the realization of an old wish to be loved in her illness.... Then, in the sanitarium, she became restless during the night because of an unconscious wish to entice me to go there, and since I did not come during the night, she renewed the bleedings, as an unfailing means of rearousing my affection.[23]

In another letter, dated June 4, 1896, Freud writes "Her story is becoming even clearer; there is no doubt that her hemorrhages were due to wishes."[24]

The series of events finally overwhelmed him. Emma's operation took place around the first of March, 1895. Freud wrote one of his first letters of concern to Fliess on March 4, 1895. On April 21, 1896, Freud presented his thesis associating neurosis with child abuse, only to be soundly rejected by his peers. On May 4, 1896,

Freud begins to explain his new theory to Fliess. In a letter dated June 4, 1896, he states that Emma's hemorrhaging was due to her wishes. If hysterical individuals can develop blindness and paralysis from subconscious wishes, then why not hemorrhaging?

It is impossible to know the kind of pressure that Freud endured as he began to face the truth of the origin of emotional disorders. For thousands of years, the symptoms associated with mental illness had, in one way or another, been blamed on the mentally ill. For Freud, it was just too big of a jump to blame some of these disorders on the abuse of others. In 1905 Freud publicly retracted his seduction theory and put forth his psychoanalytic theory. By 1908 many respected psychiatrists had followed him, thus giving birth to the psychoanalytic movement.

WHAT CAN FREUD'S STORY TELL US?

What do we need to learn from these three men? Both Pinel and Breggin, by getting to know their patients personally, and becoming close enough to them to feel their pain, began to see the truth behind their often bizarre behavior. Out of a simple act of caring, affirmation, and the unconditional love of their patients' basic humanity, both Pinel and Breggin created results that amazed the professionals of their day.

Freud started on the same path, listening to his patients and beginning to see a definite connection between their emotional pain and their corresponding symptoms. To stand by what he believed, however, he would have had to give up a great deal. It would have become necessary for him to embrace the belief that there was no biological or neurological basis for mental illness, confront the issue of child abuse, and give up his own need for a father-authority figure in his life. When his peers began to reject him as a colleague, ceasing to send him referrals, his courage and convictions began to dwindle. Freud chose to solve his dilemma by blaming Emma. After all, she was the one with the "crazy" symptoms.

Like so many professionals before him who were in denial about the basic emotional pain model, Freud became stuck between two "fault-finding" models, vacillating between:

* Blaming the patient by claiming that the symptoms were the result of subconscious wishes, or
* Blaming the symptoms on a biologically broken brain.

Instead of finding the courage to address the issue of child abuse, at the same time facing his own personal issues surrounding his need for a supportive father figure, Freud created a psychoanalytic model that allowed him to place the blame on Emma.

Freud was a brilliant and dedicated doctor who, to do him justice, *did* stress the role of the subconscious and early childhood trauma. But he stopped short, as Masson claims, "to explain away his own bad conscience."

In a way, the emotional pain model is the easiest model to understand. It has three main premises or core issues:

1. We all hurt each other at times, both unintentionally and intentionally.
2. We all need others to heal those hurts.
3. We all deny to some extent how we hurt others, and how we need others to heal our hurts.

People create exotic theories about the causes of strange behavior and emotional disorders, because it's too uncomfortable to admit our basic human need for each other, and because we don't like to face the fact that we can hurt and be hurt by our fellow humans.

Abuse does occur in some families, and many children suffer emotionally as a result. But abuse also occurs outside of the family, often in very subtle ways. It is the emotional pain of being a vulnerable human being that results in emotional disorders, and we need a model that starts at this point. We do not need models that start from a position of hysterical lying, a chemical imbalance in the brain,

116

or a defective gene.

It's time to take the courage that others have shown and move forward, taking an honest look at the human condition. Let's not hide any longer behind our fancy theories and our often abusive cures. Let's learn what it takes to attend to and heal wounded hearts.

PART TWO

THE EMOTIONAL PAIN MODEL

CHAPTER EIGHT

THE EMOTIONAL PAIN MODEL—AN
INTRODUCTION

To a gain proper understanding of the origin of emotional disorders we must start, not with our biology, not with our instincts, but with that which makes us unique as human beings. As we examine emotional disorders, the most relevant factors are: (1) human consciousness, and (2) the intensity of how we feel pain. Let's look closer.

THE INTENSITY OF EMOTIONAL PAIN

Perhaps the most denied aspect of what makes human beings unique is the intensity with which we feel pain, particularly emotional pain. Whether it be an infant emerging from the womb, a child not getting his way, or an adult losing a loved one, pain can come suddenly. In some cases it has the potential to destroy us emotionally, quickly slicing to the very core of our being.

Some friends of mine recently lost their oldest son to an overdose of cocaine. Three months before graduating from college with honors, the son wanted to try it just once to see how it felt. Although he was a clean-cut young man who hardly ever took a drink, he had a congenital heart problem. That, coupled with the use of the drug, is probably what killed him.

When his parents found out about his death, the shock of the news stung them and was felt in every nerve of their bodies. As hard as their natural psychological defenses tried to help them minimize the intensity of that pain, these defenses were not strong

119

enough to protect them from it.

Not only do such experiences give us intense pain, both emotionally and physically, they also cause us to feel a violation of our selfhood, our very identity or sense of self. The father especially, struggled with his son's death in terms of his own responsibility. "What did I do wrong in raising him?" "What could I have done to better be there for him?" "Should I have called him more, visited him more?" "Did he die because I was not a good father?"

I know that my friend was a caring and responsible father, but the death of his son made him seriously question his self-worth. So much of who he was as a person, how he saw and defined himself, was wrapped up in the image of himself as father and the protector of his family. In an instant, a major part of his identity was destroyed.

Our vulnerability to pain has its origin in human consciousness. Because we have the ability to be consciously aware and to *invest* our hearts into whatever we choose to focus upon, we have the potential to open ourselves up to becoming deeply hurt. As we make such conscious choices and expose ourselves, the choices become a part of our total selfhood.

It is not simply that we are conscious beings. As we choose to be aware, we can't help but invest ourselves or our sense of self into our choices. As a result, each choice becomes a part of our identity, our self-worth, our overall view of ourselves and life.

For example, when a child enters a store and sees a toy that he likes, he invests part of his heart in it. He "falls in love with" that toy to a certain degree. He chooses to develop a bond with it based upon how it may make him happy or bring meaning to his life.

When his parents tell him that he can't have it, especially when he is young and does not yet have a strong set of defenses to deaden that pain, he can feel the hurt of the loss slice all the way through him. As a result, he may cry out in deep distress, and even act angry to defend himself from the suffering that he is feeling.

We, as adults, may not think there would be that much pain associated with the loss of a toy, but to a child there is. The loss is heavily felt, not just because the child's defenses are not yet adequately developed, but mainly because he placed the innocence of his heart into what he wanted. At that moment his whole world, his immediate future, was wrapped up in possessing that toy. Wanting and having this toy and the meaning (to him) that went along with the toy becomes a part of his selfhood at that moment.

Consequently, the process of maturing is often the process of learning how to best invest our hearts, our joy, and our dreams into meaningful projects, while also developing the ability to absorb life's painful moments. We never want to lose our creative, enthusiastic energy for living, but we also must learn to deal with our pain so that we don't feel the raw hurt that a child does over the loss of smaller things.

Nevertheless, when adults who are invested in their world experience great losses, the overwhelming pain that they experience can bring on the classic symptoms defined as mental illness. Extreme depression is often the result of a great loss. A person whose marriage breaks up, or whose parent dies, or who loses his or her job, can feel immobilized by the pain, drained of all energy. If the person chooses to live in denial of the enormity of such a loss, he can become increasingly manic or delusional. He may attempt to trick himself into not believing in the loss, or in believing that he will succeed the next time.

If a person loses a loved one, as did my friend who lost his son, he could even begin to hallucinate, hearing and seeing the person he has lost in an attempt to "keep him alive" to avoid dealing with the deepest level of pain associated with the loss.

If a person's marriage or love relationship breaks up, she may experience anxiety and/or panic attacks when she thinks about the possibility of seeing her "ex" at church or at a particular store. The anxiety is there because the person is responding to an inner woundedness created by the loss. On a subconscious level there is an awareness of this vulnerability, which is where the defense mechanism of anxiety comes from.

Our emotional pain is a natural consequence of our human nature. We can't help but invest, hope for, dream, and desire the best for our lives. The more we invest, however, the greater the possibility of intense pain.

Unfortunately, because of this basic vulnerability and our need to be accepted by other people, we unintentionally give over our *power* to others, opening ourselves up to being hurt by them. If Billy, on his first day at school, wants to look sharp and be accepted, he may spend extra time picking out the shirt he will wear. By doing so, he has both invested his heart or innocence into that choice, and become dependent upon the acceptance of others. Both his choices and his dependency on others become part of his selfhood at that moment.

Because of the nature of human consciousness, as Billy chooses that shirt, he becomes aware of that choice and his vulnerability to that choice. At that moment, the shirt that he has chosen, the value he has put on that shirt, how others will receive that shirt, how he will react to their reception, all become a part of his "existential" selfhood at that moment.

His choice of clothing certainly could have been partially due to an inborn personality factor due to his genetic makeup. But the choice of the shirt could have been made based on past events that have become a part of his selfhood. For example, a popular kid at school might have worn a similar shirt. As Billy chooses his shirt, he may be investing (consciously or subconsciously) in the hope that he and his shirt will be received similarly to the popular kid.

The starting point in our understanding of Billy's selfhood is his set of choices, his awareness of those choices, the value he has placed on those choices, and the affirmation or rejection that may follow those choices. The next time he looks into his closet at the shirt, choosing it will be dependent on his past choices and his awareness of those choices. It is the conscious set of choices and the corresponding feelings resulting from those choices that make up a person's self awareness or selfhood: not his genetics or his chemistry. Billy is aware consciously or subconsciously, of making a deliberate choice for a particular reason, and that is part of who he is at any particular moment in his existence.

We are created or come into this world with the ability to be conscious human beings, and from that sense of consciousness, we make a set of choices that we are aware that we are making. The choices that we make and the way those choices are affirmed become our selfhood. We may inherit different personality traits or even physical characteristics that may influence those choices, but it is the choices we make that become our selfhood, our identity or how we view ourselves. Thus we can have an image of ourselves that is quite different than how others would view us from the perspective of certain personality traits. We could be emotionally dying inside with loneliness while others would still see us as having a "cheerful" personality.

Because Billy depends on others to form part of his selfhood by the way his choices are affirmed or disaffirmed, classmates may hurt or crush him if they make a negative remark about his shirt, even accidentally. One of Billy's peers, might hurt him more deeply by intentionally attacking his innocence, saying "What a stupid shirt." Thus there are two ways that a person can be hurt—unintentionally (Father says "no" to a toy) or intentionally ("stupid shirt").

Whenever a person chooses to invest his heart or innocence, he becomes dependent upon the unconditional acceptance or love of others, and places his trust in that acceptance. If Billy chooses a shirt and is rejected by his peers, he feels the hurt at a certain level. If he goes home and shares his story with his father, who says, "They're right. It is a stupid shirt. I told you it was," his hurt will penetrate even deeper because of his need for the unconditional love of his father. If this is a single incident in an otherwise warm relationship, Billy will have the resources to overcome his father's rejection. But if his father has made a habit of belittling Billy and the choices he makes, Billy's woundedness will grow and result in emotional problems later in life.

These brief examples of the emotional pain model, show how emotional pain can eventually become responsible for all kinds of emotional disorders. These disorders result from our basic human condition, our need to invest our innocence into a world that can and will bring us great pain at times.

We can also see that, even though a parent might be responsible for some of the pain in his or her child's life, there are unlimited sources of pain outside the home. For example, children on the school ground might begin to excessively pick on a child, and if these violations are coupled with other violations, severe emotional damage could result.

I had a friend of Mexican-American descent who lost his first wife to an illness. For a while he was a single parent to his daughter; later he married a woman of Asian descent who would often take his daughter to school. Even though I thought the daughter and stepmother had a lot of similar features, the children picked up on the ethnic differences between them and started teasing the daughter for having a "slant-eyed" mother. After losing her biological mother, the girl was now being rejected for having a step mother who looked different than she did. This is typical of the kind of event that can emotionally injure a child without the parents ever becoming aware of what is happening.

AN ELEMENT OF CHOICE

Even though emotional violations (death of a love one, teased at school, etc.) can bring an instantaneous, automatic reaction, it is important that we also recognize that an element of choice eventually enters the picture. Choice is and must be present because we are conscious human beings. The choice is not always a conscious one; it may be a choice forced upon us by our subconscious, but there will still be *some* element of choice involved. It is important that we understand and accept this element to properly grasp the most mysterious aspects of emotional disorders.

For example, a young boy growing up with a verbally abusive father may learn that looking past his father's eyes at some other object is the best way to minimize the intensity of his pain. The very first time that he saw anger in his father's eyes and looked away was simply a natural reaction. But if, somehow, he had found the "supernatural" emotional strength, he could have looked his father straight in the eyes and said "Dad, I will not listen to you until you learn to talk to me properly."

This is not something I would expect a child to be able to do. But it's clear that when this child displays "poor eye contact" as he grows up, this behavior had its origin in his early choice to avoid contact with his father to protect his selfhood. Although, for this reason it is what I call a *forced choice*, with proper emotional strength, he can become consciously aware of this behavior and *choose* to change it. Later as an adult, he may realize that his communication skills greatly suffer because of the way he was forced to choose to deal with his pain as a child. With this new awareness, he can begin to take charge of his fear and his choices about eye contact.

In an example like this, we can see that the emotional pain model does not lay blame on the individual, but eventually opens the door for him to take charge of his own life and set of choices. The medical model, on the other hand, suggests that the person has no choice of possible behaviors because of some biochemical defect. While this idea may initially be freeing and relieve guilt, it ultimately becomes incapacitating because the person never deals with the root cause of the emotional disorder and because the treatment methods generally employed by medical practitioners (medication, ECT, forced hospitalization) limit the person's ability to function without solving the person's emotional problems.

The emotional pain model does not blame the person, nor does it necessarily blame the parents. In developing a proper understanding of the pain model, it is important to realize and accept that emotional disorders can originate even in good, loving families— not because there is something wrong with the parents, which we traditionally have been taught to believe, but because each individual begins to choose, consciously or unconsciously, his or her own way of dealing with pain at a relatively early age, perhaps even from birth.

A child who is very sensitive to emotional pain may begin dealing with her pain by choosing to please others, perhaps trying to

become the "ideal" child as a way of avoiding the distress associated with hurting the feelings of others. Thus, even though this
child may come from two loving and caring parents, she may subconsciously begin to strive more and more toward perfection as a
way of avoiding any pain of rejection or disappointment from others.

What happens, and it happens quite innocently, is that this kind
of behavior only gives the parents an opportunity to affirm the child
when she does well. They may attempt to love their child unconditionally, but if she begins to use "good performance" more and more
as a way to avoid pain, greater and greater emphasis will be centered around achieving. The more perfect the child becomes, the
less chance the parents get to affirm her when she does fail. Thus,
she seldom or never experiences the unconditional love her parents could offer her when she made a mistake or did something
wrong. Obviously, if a child only gets straight A's, the parents never
get an opportunity to affirm her in the face of a failure (or even a
"B").

When this child grows into an adult, and failure eventually comes,
it may throw her into a severe emotional crisis. In fact, I have seen
such situations lead to severe panic disorders, highly compulsive
behavior, and even symptoms that can be labeled as schizophrenia.

Betty, whom I mentioned in Chapter One, is a good example of
this type of person. Striving to live a near-perfect life, she had little
capacity to handle the pain and shame of a failing marriage.

All emotional or so-called "mental" disorders, whether they be
schizophrenia, depression, mania, panic attacks, or compulsive behaviors, are defense mechanisms that the mind creates to deal with
an overload of pain. This is the central difference between the medical model and the emotional pain model. The medical model presents the brain as broken or defective. The emotional pain model
declares that nothing is wrong with the brain and, in fact, shows
that the brain is often working *brilliantly* as it helps creates strategies to deal with the emotional pain of an investing heart. From this
standpoint, schizophrenia is one of the easiest conditions to understand, because the mind of the person diagnosed as schizophrenic

is often working brilliantly to protect itself from emotional pain. Let's look at an example.

JACK

Jack was referred to me many years ago by a local minister. Jack truly believed that he was half man and half woman. He knew he was born into this world as male but he constantly walked around telling everyone that he was changing into a woman. He would say things like "See, my breasts are getting bigger. My voice is higher" and so forth. At times he also believed he heard voices coming from the TV telling him that he was half woman and half man.

Prior to the time I began working with him, he had spent twenty years taking a multitude of psychiatric medications. Finally, when he came to the realization that the drugs were killing him, he suddenly stopped taking all his medications. **This is a dangerous practice and any reduction in medication should always be monitored by a physician.**

Once off the medication, however, his hallucinations and false beliefs started becoming stronger. At this point, most psychiatrists would have concluded that this increase in symptoms only substantiated Jack's mental illness and his need for the medication. I approached him from a different perspective.

This is an interesting case because, even though Jack had been in and out of different psychiatric facilities for over twenty years with no improvement, it was quite simple to discover the root of his problems. Jack grew up as an only child in a family of two very emotionally withdrawn parents. As a result he does not remember feeling any physical love or touch. In addition, his father was quite verbally abusive, telling him that he would never amount to much.

When he was about seven, an older cousin came to visit, and molested him. The affectionate touch of the cousin overwhelmed Jack with warmth, creating a deep contrast between this warmth with all his deeper feelings of coldness from his childhood. After molesting Jack a few more times, over a period of weeks, the cousin left. Jack remembers feeling both good and bad about the experience. He felt a hunger for the touch but he also felt violated and dirtied by the touch.

Some time later, a younger cousin came to stay. Jack saw this as an opportunity for touch. He was unable to resist the desire to molest the cousin. Though he felt terribly guilty afterward, his need for warmth was so great that he molested him a couple of more times. Finally, his sense of guilt stopped his behavior.

Jack and I discovered that the reason he needed to believe he was half-man and half-woman was to give him, or his selfhood, a way of dealing with the shame of those incidents. He had received very little physical affection from his parents and no verbal affirmation. Thus, when he performed the shameful acts of molestation, he did not have the inner strength, warmth, or love to help him deal with the shame of these actions.

When the older boy molested him, Jack invested his innocence into the good feelings of the relationship as it filled a previously unmet need. When the boy left him, Jack was left with the cold feelings of loneliness and shame. With the younger boy, he felt even more shame because of the increased responsibility associated with his choice to molest him. Although there may have been little or no choice with the older cousin, Jack's need for touch grew into a *forced choice* with his younger cousin. At first he had lost control over this action, but as he began to feel the guilt of his actions, he eventually regained control and stopped molesting his younger cousin.

Jack's mind was not defective. It had created a brilliant solution by deciding he was half-woman. As half-man and half-woman, there would be no shame in having a sexual encounter with either sex. Obsessively believing in and concentrating on this identity issue helped keep his mind away from his feelings of shame and to believe that he was worthy of warm affection. To make this solution work, however, Jack had to absolutely believe in it. To disbelieve would be to allow all the shame of what

128

he did, in addition to the new lies about himself, to overwhelm his selfhood.

The tragedy of Jack's life is that he spent nearly 20 years being told that he had a defective mind, when his mind had actually created a highly efficient solution to the problem of his loneliness and shame. Once Jack was off his medication, he was able to discover the truth about himself as the pain of his past began to surface. It was the surfacing of this pain that brought back his symptoms, not some defective part of his mind that needed further medication.

DIFFERENT OPTIONS—NOT DIFFERENT DISEASES

The medical model creates further problems when it attempts to associate different symptoms with different so-called diseases or defects. Under this system of thinking, schizophrenia is supposedly caused by one kind of chemical imbalance, while depression is the result of a different chemical imbalance. Instead of trying to neatly categorize all the different disorders and then labeling them as diseases, it is more important to see the different behaviors or symptoms as different sets of options or choices that the mind is making to deal with pain.

The human subconscious can create (choose) a variety of different strategies for dealing with emotional pain. A person with multiple personalities will often create a separate personality to deal with the shame of childhood incest, or a person may create a same-sexed personality that does not feel any sexual shame. As an adult, when this person must make love to his or her spouse, the personality that does not feel shame will come out, allowing the person to make love without the felt shame. As an alternative, a personality of the opposite sex may be created that allows the person to be in a same-sex relationship.

Other sexually abused individuals will become obese, putting on weight to make themselves undesirable and unattractive to the opposite sex. Others may become dangerously thin, or very promiscuous to hide from their shame. Some will become addicted to drugs or alcohol as a way of dealing with the pain. Others may just feel no desire for sex at all.

As an example of the different options available, the basic emotional pain model for sexual abuse is illustrated in Figure 8.1.

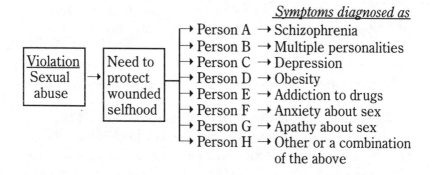

Figure 8.1: The basic emotional pain process for a victim of sexual abuse.

We could also create a set of possibilities for the person who comes from a good family, yet is over-sensitive to pain or to hurting others. These possibilities are shown in Figure 8.2.

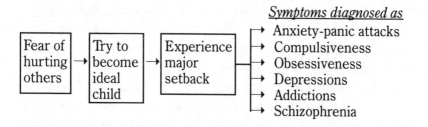

Figure 8.2: The basic emotional pain process for the "ideal" child.

These figures are an over-simplification of the process. What the diagrams do illustrate is that we all have been hurt and we all

130

consequently have developed ways of coping that the medical model often labels as symptoms of mental illness. In fact, with the stresses of contemporary life, most individuals will have experienced almost every symptom associated with the above so-called disorders of mental illness. Who hasn't distorted reality at times? Who doesn't talk to themselves as if they were another person at times? ("Why did you do that?") Who hasn't felt depressed or anxious, or used food and drugs to deal with pain?

Even though the above symptoms or syndromes may be dependent upon other factors, they are all *primarily* called upon by the mind to protect the person against overwhelming emotional pain. Thus, one person may subconsciously choose one set of behaviors over another based upon an inherited personality factor, such as intelligence or age, or based upon the type and degree of the abuse or the behavioral modeling that goes on within the family. Nevertheless, there is always a choice involved and that choice becomes a choice primarily made to protect the woundedness of the person.

SUMMARY OF THE EMOTIONAL PAIN MODEL

In this short overview I have stressed that, instead of seeing the mind as sick, diseased, or disorganized, we must view the mind as operating subconsciously to protect the wounded part of a person. The more wounding and subsequent violation of trust that the person has undergone, the more the subconscious mind will act to develop ways of coping.

Jack had so much shame and so little self-esteem, that he could not feel good enough about himself to find the resources necessary to deal with his deepest pain. He needed a solution and his mind developed one; but he could not accept or believe that part of him created this strategy, because then he would feel like a fool. So his mind became even trickier by creating voices. That way the power or the permission for his behavior was coming from a separate God-like place of authority. Because of this belief, he did not have to trust others. If they rejected his voices, they were rejecting God, not him or his method of coping.

Cases of child abuse such as Jack's bring us great clarity because of the severity of the emotional distance of his parents and the molestation. But, as I have said, emotional disorders can also originate in non-abusive families, because that is where the person first begins to invest his innocence, experience pain, and subconsciously *chose* how to deal with that pain. A child full of love and sensitivity to the feelings of others may never feel right about expressing her feelings fully to dedicated and loving parents. In fear of hurting her parents' feelings, she may make a million and one little choices not to allow her needs to be voiced.

With each one of these small choices, she fails to correctly identify her feelings or make her own needs heard. Once away from her parents, and living in a violating world, she may find herself incapable of taking care of herself.

Are the parents to be blamed for this? The answer is no. Parents who try to do their best must understand that they will never be able produce a pain-free world in which a child will not need to develop his or her set of defenses.

To see the diagnosed disorders of schizophrenia, depression, mania, and addictions as a chosen defense against pain is not to cast blame. It is only to admit to our humanness in a painful world. It is to admit that there is nothing wrong with the mind, outside of the fact that our hearts have been broken and we are all hurting.

CHAPTER NINE

HUMAN CONSCIOUSNESS AND MULTIPLE PERSONALITIES

It's natural to believe that there is something defective about a person's brain when he or she behaves in a difficult-to-understand manner. In fact, most of us have asked ourselves "Why did I do that?" when we have done something we considered foolish or destructive.

Consequently, it has been all too easy for the medical model to attempt to reduce behavior down to the most simplistic terms possible. A person's behavior is seen as being determined, not by a conscious choice, but by his genes and chemistry. Because this model has a deterministic basis to it, it can be used to control the lives of others. Most importantly, the medical model fails to properly explain the element of human choice. It fails to show that the behavior is there for a productive reason, as a chosen strategy to protect a person's delicate selfhood.

When we do not understand the full nature of our ability to make conscious choices, this can result in catastrophic results for us and others. These points will become more evident as we delve deeper into the emotional pain model.

Cases such as Bob's and Jack's, as well as our own understanding of how we make choices to avoid pain, help bring clarity to the difference between deterministic and emotional pain models. There is nothing, however, that allows us to understand the workings of human consciousness and its relationship to emotional disorders better than the study of people with multiple personalities. Just as

133

Bob's and Jack's stories have become a great help in understanding
the nature of schizophrenia, so individuals with multiple personalities are quite helpful in understanding emotional pain in general.
Let's look at one particular case that will help give us a true starting
point to understanding emotional disorders.

JAMIE

Dr. Joanne Crawford, an associate of mine, is working with a
client with multiple personalities. As best as we have been able to
ascertain, Jamie first formed a new personality at the age of one
month. At this time we believe that her mother tried to kill her by
suffocating her with some object, perhaps a pillow. Since I have
done work with multiple personalities in the past, Dr. Crawford and
I often collaborate.

What has personally fascinated me about this case is the confirmation it has provided that a person's consciousness is well enough
developed at this age that a split into two different personalities can
take place. To give you an introduction to the topic of multiple personalities and the significance of human consciousness, let me show
you how we figured out that Jamie's personality split at the age of
one month.

Jamie knows that something traumatic happened to her at one
month. At this point in her life, her grandmother was brought into
the home to take care of her, and her mother was kept away from
her as much as possible. Later on, for whatever reason, her mother
was allowed to be around her again, and the abusive behavior continued.

Jamie's crying (at later ages) always triggered the worst possible response in her mother, often pushing her into a state of emotional confusion and fiery rage. When this happened, Jamie would
be punished, beaten and pricked with pins every time she cried until she learned not to. Together, we and Jamie have figured out the
most likely scenario for the events that transpired in her early life:
We believe that when one-month-old Jamie was crying, her mother

134

came in, grabbed something like a pillow, and tried to suffocate her. She also tried to kill Jamie on several later occasions.

At this point, the part of Jamie's consciousness that was present and needed to cry, split off and went to a subconscious level, leaving behind a new awareness or consciousness that did not need to cry.

As strange as this may seen, this splitting off is actually a very common process that we all go through as adults. Time after time I will see clients come close to crying, then, for one reason or another, take that part of them and "push" it into their subconscious or out of their direct awareness. They do not create a new personality when this happens, but they do split off the need to cry from that moment in time, often without consciously realizing it.

The key to understanding emotional pain is realizing that each of us is born with a need to be nurtured, fed, and loved; but because an infant can't talk or share, and because none of us can distinctly remember events at the age of one month, we have a tendency to minimize the role of consciousness at that time. Instead, we associate the development of consciousness with our cognitive or intellectual development.

Consciousness, however, is something that just *is*. The special awareness of one's self is just as present in an infant at birth as at any later age. What is limited is not human consciousness, but the concept of self, language, and a more complete understanding that one is a separate being from other beings.

Thus, Jamie, at one month, does not just cry for some basic need such as hunger. She is also consciously aware at some level, and she invests this awareness into her need to be affirmed. At a non-language or pre-cognitive level, she is saying "I, Jamie, hurt and need to be loved back." By picking her up and cuddling her, feeding her, or changing her diaper, her caregiver affirms that she is a worthy and valuable person.

When her mother tried to suffocate her to death, Jamie experienced the act, not just as a violation to her physical body, but to her conscious sense of self. With no psychological defenses yet developed, baby Jamie had to do *something* to protect her selfhood, the part that she had chosen to invest at that moment.

To protect herself, she took the awareness of being violated when she needed assurance, and pushed that awareness into her subconscious. To do this, a new awareness or consciousness had to split off from her core self.

Our selfhood, at any particular moment, represents that which we choose to identify with or invest ourselves in. For instance, if I choose to root for a particular sports team, then that team becomes part of "who I am." I am Ty Colbert, who likes the Los Angeles Dodgers. If someone puts down my favorite team, I feel defensive; if my team wins, I feel a part of their victory.

Even if we do not choose to acknowledge a particular identity, others can force us to become aware of that identity. For example, a child in his earliest years will be oblivious to his ethnic identity. Others may then force him to be aware to know that he is a member of a particular group whose skin color, belief systems and customs are either desirable or undesirable. Consciousness forces us to become aware of ourselves, even when we don't want to choose to be aware.

When someone is shamed by another because of her ethnicity, the person may not want to be "who she is." She may feel like disappearing or splitting from that aspect of her identity. For example, many Asian women undergo painful plastic surgeries to "fix" their eyes. On a lighter issue, I might not want to be a "Dodger" if the Dodgers were to become the laughing stock of professional sports.

At one month of age, Jamie's sense of self and awareness of the world were just barely taking form. Her whole sense of selfhood at any moment was invested in her particular needs.

However you choose to define the source of consciousness, a debate that leads into religious and philosophical issues, it is only important for our discussion to understand that it is complete even in infancy. As soon as we are born, we have the potential to consciously invest in any given moment and to be aware of that investment at some level. Thus, when Jamie's mother tried to kill her,

her awareness of her self felt violated.

When we fail to understand that consciousness has full potential at birth or even before, we fail to see others as fully human. It is this very act of lowering the level of humanness that allows us to judge and treat people as less than human. For example, when we see an emotionally troubled person, we might give ourselves permission to be abusive or degrading to him because we might judge him to be less than fully human in full use of his capacity to be conscious. While our society does not openly admit to such a position, this is often what we do.

Yet as I have shown you with Bob and Jack, their symptoms, or assumed diseases, are not proof that their consciousness is less than whole. Their consciousness is just as whole as that of any "normal" person.

When you look at individuals who are full of psychiatric drugs or have recently been through shock treatment, they may not seem to be "all there." The mental, cognitive aspect of their minds may be less than fully functional, but that does not mean that part of their consciousness is missing or diminished.

Seeing a difference between human consciousness and a person's level of functioning is an absolutely necessary requirement if one is to understand the origin of emotional disorders. Even those professionals who openly criticize biopsychiatry as being deterministic often do not fully acknowledge the separateness of consciousness, leaving the door open to a deterministic view.

Consciousness is not something that starts at a particular point and continues to grow, as if it were a plant. Outsiders can affect a person's degree of full awareness, but they are always separated from complete control by the fact that the person chooses to what degree to be aware. Jamie's mother could punish her daughter enough to get her to stop crying in her present awareness, but she could not control her child's need to cry and to be affirmed, even at the age of one month.

To protect Jamie's investing self at that moment, her original self went "underground" to a place where it could continue to cry, but not be harmed. When it did so, it took with it both a hope and a need to later be nurtured or healed. The one month-old, as well as other later splits, stayed "inside" on a subconscious level waiting for a safe enough situation to emerge and be nurtured and healed. After thirty years of hiding, when Dr. Crawford had finally established the necessary trust and safety, these split-off personalities surfaced. When they did surface, Dr. Crawford was suddenly in the presence of a one-month-old child with the *exact* needs of any one-month-old traumatized in a similar way.

Again, if we look closely enough, we can see that all of us, at one time or another, act in a similar manner. For example, a man who is being violated by a boss in whom he has trusted may block out the awareness of the violation, or the intensity of his pain, because he does not want to admit the degree to which he is being violated. Upon arriving home, where he feels safe, he may seek the nurturing of his family either directly or indirectly.

The part of his selfhood that was violated and needed to be expressed at work was split off and pushed down to a subconscious level for protection. But just as Jamie's one-month-old split later needed to resurface and be affirmed, so does this man's split-off part. Whereas Jamie had to split off her total self at that point and start a new personality, this man only had to split off a moment of his life.

What we must understand as we study individuals with multiple personalities is that there is no primary difference between what they do and what you and I do every day of our lives. There is no fundamental cognitive or biochemical difference between you and such a person. It is also important to see how the element of choice is involved.

At the point of her first split, Jamie had two personalities. Her original personality, the infant who needed to cry and be nurtured, was pushed down into her subconscious, and a new compliant personality who did not need to cry emerged. Later, as an adult, Jamie was often told how sweet and obedient she had been as a little girl. "You never cried," people told her.

As Jamie grew up, some of her older child personalities that eventually emerged also cried, but after being punished by her mother, they too stopped crying. These older personalities were able to learn not to cry more quickly because the original need to cry had already been split off.

It is important to note that Jamie's need to cry did not go away; instead, it was violated and shamed. When she reached out to her mother with her conscious, investing heart, that part of her was shamed by the person who should have loved her the most. In response, she had to go "inside," a term used to describe this coping process, to the place where she could cry without feeling shamed or punished.

Many of us feel ashamed or embarrassed about crying, which leads us to go off by ourselves and cry when we need to. Jamie couldn't remove herself physically when she was first violated, so she buried that part of her and did her crying inside.

As Jamie's new compliant personality stayed "out," it began to age as her body aged chronologically. The first or core personality stayed split off inside her, not aging. One of the reasons we knew this was that Jamie shared with her therapist that all her life she had heard the distant sound of a crying infant inside of her. The fact that such split-off personalities do not age until they resurface helps give credence to the idea that consciousness is a separate entity from the physical-cognitive aspect of our total being.

When Jamie was three, her mother's brother, who may also have abused her mother when young, began to hang around the home. He started fondling Jamie whenever he could. This sexual abuse caused Jamie to feel a deep sense of violation within herself, accompanied by an overload of shame. This new feeling was not the same as being rejected when crying, but a felt bodily shame.

If we examine our own feelings for a moment, we can tell the difference between these two kinds of shame. There is one part of us that might feel embarrassed about crying in public. This shame has to do with our sadness and with not feeling okay about letting that sadness be known. When someone tries to touch, kiss, or hug

139

us when we don't want them to, however, an entirely different set of feelings of shame and anger result. Instead of feeling embarrassed about our sadness, such advances can cause us to feel bad or dirty about ourselves or our bodies.

As adults, we can choose to avoid or reject someone's advances. When dealing with older relatives whom we might not want to touch us because they approach us in a clingy, needy way, we are able to allow the physical contact, but not feel overwhelmed by it. In the case of a child, who really has no choice in the matter, the feelings of shame must often be split off into a separate awareness.

When Jamie was fondled by her uncle, she split again, creating a new personality who did not need to feel guilt or anger when fondled. This third personality was needed to help protect her overall selfhood from the shame of her uncle's abuse, just as the second personality was needed to help her stop crying when her mother abused her.

As adults, we don't create separate personalities when we feel violated, but we do create separate "false selves" as a way of operating in a violating world. For example, if someone is touching us inappropriately and we do not let that person know our boundary needs, we may laugh or pretend to accept the touching as a way of creating a protective distance.

At this point you may be wondering how the conscious mind can split off or block out certain segments of awareness. Inherent in human consciousness is the ability to make choices about what we will allow ourselves to be aware of. It is this ability that allows us to invest "who we are" into life, feel alive because of that investment, and feel loved or affirmed back. When someone affirms us, and we are able to receive that affirmation, it can fill our souls and hearts, causing a warm physical sensation throughout our bodies from head to toe.

Along with our ability to be aware, we also have the ability to choose not to be aware, and then to hide from ourselves the fact that we have done this. This double act of denial blocks out all present conscious awareness, both of the event we want to avoid, and of the fact that we are blocking it.

If a person walking down the street happens to see several bullies beating up an elderly woman, and then turns his back and walks off, he may be doing this to give the appearance that he is not aware of what is happening. If the police were to stop and question him, he could simply say "I didn't see anything," making him appear innocent of ignoring his responsibility to society or to the woman.

If he also chooses to deny to himself that he saw the woman being beaten up, pushing the awareness of the event down into his subconscious, he could also free himself from his *full* awareness of the responsibility.

This double choice of denial is all that is needed to *push* awareness into the subconscious. The guilt and fear that accompanied not helping out the woman may not be sufficient to blank out all of the man's memories, but it might enable him to blank out enough to give him permission to consciously not feel bad about it. For Jamie and other severely abused children, this double choice is made almost instantly to protect the purity of the original selfhood.

It is easy to see this choosing process taking place in a young boy trying to stay out of trouble. At first, when he says "No I didn't do it," you can look into his eyes and see that he *knows* he did. As you proceed to question him, however, you can actually see the process of choosing not to be aware of the act himself going on in his mind. The more he can convince himself that he did not commit the act, the more he can stand there stone-faced and deny his actions to the world.

This boy trying to protect his selfhood by denying his act also helps us to understand the concept of a "forced choice." As his fear and shame began to surface, these feelings *forced* his subconscious to take over and begin to block out the awareness of the behavior in question. Thus the fear and shame, and the threat of further injury to his selfhood, forced him to choose to not be fully aware.

Any parent who has found herself in such a situation knows how careful she must be to help the child tell the truth without overloading his selfhood. By helping him to tell the truth and not feel shamed, she helps him build the inner strength to tell the truth later on. A child's selfhood is terribly vulnerable, and must choose to split off an experience if it becomes too threatening.

Because of Jamie's ability to choose to be unaware of what was happening to her, by the age of four, she had three personalities—three separate segments of consciousness as shown in Figure 9.1.

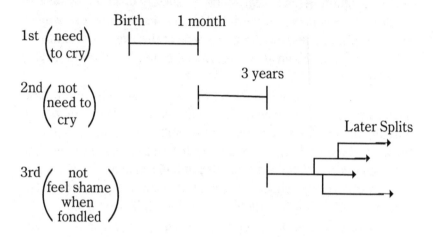

Figure 9.1: Diagram of Jamie's first three personalities.

The original birth personality split off and stopped aging at one month. Later when it came out at full consciousness, it was at the exact same age it split off: one month. The next split-off personality lived in the time period of one month to three years. The third personality remembers nothing before the age of three but remembers from age three on until other splits occurred due to later abuse.

It took nearly ten hours of therapy a week for six months for Dr. Crawford to establish the necessary trust and safety to work with Jamie—a very delicate and difficult process. After some of the older personalities (other than the original three) had emerged, shared their traumas, gone through an emotional healing, and integrated, the younger ones started coming out to full consciousness. When Jamie's second personality appeared, she knew what age it was because this part of her had no memories after the age of three and, unlike her other personalities, remembered events and feeling from a very early age to three years old.

The second personality could talk, but would naturally be limited in what she could communicate when she was one month old. Talking to Jamie when she was in this personality was similar to trying to ask any three-year-old what she remembered about herself at one month old. This personality could remember and communicate some of the trauma Jamie had experienced, but saw events in pictures. She described her first or original memories of being behind something that looked like white bars and seeing dots, as depicted in the Figure 9.2.

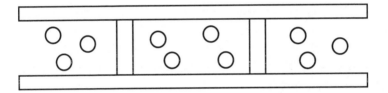

Figure 9.2: A picture of Jamie's early memories behind bars.

Jamie has a photograph of her mother holding her soon after she was brought home from the hospital. In this picture, her mother is wearing a white dress with blue polka dots. Thus, we are making an assumption that the earliest memories of the second personality are of Jamie inside of her crib looking at her mother's dress. Jamie also remembers, in the next instant, an object coming down onto her face.

When the original personality comes out in the therapist's office, the one who is one month old, Jamie's body becomes that of an infant. Although she is physically an adult, Jamie is unable to hold her head up when in this state. Dr. Crawford has to use pillows to prop her up, and can communicate with her only through eye contact and touch, as any parent would communicate with a one-month-old child.

143

To summarize, Dr. Crawford knows that she is working with one personality who is not old enough to hold her head up. She knows that the three-year-old personality has earlier picture-memories of a crib. And Jamie knows from her cousin that at about the age of one month, something terrible happened, and her grandmother had to go to live with the family to keep Jamie safe from her mother. In addition, the one-month to three-year-old's Jamie's earliest memory is of something being forced onto her face. Because of this evidence, we can be fairly sure that Jamie had her first split at about the age of one month.

WHAT HAVE WE LEARNED?

In the emotional pain model, the full potential of human consciousness exists at birth, and most likely before. One of the primary qualities of human consciousness is a "purity of the soul," a special ability and need to invest one's heart and self into all that we become conscious of.

Out of this investment comes a need, not just to be fed, clothed, touched and nurtured, but to be affirmed as a special and distinct person. When a person is not affirmed in this manner, that person feels violated; and the hurt, loneliness, and shame of that violation can *crush* the part that the person chose to invest. If the loss is a loved one, then such a loss can crush the part that the person invested into the loved one.

At one month, baby Jamie does not just require that her biological needs be met. She also needs to be affirmed as a special person, and she can't help but invest the purity of her heart and soul into that desire. Violations of that investment will result in her crying, like any infant. If nurtured within a short period of time, that small wound to her selfhood will feel healed. When a mother is properly nurturing her infant, she rocks, cuddles, strokes and talks to that infant. During this time it is important that the warmth of her eyes make contact with the need to be affirmed that she sees in the eyes of her child.

144

When Jamie's mother tried to kill her baby at the age of one month, Jamie was not just struggling physically to live, she also needed to defend her selfhood from that violation. A protective part of her consciousness took over and made a forced choice to split, taking this violated piece of her and hiding it in a safe place.

When Jamie invested her heart or innocence, needing to be affirmed, and was violated instead, this piece of her total selfhood became dependent on an outside source of love to heal this pain. When this one-month-old personality comes out during therapy, Jamie's therapist holds her and rocks her, allowing her to release the pain and the crying about this event in order to heal this part of her life.

If the therapist can provide enough warmth and trust, then a healing may proceed and this core personality will integrate back into the other parts.

SUMMARY

The study of multiple personalities—how Jamie specifically chose to take care of her selfhood at one month old—is a gift to us because people with multiple personalities show us the clearest picture of what it means to be a conscious human being. When we study this phenomenon, and especially when we work with such clients, we get a glimpse of the unlimited nature of human consciousness and the power it can exercise over the mind and body. For example, if a person with multiple personalities is intoxicated from the use of alcohol, a new, completely sober personality can come out, allowing the person to drive home safely, free from the chemical effects of alcohol.

Individuals with multiple personalities not only allow us to get a sense of the almost unlimited capabilities of human consciousness, but also of the absolute vulnerability of the human soul. Even though Jamie's physical body was not injured at one month of age, her soul and identity were wounded. On her own, Jamie was not capable of healing that part of herself, and the one-month-old stayed hidden,

CHAPTER TEN

CRAVINGS, ADDICTIONS AND COMPULSIONS

After finishing the last chapter, I gave it to Dr. Crawford and Jamie, to make sure that they felt comfortable with what I had written; and I assured Jamie that her identity was well-protected (although she openly shares her life story with many individuals and in college classes). Later I spoke with Jamie over the phone about her response to the chapter. Our conversation just happened to take place after her therapist had been working with Jamie's one-month-old personality in therapy, which meant that her feelings were still close to the surface. This would be analogous to talking to someone within a short time after the loss of a significant loved one, when her feelings for that person would be very close to the surface of her awareness.

After talking about the chapter in general, I asked Jamie if she believed that the split had to take place because her infant self had felt personally violated. "Yes," she quickly replied, then said, "It felt as if I had done something bad or was bad."

The one-month-old Jamie would certainly not be able to put those words to her feelings. As these same feelings filtered into adult awareness, however, the present-day Jamie could express them with words. As an infant, she had felt as if she had done something *bad* when she reached out through her crying and was literally stifled. Not feeling worthwhile enough to receive someone's love and affirmation overwhelmed her sense of self to the extent that she had to split off. The violated part of her personality (her whole self at this

147

point) felt so shamed that it had to remove itself from any further contact with the outside world. It had to hide some place where it was safe, even if that meant secretly crying for the next thirty-five years.

Each of us has parts of our lives that we feel bad or shamed about. These areas might include the ways in which we have hurt others, or the ways we have failed ourselves or our God. There are also parts of our selfhood where others have made us feel bad about ourselves.

If we stop and dwell on these areas, we can feel the need to get away from them. Because of the shame associated with these parts of ourselves, we experience a discomfort about being present with these areas. The greater our feelings of shame or badness, the more we need to keep these areas separated from full awareness. In fact, if we are conscious enough, we can catch our mind focusing on these areas for a moment, then quickly drifting away. As we choose, subconsciously, to avoid contemplating these areas, we block out the awareness of these areas of "felt badness."

Jamie, at one month, had a fully functioning consciousness, but a very small and limited sense of self. She did not have the multitude of adult experiences that would allow her mind to drift off to some other awareness. When shamed for expressing her needs, she could not let her mind drift away from the shame to a good meal, or a shopping trip. Her whole self had been shamed; thus she had to start over, creating a new personality that could exist without crying.

To properly understand emotional disorders, we must realize that there is no fundamental difference between how we split off daily from painful, shaming experiences, and how Jamie or diagnosed schizophrenics split off from their experiences. The difference lies in the *degree* of the person's reaction to the felt violation. The root of all emotional disorders is each person's need to feel loved and worthwhile.

Jamie did not just reach out to her mother to be fed or to receive physical contact. Even at one month old, her consciousness or sense of self was saying, in effect, "This is me. Please love me for who I am."

Like Jamie, each of us lives with a certain *desperation* deep inside: the fear of not being thought worthwhile. This desperation is analogous to the terror we would feel if we woke up one morning and discovered that we were unworthy of being loved, not even by ourselves.

When others accept or approve of the choices we invest ourselves in, we feel affirmed. When others shame or violate our life choices, we feel unloved, worthless, and empty. If we are shamed too often, eventually, an inner sense of desperation will develop, and the protective part of our subconscious mind will take over, beginning to *rule* our lives by making choices for us.

Theoretically, if we lived in a perfect, non-violating world, where we were always unconditionally accepted, we would not need to hide from our inner desperation. In the absence of such a world, our minds attempt to keep the violations of our selfhood away from full awareness.

As adults, we all have a million and one ways to dodge these feelings. Rejected by a woman, a man may quickly say "Oh, she was not what I wanted anyway." A student who fears failing and being seen as dumb, may say "Why go to school? They don't teach you anything that you can use."

Fearful of letting the pain of rejection penetrate too deeply, the man and the student split off their full awareness of these events by rationalizing away the rejection. The person standing on a street corner believing that he is Jesus Christ and hears messages from God is likely using these beliefs to protect the vulnerability of his fragile selfhood. An extremely depressed person has most likely been using her mind and body for most of her life to deaden and avoid feeling her pain.

Regardless of which strategy we choose to shield ourselves from the pain and accompanying shame that constantly tries to say to us "You're not lovable," or "You're not as lovable as I am because...," the accompanying symptoms are created by the protective part of

149

our subconscious mind.

Jamie, at one month, consciously reached out to be loved and affirmed. When her mother tried to kill her, she was consciously aware that her need to be loved, to feel worthwhile, was being rejected. As a result she started to feel *bad* about herself. She was aware to some degree that someone did not feel she was worthy of living or being loved as a human being.

CRAVINGS, ADDICTIONS, AND COMPULSIONS

Perhaps the most puzzling aspect of human emotional disorders is what causes the *craving* or the push behind out-of-control behavior. If not a gene or a chemical imbalance, what produces the craving in a person who, once he chooses to pick up a drink, seems to have little or no power to stop drinking? What forces a person to lose his ability to choose to eat in what he considers to be appropriate amounts? What is this secret force that can drive a person to become a workaholic? Why do some people compulsively wash their hands, or rape, or abuse, or even compulsively feel the need to kill?

When Jamie reached out for affirmation at the age of one month and was violated, she was left with a sense of coldness or inner desperation instead of the warmth of being affirmed. It is this feeling of *inner desperation* that lies at the basis of all out-of-control behavior.

Most of us have experienced some significant loss that has left us with a sense of desperation. At the time, we have also felt the need, a push or a pull to do whatever was necessary to stop this terrible feeling. Our minds may have even become a little "tricky" at this time, trying to convince us to do something against our better judgement.

For example, if our lover breaks up with us, we may feel a real need to call her or write her a letter in the hopes of getting her back. Even if our "ex" has said that the relationship is definitely over, our minds may have tried to convince us that we still have a chance to make things right.

We may feel the need to drive by that person's home, call just to hear her voice on an answering machine, and so forth. Obviously some people become so afraid to face their desperate feelings that they will stalk the person or become violent in attempts to force the person to come back.

The force behind the phone call, the letter and the belief that the relationship may still work out is the need to make the feelings of desperation disappear. Just getting a glimpse of the person may be quite seductive, if that glimpse can temporarily take away our inner desperation by restoring memories and making the relationship seem possible.

To properly understand the overpowering craving force that can develop in any of us, it is fundamentally important to realize that (1) we can't be alone with our desperation for longer than a second or two, and (2) our mind will do anything, creating any kind of craving or behavior, to rid us of the feelings of desperation. Let's look at each of these points individually.

The reason none of us can sit very long with deep feelings of desperation is that, when these feelings are allowed to interface with our selfhood directly, they begin to destroy or disintegrate our selfhood. Since our selfhood is ultimately dependent upon the affirmation and love of others, the violation by others leaves us with a desperation that begins to literally eat away at our selfhood as an emotional cancer.

When I have counseled individuals similar to Jamie's degree of abuse, they have been quite clear about just how scary that desperation is. At times they feel as if it will annihilate them. These desperate feelings are so strong, it seems as if they have the power to rip and tear their selfhood apart.

Why is this inner sense of desperation the fundamental element in understanding the true origin of emotional disorders? As we invest in the world, making choices, we become dependent on the affirmation of others. If affirmed by others, we then feel a sense of warmth surrounding those choices. When a child is properly affirmed you can see him glow inside with warmth.

For example, how often will a young child come to a parent and say "Mommy, look at what I made." He has invested his creative innocence into his project and now is seeking affirmation. The warmth that he felt from making the project will *only* penetrate so far into his selfhood. If he is properly affirmed by a person he feels bonded to, you can see the glow of his investment penetrate much deeper.

On the other hand, if the child's efforts are rejected, then his investment is now surrounded with feelings of coldness. If his sense of self is strong enough or his defenses solid enough, the coldness of the rejection will not penetrate that deep. But if he invests his heart unprotected, he will feel a sense of desperation as the cold- ness of the rejection literally begins to erode away the part of his selfhood that was involved in the choice. The greater the invest- ment and the greater the violation, the greater the desperation and the greater the need for the mind to take over and create a craving for something to help keep the feelings spit off from full awareness.

Understanding how this inner desperation creates a need to crave certain behaviors or substances also allows us to understand the craving behind our need to hurt others. When others strike out at us, we are left with a desperate need to reaffirm the part of our selfhood that was disaffirmed. Just as a craving for alcohol can tem- porarily block out the desperation associated with loneliness, the need to hurt back can block out the need to recapture our lost dig- nity by robbing others of theirs. As we hurt others there is a tem- porary sense of relief from our inner desperation. That's why we often "feel good" as we involve ourselves in gossiping about others or hearing about tragedies that have happened to people we don't like.

Most of us never experience the very depths of our desperation because our mind takes over the instant we are violated, creating the necessary defenses to avoid any conscious contact with our over- whelming innermost distress. It is only in events such as the sud- den loss of a loved one or severe abuse, that we are suddenly hit with an overload of desperation.

Our protective subconscious is always on guard. When we get a little close to a situation that may expose us to our inner desperation, we may begin to feel a little anxious, or perhaps we experience a small sense of panic. This anxiety is not indicative of the danger of an external object, but of the degree of our inner vulnerability.

For example, many years ago I went through a fairly rough breakup with a girlfriend. We both lived in the same town, had the same friends, and attended the same church. I remember that for a few months afterwards, if I thought I saw her car, my whole insides would suddenly jump.

Was I afraid of her physically? No, of course not. I was afraid of being further wounded by the situation. When we finally had a chance to sit down and heal our relationship, the *compulsive* part of me that was constantly on guard went away.

When a person is full of shame, her protective subconscious may pick hand-washing as a means of trying to feel clean, or alcohol or drugs to numb the pain and make her feel good. Someone else may turn to hate to reclaim his lost dignity.

This element is also what is behind most, if not all, hallucinatory behavior. I once worked with a person who had begun to see bugs that were not real. She would see bugs all over the office coming at her and beginning to crawl up onto her. Her reaction to them was so real and she looked so terrified that I would find myself glancing around to see if the bugs were real.

What caught my attention about the hallucinations was that she would begin to see the bugs right as she was about to get in touch with her deepest pain. After working with her for a while, I realized that the bugs were there as a way of protecting her from this inner desperation. The pain of her desperation was so intense that her mind would create the bugs to distract her attention away from her fear of her deeper feelings. Because she believed the bugs were real, she became fearful of them, and this trick of her mind successfully separated her conscious mind from her deeper feelings.

THE CHOOSING PROCESS

At the root of all our cravings, addictions, compulsions, and out-of-control behavior is our subconscious *choosing* to use these behaviors to stay away from our inner feelings of desperation. The woman who saw bugs may have once mistaken a shadow or the black top of an ink pen for a bug. As she became startled by her false interpretation, her subconscious learned how to suppress her feelings of desperation, as well as hurt, loneliness, shame, and anger, by imagining the bugs. In the future, as her feelings began to surface, her mind would quickly sense these feelings coming up and create the bugs to facilitate pushing the feelings back down.

An alcoholic who has successfully gone through several years of recovery and is in touch with his feelings, will tell you much the same. For example, one client of mine, Alfred, told me that when he was actively drinking, all he was aware of at first was a slight urge to drive down the street where his favorite bar was located. Actually, he was not even consciously aware of the urge—he would just find himself on that street.

In recovery, he became aware that the process of taking that first drink often resulted from his need to suppress his feelings of inadequacy at work. When these feelings would begin to emerge, Alfred's mind would come to his rescue, eventually getting him to the bar through a series of small choices.

Often the process would start when his boss would come into his office and throw a degrading remark at him. Alfred would first try to suppress his feelings by taking his mind off his job and focusing on quitting time. This would allow him some relief. Once he was off work and on his way home, he would convince himself to drive down a particular street; not because it was where his favorite bar was located, but because it was a "better" way home. Once on the street his mind would then begin to convince himself that he ought to stop to check up on his old buddies.

It is important to realize just how clever our protective subconscious can become. In Alfred's case, each little step was highly calculated, designed to reduce the anxiety that signaled his deeper feelings beginning to emerge; yet each step was still seemingly innocent enough to convince Alfred's rational side that nothing threatening was happening.

When deep feelings of desperation, loneliness, hurt, shame, and anger begin to push their way up to awareness, anxiety is created. This anxiety is a signal to the person's protective subconscious to do something quick to push the feelings back down. The creative part of the mind then kicks in, creating a hallucination, or a need to drink, eat, stay busy, become manic or any other number of behaviors.

The subconscious mind is utterly brilliant at not only designing what actions will work best for which person at that moment, but at creating a series of actions that allow the subconscious to become increasingly powerful. With the alcoholic, the compulsive eater, the hand-washer, or the person who feels a strong craving to hurt others, the act doesn't suddenly come upon him out of the blue because of some mysterious chemical imbalance. His actions result from a complex process, a series of subconscious choices that become increasingly powerful and directional until the final conscious act ceases to be a free choice. Figure 10.1 shows the time graph of Alfred's choices leading him to the bar.

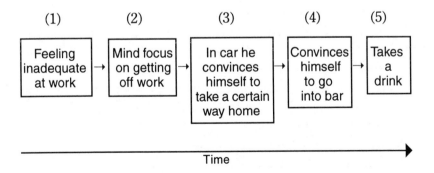

Figure 10.1: A time graph of Alfred's set of choices.

Once the first drink is taken, the chemical effects of the alcohol (or drug, food, sex, etc.) may then take over, increasing the person's craving even more. Because the fear of withdraw symptoms may also be involved, the chemical effects of a drug may play a major role in keeping the person on the drug; but the basic craving process is not the result of a biological mechanism, but a series of small decisions or choices that the subconscious makes in its attempt to keep painful feelings away from the selfhood of the person.

SUMMARY

Jamie has taught us that our consciousness starts making choices to protect our wounded selfhood at a very early age. The behaviors that we choose are not simply conditioned reflexes based upon a deterministic or biological deficit model. They are conscious choices.

We have learned that, the more wounded the selfhood, the more the protective side of our subconscious must take over and make choices that are based solely on the immediate protection of the selfhood of the person. Even if the long-term consequences might be disastrous (being arrested for drunk driving or becoming extremely overweight), the mind will block out such a consequence to give itself permission to choose the most efficient solution.

This narrowing of choices and loss of control over our lives is what we see gradually happening on a massive scale in our society. When parents reach the end of their day feeling violated, burnt out, and emotionally exhausted, they feel more of a need for isolation, finding refuge in self-absorbing activities such as drinking, television watching and over-eating. As parents have less of themselves to offer to their children, their offspring will feel even more alone and isolated, and will feel more of a need to split themselves off from these feelings through such activities as eating, television, Nintendo, or acting out for attention.

More and more, the medical model tries to convince us that some sort of physical defect is involved in the growing amount of emotional dysfunction in our society. The more we use this medical

156

model to become oblivious to our inner choosing process, however, the more we will see people in our culture gradually losing control over their ability to act in a moral and responsible way. Under the medical model, as people become more out of control, our society will become more dependent upon using medication to control people. The long-term effects of using psychiatric medication can only parallel the devastating effects of street drugs. If this pattern continues, a generation from now we will have a society held together, not by love and cooperation, but by the pharmaceutical chemicals running through our veins.

In fact, such a scenario is clearly taking place today. On March 1996, the *Child and Adolescent Behavioral Letter* published by Brown University in St. Providence, Road Island, states that it is estimated that 10 to 12 percent of all boys between the ages of 6 and 14 are on Ritalin. The article goes on to state that a major influential parents' group, Children and Adults with Attention Deficit Disorders, supports the drug's use, also receives funding from the company, Ciba-Geigy, that manufactures Ritalin. This article further states that there is a growing use in illicit Ritalin among teenagers who seek the energizing effects of the stimulant.

If we can begin to see our out-of-control behavior from the standpoint of our inner woundedness, we can begin to turn away from the medical model and toward an emotional healing model. Alfred lost his ability to choose because of the violations to his selfhood, but he gradually recaptured his ability to freely and responsibly choose through the healing of that part of himself.

Our cravings and our out-of-control behavior represents our need for love and dignity and the healing of our inner desperatation as individuals and as a society. If we allow our society to collectively become more violating and less nurturing, we will gradually lose our freedom to make proper choices. More and more of our life and interactional choices will be made from a place of inner desperation.

CHAPTER ELEVEN

EMOTIONAL PAIN MODEL—FUNDAMENTAL ELEMENTS

As bizarre and unpredictable as our behavior and thinking processes can become, there is one aspect of the human emotional process that operates in a very precise and predictable way: the feelings that are always experienced immediately after a violation. This basic feeling reaction comes into play before the protective part of the mind becomes involved. Once a person's subconscious begins to create ways to protect the selfhood, the possibilities and corresponding behaviors become unlimited.

Understanding this consistent aspect of how the human being reacts to pain will give us not only a fuller understanding of emotional disorders, but a greater knowledge of the origin of self-hate and violence toward others. As we come to a true understanding of the more severe forms of emotional disorders, as well as the "darker" sides of our own behavior, we will see that they all stem from an emotionally wounded selfhood. The behaviors of someone like Bob or Jack, and people who need to inflict serious harm upon others are the result of the significant violations to their selfhood that these individuals have suffered over a long period of time.

To help bring clarity to the fundamental elements of the emotional pain model, I want to first take a look at the life of Charles Manson. My goal is not to solicit sympathy for him, but to give you an example of the longstanding pattern of violations required to produce a criminal mind such as his.

CHARLES MANSON'S CHILDHOOD

In August of 1969, several individuals under the cult-like influence of Charles Manson, went on a rampage killing eight people in the Hollywood area of Los Angeles. One of those murdered was the actress Sharon Tate and the murders became known as the "Tate-LaBianca Slayings."

In addition to the accounts we have of his life in the book *Helter Skelter* and its film version, Charles Manson also wrote a small autobiography mainly about his childhood. Far from a self-pity or "let-me-blame-others" type of book, this volume seemed motivated by his need to share the pain of his early life with others.

Manson starts his story by describing a little of his mother's past, stating that her childhood had been completely dominated by a mother who was fanatical about her religious beliefs.

> My grandmother was stern and unwavering in her interpretation of God's will and demanded that everyone abide by her views of God's wishes. According to Grandma, the display of an ankle, or even an over-friendly smile to one of the opposite sex was sinful.[1]

He also stated that when his grandfather attempted to show any affection toward his mother, he was chastised by Grandma for his "vulgar" behavior. Continuing, Manson writes:

> Grandma was constantly on my mother's back, "That dress is too short, braid your hair, come directly home from school, don't talk to any boys, and 'no' you can't go to the school dance."[2]

At the age of fifteen, Manson's mother ran away from home, and "exploded" into her newfound freedom. "She drank a lot, loved freely and answered to no one." She gave birth to Charles at the age of sixteen. He saw his father once when he was young, but does not remember his face.

Not ready to make the sacrifices necessary to raise a child,

Manson's mother placed him with one relative after another. Often, while his mother disappeared for several days, he would be left with a sitter until a relative came to get him. Once, he claims, his mother even sold him to a waitress for a pitcher of beer. Several days later, his uncle had to search the town looking for the waitress to get him back.

When Manson was six, his mother was arrested for robbery and sent to jail. Again he was tossed around from relative to relative as an unwanted child. He remembers his family members referring to him as the "little bastard," and his peers telling him "Your mother's no good; she's a jail bird."

At Christmas when he was six, his only present was a hairbrush from his grandmother. She told him to use it to keep his hair in place. The kids in the neighborhood teased him about his one present by showing off all their new toys in front of him. Again, he felt humiliated, like an outcast.

Manson was eight years old when his mother was released from prison, one of the happiest days of his life. She came and got him and appeared to have missed him, but it wasn't long before she was back into her old habits, pulling him along for the ride. He was now old enough to live with her full time, taking care of himself while she was out running around.

By the age of twelve, he wrote that he had "missed a lot of school, seen a few juvenile homes where she temporarily put me, and no longer believed all my mom's lovers were visiting uncles."

About this time, his mother's current lover started threatening to leave her, stating that he could not stand her kid. He overheard his mother say, "Don't leave, be patient. I love you and we'll work something out."

The next thing Manson knew, he and his mother were standing before a judge, and she was saying that she could not afford a proper home for her son. Manson was made a ward of the court and placed into a boys' home.

Being checked into the boys' home was devastating to young Manson. He wrote:

My head and stomach started going wacky. I felt sick. I couldn't breathe. Tears ran down my cheeks. Some invisible force was crushing my chest and stealing my life away from me. I loved my mother. I wanted her. "Why, mom? Please, come get me." I was lonelier than I had ever been in my life.[3]

Even though Manson called it a "good boys home," he was exposed to a lot of things the average kid doesn't experience. He saw kids forced into homosexual acts and he was told how to beat the law. He also learned how to keep his feelings to himself because, he said, if a person cared too much, others would take advantage of him.

Once in a long while his mother would show up and tell him, "Pretty soon I will be taking you home." He wanted to believe in her but she never kept her promise.

Sick and tired of waiting for her, he ran away, straight to his mother. She took him to the judge who put him right back into the boy's home. This second abandonment was a painful turning point for Manson:

This time there were no tears. At least, none ran down my cheeks. I also knew I could no longer smile or be happy. I was bitter and I knew real hate. The trip back was a waste of time. I split the very first chance I got. Goodbye, boys' home. Goodbye, Mom.[4]

At this point, only twelve years old, he began to steal to support himself on the streets. Soon he met a friend who invited him to live with his uncle, who forced both children to steal for their keep.

Eventually Manson was caught and put into a bonafide reform school, "full of warped, sadistic people." He wrote that this place turned out many hardcore criminals, mainly because of the type of person who sought employment at such places. The children were often whipped and physically beaten until they passed out. Homosexuality was rampant, forced on most of the kids either by those who worked there or the older inmates.

It was not uncommon to get raped in the rear then beaten... At an age when most kids are going to nice schools, living with their parents, and learning all about the better things in life, I was recuperating from the wounds of a leather strap and learning to hate the world and everyone in it.[5]

At the age of sixteen, he finally escaped with a friend. They stole a car and headed for California. Upon crossing the Utah border they were caught. Since they had crossed the state line, he was sent to a federal reformatory for three and one-half years.

After Manson was released, he fell in love and married. He says he felt loved for the first time in his life.

When she would whisper "I love you" I would feel goose bumps all over my body. Her love was filling a huge void. For the first time in my life I felt I could conquer the world.[6]

To support a wife and then a child, he started to steal and was soon back in jail. In prison he began to realize more deeply than ever the meaning of his wife's love and the pure love given to him by his child. He started to understand what a fool he had been for most of his life. For the first time he felt truly motivated to do what was necessary to develop a positive attitude and the skills to become an honest person.

His wife wrote him daily and visited as often as she could. Manson felt inspired by the love he now felt, something he had never known as a child, and his own child and the future support of his family became his one and only goal. Unfortunately, the emotional supports that were sustaining him were suddenly removed when his wife stopped visiting and his mother told Manson that she had run off with another man. When he realized that he had been abandoned by the only women he had ever loved, Manson fell apart. "I flipped. The whole world caved in on me. I never saw her or my child again."

In spite of this, Manson still tried to find some meaning and

163

purpose in life. Although he was still imprisoned and bitter about his wife's betrayal, he discovered that he had some musical talent and began to put his energy into developing it. He fell in love with playing the guitar and writing music.

One day when his mother was visiting him, he asked her if she could possibly find the money, about two hundred dollars, to buy him his own guitar. She said that she was broke and could not even afford food. Because he desperately needed her love, Manson told her that he understood and that it was all right.

About two months later, however, his mother showed up for a visit with a little girl in her arms. Greeting him with the words "Meet your little sister," she told him that she had spent well over two thousand dollars to adopt the child. Reacting to the situation, Manson wrote:

> I felt a jealous rage building inside of me. I flipped and said some pretty nasty things to her telling her I never wanted to see her again.[7]

He still believed in his music, and spent his final year in prison writing as much of it as he could. When he was finally released, he was determined to find his way into the music world and live an honest life. After several disappointments, and a few broken promises within the highly competitive music industry, Manson found himself on the streets of San Francisco during the sixties. After a life of disappointments, failures, and emotional abandonment, he went on to become one of the most feared and notorious killers of our time.

When Manson became a criminal, he made choices that he must be held accountable for; but he was not the only one responsible for the path his life took. Almost every aspect of society had a part in the development of this criminal mind: his parents, his grandparents, the church, the community, the courts, jails and the juvenile system.

Manson did not just suddenly become a killer. Time and time

again, as an innocent child, he invested his heart and then had his innocence crushed by rejection and neglect.

In fact, if we think back to some of the other case studies I have shared, we see the same pattern. Bob, the person who stood up against the wall in my office was not violated as violently as Manson, but daily sought to be accepted by his father and peers. Every day that he faced, he had to anticipate more rejection. Jack, who firmly came to believe he was half man and half woman, entered each day dreadfully alone, deeply desiring the need for human touch.

Because our own subconscious mind has become so efficient at blocking out our pain, trying to help us forget or deny the thousands of times we have been hurt, we fail to understand the immensity of the build-up of pain that goes into creating behavior such as Bob's, Jack's or Manson's.

Over a period of time, Bob's emotional pain was so intense that it forced him up against the wall as his only means of taking care of himself. Jack felt so desperate for touch that he couldn't resist the sexual involvement with his cousins. Manson had been so deeply robbed of his dignity that it soon resulted in a compulsive need for control, power, and violence toward others.

THE EMOTIONAL PAIN DIAGRAM

How can we begin to understand the behaviors of someone like Bob, Jack, or Charles Manson? We can begin to develop a proper understanding of emotional disorders, and answer our major questions about them, by first understanding how our mind reacts to the violations of our selfhood. Figure 11.1 illustrates the basic emotional pain diagram.

As I mentioned at the start of this chapter, there is a consistent and predictable aspect to the manner in which we all react to emotional pain. This consistent and fundamental process that we use to deal with human violation is shown in the first half of the diagram, in Points 1 through 4. Let's start with Path A, the path we follow when we have been violated by someone else.

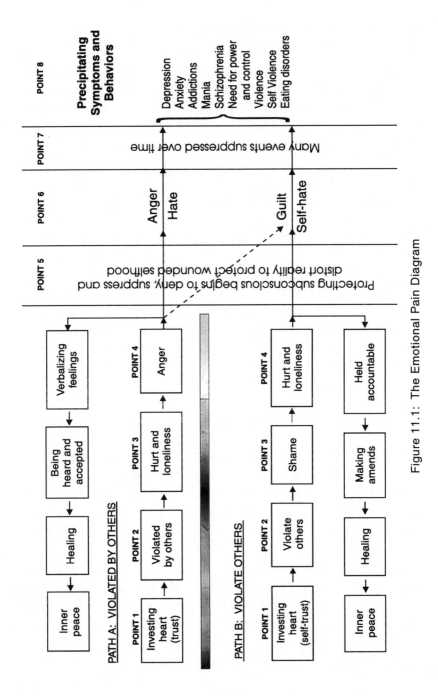

Figure 11.1: The Emotional Pain Diagram

166

PATH A

Every time we choose to participate in life, investing our heart into something or someone, we expose ourselves to the possibility of being violated. In fact, we take on that risk by simply walking out our front door or getting out of bed in the morning.

Do you remember times as a child when you were just innocently looking around at school and some smart-aleck kid would throw you off guard by saying something like "What are you looking at, ugly?" Although he might not have been able to articulate it if asked, he somehow knew that just by being present in the same room with him, you were making an emotional investment, and that he could take advantage of that investment.

When we are violated, it is fundamentally important to realize that whether the violation is accidental or intentional, we *immediately* and *always* experience feelings of hurt and loneliness (Point 3). When this happens, the cognitive-conscious part of our mind often quickly steps in to keep us from being aware of these first two feelings, but in spite of this defense mechanism, we always experience them.

We feel hurt because a part of our selfhood has been violated or "stabbed" emotionally. We experience loneliness because there is now a felt distance between us and the violator, and any others who are involved in this particular incident. For example, if someone were to make fun of us in the cafeteria in front of our peers ("What are you looking at, ugly?"), we would feel hurt by the violation and momentarily alone or isolated. Our mind might quickly come to our rescue, laughing, or perhaps replying with something aggressive such as, "Your ugly face," but the hurt and loneliness will have still been experienced.

Sometimes the dominant feeling we have is loneliness, such as when we lose a loved one. If the violation happens because a sibling takes a toy from us as a child, we may have felt more hurt than loneliness.

Regardless of the relative intensity of these two basic feelings

Regardless of the relative intensity of these two basic feelings or the effectiveness at which they can be blocked out, this is where we must begin: when violated, we always experience some degree of hurt and loneliness.

Soon after the hurt and loneliness, we will begin to feel some anger (Point 4). Anger is a natural protective reaction to being violated, even if the violation is accidental or unintentional. For example, when I am suddenly awakened in the middle of the night by my son crying out, if I pay close attention to myself, I will discover that, at times, I feel violated. Of course my child did not intentionally want to hurt me, but I will still feel violated because of my need and desire for rest.

If I stop and take a moment to think about my late-night feelings, I will be able to identify some hurt, some loneliness, and some slight anger or irritation. These feelings are so small that, after a second or two, my love for my son quickly absorbs them, allowing me to fully attend to his needs.

If I happened to have a bad cold, knew that I had to get up early, or felt that my wife was not sharing her part of the responsibility, then my felt love or dedication might not be enough to absorb my hurt, loneliness, and anger. I might then begin to slip past Point 4 to a place where I might feel anger at my son for awakening me. (Point 6).

It is important for us to realize that, when we are violated, feelings of hurt, loneliness, and anger are always present. If our love for our self or the person we are interacting with is sufficient, or if we can correctly identify our feelings and defend our selfhood (e.g., "Your words hurt me,") then we will be able to stay within Points 1 through 4. If we do not have the inner strength or love to absorb the violation, then our mind or protective subconscious will come into play. This is the moment when we all start to become a little "crazy."

For example, let's say that I had to get up three times during the night, but managed to suppress my growing anger because I wanted to be there for my son. The next morning I might snap at my wife,

168

expensive? Why do you continue to waste our money?" As my denial system split off and repressed the feelings I had during the night—the ones that I didn't have enough inner strength to absorb (Point 5)—my unhealed pain would feel a need to act out the anger in some way (Point 6). Notice, however, that my act of anger does not heal my wound, but was an attempt to affirm my sense of self by attacking the dignity and innocence of my wife.

If I had stayed close to my feelings, perhaps saying to her, "I feel some irritation at you for not helping out last night. I need you to get up some of the time," I would have given her an opportunity to affirm my need directly, perhaps by saying something like, "Oh, I'm sorry. I slept right through it all. Please feel free to wake me up next time."

Let's now take this scenario one step further. Let's assume that, as a child, I was neglected; that when I cried out at night, I was either ignored or punished. As an adult, I would be harboring a lot of pain in this area that my protective subconscious had to deny as a child. Along with this pain, I would also have a lot of repressed anger. Now, when I was awakened at night, the little bit of irritation caused by my son would begin to trigger the rage from my child-hood. Since my parents re-claimed their dignity by beating me, I might feel a strong urge to beat my son.

The reason that child abuse is passed along from one generation to the next is not because of defective genes, simple condition-ing, or modeling. It is primarily the result of a violated selfhood—the need to inappropriately affirm oneself by violating another per-son back. We don't just passively model violating behavior. There is an inner emotional *drive* to hurt others. If I had been severely neglected as a child, and had repressed that pain, then it would ap-pear to me that my son was responsible for triggering it. By becom-ing angry at him, I would not only punish him for triggering my own pain, but use *his* innocence in an attempt to reclaim some of *my* lost innocence. Subconsciously I will believe that if I can hurt him in the same way that I was originally hurt, then I will be able to re-claim that aspect of my own violated innocence.

To summarize Path A, Points 1 through 6: When we are violated, we will experience feelings of hurt, loneliness, and eventual anger. We may not be fully aware of these feelings, but they are always present. If these feelings are not dealt with properly at the time, their suppression might eventually emerge in the form of more intense feelings of anger, rage, or the need to get even and hurt others.

Also notice that, beginning at Point 4, our feelings can switch over to guilt and/or self-hate at Point 6. Before we consider this aspect of our diagram, let's turn our attention to Path B.

PATH B

We travel Path A when we feel we have been violated by others. Path B represent the feeling-emotional path that results when we violate or hurt another person, animal, or any other aspect of our environment.

When we hurt others, and are made aware of that fact, we realize on some level that we have violated the innocence of that person. Consequently, when we feel some shame at what we did, this shame results in the violation of our own innocence or goodness. This causes feelings of hurt about the violation of our own innocence and a felt separation from our own selfhood. We not only feel sorry for hurting the other person, and alone (separated from them), but, most important, we feel hurt and isolated from our own innermost innocence.

For example, let's say a five-year-old child is playing around at the dinner table and accidentally spills his milk. Although he did not do this on purpose, he is also aware that he was being careless or irresponsible to a degree. If you watch his body language or facial expression carefully, you will first see some shame, then some hurt and a sense of aloneness within himself as well as with everyone else. We experience this aloneness because, when we have done something wrong, our shame literally turns into a need within ourselves to get away from ourselves. This is why we say things to ourselves such as, "Why did I do that? How could I be so stupid?"

The natural reaction to the violation of others is to feel some slight shame. This slight shame may be present as a natural part of our conscience or it can be the result of others letting us know that we have violated them. As I pointed out in my book *Why Do I Feel Guilty When I Have Done Nothing Wrong?*, this slight shame is a good kind of shame because it is only intended to awaken us to our wrongful act. In other words, it should not feel like a destructive shame, but only awaken us to the fact that we have hurt someone and need to apologize, ask forgiveness, and change our behavior.

If Johnny spills his milk and his mother says, "Johnny, remember I asked you to be careful. I know you want to have fun, but I must ask you to control your behavior better at the dinner table. Do you understand?" she is using the incident and his slight shame to help guide him to control his emotions better. Thus, when he begins to goof around at the table the next time, his slight shame will encourage him toward proper self-discipline.

If his mother were to begin yelling at him, telling him that he is a "bad boy," then she is taking the incident in which he violated himself, and violating him deeper while he is still in a vulnerable condition. In other words, he opened the wound, perhaps accidentally, and she is using the opportunity to stick the "emotional knife" in deeper.

If we are overly shamed, or learn to shame ourselves excessively, perhaps as a way of suppressing feelings of anger when violated by others (Point 4, Path A), then shame begins to take on a destructive, cancerous role in our lives. It is important to note, however, that when we feel a slight shame or conscious awareness, this can be a good shame. If we pay attention to it, by properly asking forgiveness or repenting, our actions will bring us back into healing-loving relationships with those whom we have violated. Unfortunately, most of us have had enough destructive shame imposed upon us that it is hard for us to separate the good kind of shame from the destructive kind.

As we shall see in the next chapter, when we go into Points 5

171

through 8 in more depth, we all begin to feel and act a little crazy when we mix feelings of guilt and anger from our past. Developing the ability to properly separate the anger of the present from that of the past, and to distinguish between destructive shame and a little bit of good constructive shame, provides us with the necessary and fundamental skills to live an emotionally healthy life.

PATH A VERSUS PATH B

Before we talk more about the right side of the equation in the emotional pain model, I will to point out some other differences between Paths A and B. Path B is more of a moral or religious path than Path A. It has to do with how we, our society and our religious or moral training define correct, ethical, good behavior. Based upon what is considered right or holy, a person should feel some shame when he engages in actions such as stealing or harming others. Hopefully, he will then attempt to rectify or heal the situation.

Path A, which this book primarily focuses upon, has much more to do with the emotional health of the person. Whereas Path B signifies the sin or harm done by the person against others, Path A signifies the sins or harm done against the person himself.

It is important to realize that, in almost every case, people who suffer from severe emotional disorders do so because they have been sinned against or violated. When Johnny spills his milk and his mother yells at him, telling him that he is a bad boy instead of constructively addressing his behavior, she is attacking the very essence of his selfhood. When she does this, she imposes Path A on top of Path B. Although Charles Manson chose to become a criminal, most likely he wouldn't have done so if he had not been so overwhelmingly violated at every step of his life.

This is the area where the church and other religious bodies often make a grave mistake. From a theological standpoint, there is a tendency to see a person's symptoms of depression, schizophrenia, or other behaviors as the result of the person's disobedience to God. In reality, just the opposite is true—others have been violating *him*. When a religious authority tells a person that his symptoms are the result of his "disobedience to God" or "lack of faith," that person is further violated.

Of course an individual's situation is never that simple. Much of Manson's behavior was the result of violations against him, but he still chose to violate others. In this sense, he still must be held accountable for the crimes that he committed.

For a person to be able to make sense out of her feelings and emotions, she must have the ability to stay to the left side of the diagram. Once the degree of violation has pushed a person over to the right side, Paths A and B begin to enmesh themselves together, creating a multiplicity of complex and difficult-to-understand behaviors. Once a person has progressed into this level of emotional dysfunction, trying to lead her back from Point 8 to Point 2, where a healing can take place, can be a difficult and complex matter. This process becomes quite difficult for Manson or any person who has used his behavior for many years as a defense against the intense pain accumulated at Point 2.

Our best solution, if we as a society want to avoid these "worst-case scenarios," is to build an emotional health program between Points 1 through 4. Unfortunately, this isn't what our culture does. Instead, society and certain religious institutions blame the person for his symptoms, while the medical model denies the entire process that occurs between Points 1 through 7, focusing their efforts completely on suppressing the symptoms or behaviors at Point 8.

THE EMOTIONALLY HEALTHY PERSON

From the emotional pain diagram we can define the emotionally healthy person quite easily. This person has the capacity to stay within Points 1 through 4 the majority of the time. When hurt or violated, if he is not able to absorb the violated feelings, he has the courage and inner strength to address the violation in the most open and honest way possible without violating the innocence of the other person. Thus, a person will make a statement such as "I feel upset when you arrive late. I need to talk about this issue," instead of "You're a lousy worker. You're fired."

When the emotionally healthy person does, on occasion, act irresponsibly, perhaps violating the rights and feelings of others, he is able to avoid punishing himself with destructive shame, choosing instead to take his awareness of his shame and find the courage to do what is necessary to reconcile with others. In our relationships with others, the more we can learn about staying within Points 1 through 4, the more we will experience an emotionally healthy life.

CHAPTER TWELVE

HATE AND SELF-HATE

The more we can come to understand Points 1 through 4 in the emotional pain diagram and experience this aspect in our daily lives as we interface with violating moments, the more we will be able to make sense out of Points 5 through 8. When we don't understand the dynamics of the process of Points 1 through 4, we have a hard time understanding the rest of the equation, especially the dynamics of hate and self-hate.

Children, with their innate innocence and sensitivity, are especially vulnerable to violation. When a child is violated and the corresponding feelings begin to overwhelm the innocence of his selfhood, the protective aspect of his consciousness begins to play a stronger and stronger role. For example when Johnny spilled his milk, if his mother had continued to scream at him, telling him how bad he was, his protective side might have started operating in one of two ways. It might have blocked out all sense of any constructive shame to protect him from being vulnerable to destructive shame; or it might have caused Johnny to begin to worry or become tentative about everything he did. He might have come to believe that if he worried enough about every little action, then perhaps he would never do anything wrong and always be safe. Whatever path the protective subconscious chooses, the end result is always the protection of the selfhood.

Once the selfhood has been violated, it will feel unloved and there will be a need for a healing. It is important to realize that this need will never go away until this recovery takes place. We may deny that our childhood memories need healing, but we know this is a fact from our own life experiences. Every time we have been hurt by someone who is important to us, there is a part of us that feels a need to resolve that hurt. Something feels *unfinished*.

For example, suppose someone at work makes an unfair comment about me. If I don't say anything, I may be successful at pushing the event out of my mind and going on with my work, but there is still some negative energy within me. A protective part of me wants to hold that remark against the person and not trust him as much.

I can remember back in my life to several small incidents where I was accidentally hurt by someone. The incidents were so small that they have very little, if any, effect on my present life. Yet because these situations were never resolved or healed, I still feel a small amount of pain when I think about them. On the other hand, if the incident was resolved properly, then I won't feel the pain, but will feel warmth about that situation or person.

For example, my aunt once made me eat peas when I was visiting her. I held onto that event for thirty years, finally bringing it up to her in a "joking" fashion, using humor to cover up the fact that I still felt some hurt. She apologized, telling me that she hadn't realized that she had hurt my feelings. Even though she has always been a special aunt to me, and has given me more than enough love to help me handle this event, her apology left a feeling of warmth in place of the hurt of that *specific* incident.

It is important to realize that, although we need inner strength to overcome a lot of violated moments in our lifetime, each and every moment yearns for a healing. Our heart yearns for a healing because we made an emotional investment at that moment. In the case of my aunt, when I got a chance to visit her, I always saw it as a vacation. On a vacation, a person should not be ordered to eat peas, especially by a favorite aunt.

To properly understand emotional disorders, we must realize

that (a) we always have a consistent and fundamental reaction to a particular violation (Points 1 through 4), and that we have an *absolute* need for healing. With the acceptance of these two principles, let's now look at the right side of our equation: Points 5 through 8.

POINTS 5 THROUGH 8

When we are violated and not able to experience a healing or express the corresponding feelings, our protective subconscious comes into play. At first it denies our hurt feelings. If no healing occurs, however, it is only a matter of time until the protective subconscious begins an *active* search for a way to reclaim whatever we have lost.

It is important to acknowledge that this active process is going on. In the last chapter, when I used the example of pushing down my feelings at night when my crying child awakened me, and then snapping at my wife about buying "expensive" breakfast cereal the next morning, this reaction was the subconscious part of my mind actively searching for a way to reclaim my lost dignity. When violated, we all begin a searching process. The sequence is:

a) The violation
b) Repression of the feelings
c) No healing
d) Need to affirm the self by *actively* violating others or violating ourselves through self-punishment.

Even though my comment about the cereal appeared to come out of nowhere, it was the result of my subconscious searching for a way to feel good about my unidentified and unhealed violated self. Snapping at my wife is certainly not a part of my biology, nor is it simply a learned response. My protective subconscious might learn to use a particular type of behavior by modeling others, and often does, but I can't deny that an active searching process is going on.

When a violation is not properly identified, expressed, or healed,

177

part of our consciousness must begin to find an alternative way to recapture what was lost or taken away. Even through we may be able to keep the process away from our full awareness by repressing the pain or creating anxiety, addictions, or compulsions to avoid the feelings, eventually, the energy of the violation will be directed toward hating others or hating ourselves. In Figure 12.1 I have redrawn the emotional pain diagram emphasizing these aspects.

Let's start with the self-hate aspect of our equation, then we'll study the need to hurt others.

SELF-HATE

Notice again that in the normal process of experiencing the violating aspects of life, some anger will always be present. When a child is not allowed to identify and express his feelings, when he has had his innocence deeply violated or has chosen to use guilt as a way of denying his own feelings, this false sense of guilt can begin to turn into many different forms of self-hate. The process might begin with a mild form of punishing himself with guilt-ridden thoughts or statements, then move on to compulsive activities that allow him to stay away from his feelings of shame and anger. He might even start to feel the need to inflict injury upon himself.

For example, many parents who were abused as children make a supreme commitment to be the best parents possible. To keep from hurting others with their feelings of suppressed anger, they must constantly feed themselves guilt-ridden messages. Any time the smallest recognition of anger begins to work its way to the surface, their protective subconscious quickly comes into play to produce a guilty, destructive or shameful emotional response.

Many individuals have been able to suppress their lifelong anger at their parents by always feeling guilty about something. If an overbearing mother phones and asks, "What's wrong with you? You should come see me more often," the daughter doesn't consciously feel angered by this violation of her space, but feels guilty for not pleasing her mother. Such a person can come to feel "bad" or have

178

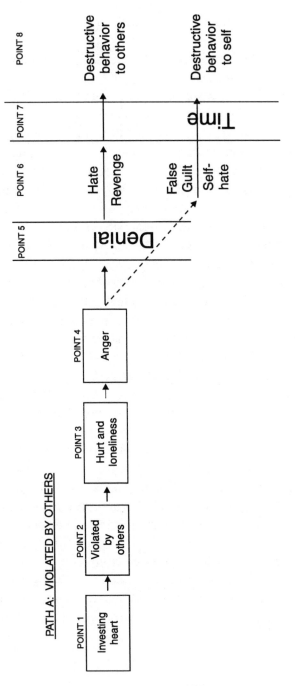

Figure 12.1: Unhealed violations turning to hate & self-hate

179

guilty thoughts about herself even if someone only gives her a disappointed look. In this manner, she obviously gives over much of
her power to others by allowing them to control her through the
use of false guilt or destructive shame.

Such an individual may also use compulsive behavior to help
her stay away from feelings of anger and shame. Let's use as an
example someone who was abused as a child, but is now determined to be the very best mother possible. If this individual is
awakened several times during the night by a sick child, she
might not even be able to allow herself the slightest feeling of
irritation, because feeling that way would trigger some of the
deeper anger and hate from her childhood. To help keep her
deeper feelings repressed, she might become compulsive in certain areas. One woman I know, after a difficult night with her
child, would clean her whole house the next day, especially if
she had received no help from her husband. To suppress the
anger she felt right after getting up and comforting her child,
she would begin organizing the next day in her mind. Dwelling
on the good feelings of having her house in perfect order would
push her anger down far enough to let her go to sleep.

Some individuals, because of their fear or distaste for any
form of anger, will begin to turn their anger into shame even if
they have not been seriously violated. I have seen this reaction
often in daughters who have been raised by very loving and caring fathers. Regardless of how loving or perfect a father may be,
there will still be moments when his child feels angry at him. If
the child does not feel free to express this appropriate anger, or
subconsciously chooses to turn the anger into guilt or self-hate
to avoid risking the loss of the parent's love, then the child will
begin to cripple herself. When she is violated later in life, instead of being able to feel her anger and protect herself, she will
blame herself instead. In reaction to an abusive husband, she
might say to herself, "If I were just a better wife, he wouldn't
get mad and hit me."

EXTREME SELF-HATE

One of the main ways that the protective subconscious can deal with unhealed pain is to turn it back upon the person who then punishes himself for being bad or having negative feelings toward others. In this way the person can hopefully remain safe and retain the love of the other person by not expressing these feelings. Unfortunately, turning anger into false guilt or self-hate can result in extreme conditions of self-hate.

Many of you have heard about people who have a need to cut or mutilate their bodies in some way. These are not acts of suicide, but for some, are acts by individuals who feel the need to punish themselves. For others, it is simply a graphic attempt to let the pain out. When someone takes a razor blade and begins making small cuts, or burns himself with a cigarette, he does *not* feel pain. He will often feel a warm glow inside of his body instead. Along with that warm glow comes a craving to harm himself which can become just as overpowering as the need to drink alcohol or take drugs. Since self-mutilation can be an extreme form of self-hatred and is often the result of sexual abuse, we will use incest as an example to help us understand the craving to harm oneself that resides behind self-hate.

Incest represents a major violation of the self from many angles. Perhaps the most significant aspect of incest is its betrayal of trust. A young child, vulnerable and needing to feel safe with an affirming parent, usually the father, will invest herself and her needs in the parent. Within this dynamic, a conscious, intimate love relationship is formed between the child and the parent.

When a child is abused, the hurt will be felt at a very deep level, perhaps all the way to the core of her selfhood. This is because, at her core, she absolutely needs to trust others, and parents are usually a child's most obvious primary choice.

A child will feel an intense sense of loneliness when her father, for example, touches her in a violating way. She will also feel shameful or dirty about herself because it was *her* body that her father was attracted to and used against her. For this reason, it is easy for her to conclude that the violation was her fault, especially when her father is in denial about his own guilt.

The intense feelings of hurt and loneliness that make up the child's feelings of desperation will begin to tear at her selfhood in a violently destructive manner. At this point, either her conscious self or her protective subconscious must come to her rescue—but how? She obviously can't go to her father; and, because of the shame and broken trust she has experienced, she will probably be afraid to seek help from other adults as well.

Addictions, compulsions, and the development of schizophrenic-type symptoms can be used as a way to deal with this desperation, but even these methods often fail because they can't suppress the intense shame.

In the face of such an extreme dilemma, self-hate often becomes the only answer. If the child can convince herself that she is bad or did something wrong, then she might try to punish herself. As she does this, perhaps by cutting or burning places on her body, she will begin to feel that she has now earned "the right" to be forgiven. The warmth of that feeling gives her a certain amount of power to combat the desperation left by her abuse.

Because this action does not result in any true healing of her desperation, the cutting only provides a temporary relief, and she soon craves more cutting, burning, or whatever method of relief is being used.

Not until that desperation is interfaced with a safe, trusting re-lationship with another human being, and the person can be affirmed by unconditional love, will the desperation begin to subside: "You were not a bad little girl. Your father was bad. You needed to be loved and touched in the right way."

Incest is an extreme form of abuse that usually results in some type of self-destructive behavior, but we should not limit our aware-ness only to cases of severe abuse. Children whose parents are going through a divorce often blame themselves because this is the best way they have found of dealing with the pain of something that they have so little control over. While they are trying to deal with the desperation of losing a parent, their protective subconscious often comes to their rescue. If they can convince themselves that they are at fault for the separation, and then find out what they are doing wrong, they believe, that by correcting their wrongdoing, they can make their parents stay together. If this could only happen, then the pain of the divorce would cease.

We see the same parallel in our society at large. As the emotional pain of our culture becomes more intense, our children will need to find more and more ways of dealing with this pain, often through expressions of self-hate. Drugs, careless sex, reckless driving—all become indicators of their need to gain an element of control over their emotions through self-destructive behavior.

A lot of young people who mutilate their bodies out of self-hate were not seriously abused as children. This behavior is simply a product of the bad feelings they have about themselves, often due to the ongoing negative peer pressure they must endure. For example, many young girls hate themselves for not being thin enough. If these young people truly loved themselves and felt a responsibility to that love, they would be taking better care of themselves.

The point that I want to make is that, if our feelings are not dealt with properly, we will eventually feel more and more of a need to hurt ourselves and/or others. As our society gradually becomes more violating and we fail to teach our children how to operate emotionally within Points 1 through 4, we will see more and more self-destructive behavior.

HATE, VIOLENCE, AND EVIL

How then does a person become a serial murderer or develop a *love* for killing? He starts on the same path as any of the rest of us, except that the intensity of his pain is much deeper. It is so deep and so intense that his protective side becomes more and more focused on a single way of dealing with the pain—hurting others.

To get an idea of the intensity of the pain someone like this feels, let me return to what Manson said when his mother turned him over to the judge to avoid losing her boyfriend:

> My head and stomach started going wacky. I felt sick. I couldn't breathe. Tears ran down my cheeks. Some invisible force was crushing my chest and stealing my life away from me. I loved my mother. I wanted her. "Why mom? Please, come get me." I was lonelier than I had ever been in my life.[1]

The intensity of Manson's pain did not stem only from a single incident. He mentions several similar experiences in his book. This feeling of abandonment and betrayal, however, must have been with him almost daily. As a child bounced around from one caretaker to the next, how many thousands of times would he have seen other kids with their parents and felt a stabbing pain? He could have turned that pain into shame, but remember, our diagram shows us that the natural reaction to violations is to feel anger.

Yet how could he ever hope to "properly" express the intensity of the anger that he felt without being further punished? Manson's only option for relief and control was to push down these feelings and gradually turn them to hate.

If we study ourselves, we can get a glimpse of what was happening in Manson's mind. When we become enmeshed in a situation where we get hurt but cannot get mad (without severe consequences), we might find ourselves *compulsively* spending time being angry in our heads. Providing the event was not that important, and that we have a sufficient reserve of self-esteem, we can eventually move back within Points 1 through 4. For example, if you were the manager of a service department and a customer attacked your team during a meeting, you might have to suppress your anger during the meeting. Afterwards, you could "blow off steam" by complaining to co-workers, or rationalize the incident away by deciding that the customer was out of line, or seek many other ways of dealing with the anger. But if you had to sit in daily meetings under personal attack with no way to fight back or get relief, your anger would eventually find some way to be expressed, whether constructively (working it out with management) or destructively (drinking heavily or quitting work).

What does someone like Manson do? By becoming angry, he might risk losing his mother, being beaten by her boyfriend, being disowned by relatives who don't want him around, or becoming the brunt of severe beatings and rape while in the juvenile homes. I am sure there were times when he did get angry, but he basically had to learn how to "swallow" it—to absorb great amounts of pain and humiliation.

His only relief, most likely, was to begin to create hateful, revengeful thoughts. He may have even had fantasies of killing his mother or her boyfriends, as a way of relieving some of his anger. Every time he had such angry thoughts, they would give him pleasure as they momentarily affirmed his selfhood, bringing back his sense of dignity. When he finally found a group of followers who would believe in his hate, this was all the more reason to hate and feel good about it.

Manson, like almost all psychopaths or serial killers, had been using hate all his life as a way of controlling the feelings of his woundedness. By fantasizing about how he would take revenge on those whom he hated, he could feel some degree of control over them and recapture his sense of dignity. Just as self-hate and self-mutilation feel good to a person full of shame, producing a compulsive desire for such activities, hating and eventually killing become a compulsive need with someone like Manson.

The more such a person uses hate as a way of reclaiming his lost dignity, the more hate, revenge, and killing become absolutely necessary for him to maintain his sense of self. When the serial killer murders, this action brings him a feeling of relief, as do all compulsive behaviors. Soon, however, he will begin to feel the need to kill again to reclaim more of his lost dignity.

Years of rage may go by as a person begins to rely more and more on hate or the thought of killing another person as a way of controlling his inner pain. Perhaps, when he kills his first victim, he will have no conscious intention of doing so. Perhaps he will acci-

185

dentally kill him a burst of anger.

The first murder may likely be followed by some degree of genuine shame. By killing a person, however, the killer has actually severely violated himself. With little capacity to be honest with himself about such a violation, he will eventually turn his genuine shame into more anger. This is illustrated by the line drawn from Point 3 in Path B, the shame he should feel for the murder, up to Point 6 in Path A as shown in Figure 12.2.

Most professionals believe that the mass murderer or sociopath feels no shame or guilt. That is not true. He has so much real shame, and so little self-esteem to help him deal with it, that he must split from it before it overwhelms him, and turn it into a rage toward others. In fact, before such a person can kill or rape an innocent person, he must transform that person into someone so bad that he can act out his anger and avoid his guilt at the same time.

Each time the serial killer takes another human life, his protective subconscious uses the killing to avoid his desperation, the anger from his past, and the genuine shame that he piles up with each new murder. Soon he develops an uncontrollable desire for evil. When he kills, he feels an extreme high, much like that experienced by a drug addict, sex addict, or any other kind of addict.

You might wonder how a person's protective subconscious can go to the extreme of murder or rape. How can the protective subconscious be safeguarding a person by driving him to such behavior?

Remember that the protective subconscious has one function and one function only. It is there to protect a person's selfhood from the feelings of desperation, hurt, loneliness, shame, and anger. Once the protective subconscious finds a solution—be it drugs, hate, catatonia, mania, or over-eating—it holds onto that solution. Since there is no real healing taking place, the person is actually further violating himself. Eventually, acting out in a particular area becomes the only way to avoid the shame of that area. If someone can justify overeating in the present moment, he can also momentarily justify his past acts of overeating. If a person can find a way to justify

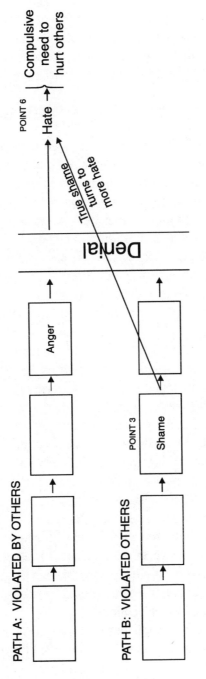

Figure 12.2: Denial of true shame and the accumulation of hate

187

killing his eighth prostitute, then he can momentarily justify killing the other seven. In this way, our protective subconscious leads us into a dead-end road where we are left with the compulsive need to use the same method of self-justification over and over again.

WHAT THEN IS "MENTAL ILLNESS" ALL ABOUT?

All of us have had our moments when we have acted a little crazy, become self-destructive, or been surprised at our anger and hate toward others. So what, then, is mental illness all about?

When we look at even the most bizarre of behaviors, we can see not a biologically dysfunctioning brain, but a wounded person struggling to find the proper identification and healing of her feelings. Behind these strange behaviors or thought patterns will always be feelings of hurt, loneliness, fear, and the need to hurt others or oneself. These elements, along with broken trust and the need for unconditional affirmation, are at the root of all emotionally troubled individuals.

When you listen carefully to the confused, seemingly rambling thoughts of a person diagnosed as schizophrenic, you can begin to pick out basic themes of anger and guilt, especially guilt. A person may feel so bad or dirty about himself that he fears going outside lest someone give him a dirty look. In this way, a person's mind might create the delusion that the KGB is after him, thus giving himself permission to hide inside where he feels safe.

Talking about space ships, or needing to save the President from an assassin, may be a person's only way of drawing attention to himself because of his own sense of worthlessness.

Often this type of delusion can be filled with anger and hate. A person might believe that certain individuals have sent the KGB after him for unfair reasons, giving him permission to be angry with anyone who does not help him—which could be related to feelings of helplessness that he had as a child.

The actual shape of each individual's stories, hallucinations, and delusions are as unlimited as their individuality, but they all have themes of guilt, anger, and fear, or they are used to help suppress painful feelings of hurt and loneliness.

Severe cases of depression are the result of the fear to express one's deeper feelings. Compulsive activities, such as hand-washing, are examples of a person's best tactic for keeping his feelings of dirtiness under control. He has no control over his deeper shame because that was put there by others when they violated him, but he can *momentarily* make himself feel cleaner as he washes his hands. This relief is soon followed, however, by the resurfacing of his deeper feelings. Before these emotions are ever felt on a conscious level, the person will experience a craving to wash his hands again. Many women who are victims of sexual abuse feel a need to scrub their vaginas to the point of bleeding, in their attempts to get that part of their bodies clean.

Regardless of the symptoms or the behavior, emotionally troubled people always have underlying issues of hate or self-hate, as well as a need to suppress deeper feelings of hurt and loneliness. To recover, we must ultimately take the path of identifying these issues and, through healing, move back to the left side of the emotional equation of our lives.

CHAPTER THIRTEEN

MINIMIZING EMOTIONAL PAIN AND VIOLENCE

If emotional pain results in the symptoms and behaviors labeled as mental illness, how then can we reduce the emotional pain in our lives and that of others? It must begin with a clear understanding of how our emotions work; Figure 13.1 emphasizes Points 1 through 4.

This simple diagram is a good model that we can use to implement changes in our society, and to raise our children in an emotionally healthy way. A person who has learned to deal with her feelings according to this diagram will have the ability to remain emotionally stable under almost any condition. The starting point must be the correct identification of one's feelings. If this skill is not taught at childhood, it often takes years as an adult to master. I may be a prime example of this lack of ability to correctly identify one's feelings.

BEING IMMEDIATE WITH OUR FEELINGS

I grew up in a semi-rural setting with four very physical brothers. We all had the ability to become angry, but our approach, which we probably learned from our father, was to suppress the early awareness of our feelings and then suddenly blow up.

That might have been all right when I didn't get my way as a child or lost at an athletic contest, but as I grew older, I soon realized that blowing my stack had very destructive results in relation-

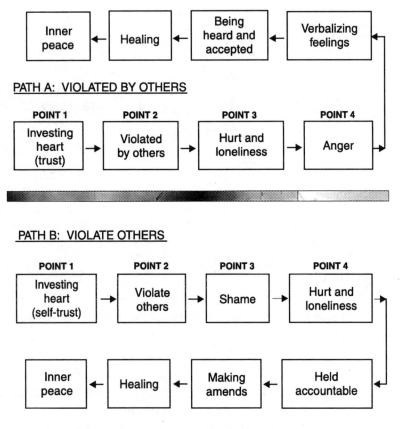

Figure 13.1: The emotional pain diagram.

ships. So I began to work on containing my anger better.

In practicum training class which was part of the course work for my Ph.D., I was confronted with one of the biggest shocks of my life. This class contained ten doctoral students, one professor, and two assistants. After counseling clients that would come into an on-site clinic, we would meet in a central room and discuss our cases. Invariably, the focus would turn away from the clients and onto our own issues.

During one class the professor turned to me and said, "Ty, what are you so angry about?" I was completely oblivious to any anger that might be in me at the moment, so I told him "nothing." Within the next few minutes the two assistants and the nine other students all told me that they saw anger written all over my face and body. Since I still wasn't actually aware of any anger and had no angry thoughts, I truly believed they were *all* wrong. In fact, I thought they were all crazy.

Five days later I was driving in my car when all of a sudden it dawned on me that I was angry, and what I was angry about. They were right! I had so effectively blocked out my anger that it had taken five days for me to notice it.

A few weeks later the group confronted me again about a new issue, but I still felt no anger in the present. On the way home in my car it came to me what I was angry about. Even though I was obviously making progress (two hours versus five days), I was quite embarrassed about my inability to be "immediate" with my feelings. I could wait until a situation became violating enough to give myself permission to explode, but I didn't know how to simply experience the small moment-to-moment violating events in my life as they occurred. I had invested so much of myself into being a "nice guy" that I had learned how to block out my anger until it reached the boiling point. Since I had been working hard on not exploding, I had further shut myself down. Later when I began to experience some depression, I also realized that this depression was the result of shutting down my feelings.

I have since come to realize the downside of not having immediate access to my feelings and not being able to experience them in my body at the moment they are developing. When I become this distanced from my feelings, I lose a lot of valuable information about what is taking place in my life, and I lose the ability to take care of myself.

Because most of us can feel our anger to some degree, we have a tendency to believe that we are always aware of all our anger. For most of us, however, because we have learned to deny the pain under our anger, we are only really aware of the "tip of the iceberg" of

193

our feelings.

This lack of awareness is true not only with anger, but with all our basic feelings including hurt, loneliness, shame, and often our need for love. Clients can sit in my office and be close to tears yet completely unaware of their need to cry or share their pain. Other clients can be talking about something painful that was done to them by someone, yet still deny that such events made them feel any anger toward the person.

Because we are all aware of some of our feelings, we tend to believe that we are aware of them all; but, just as I did with my anger, we all block out a certain amount of our feelings; this blocking prevents us from being fully present in our world and with ourselves.

Along the same line, I remember times when I was younger when I knew I had hurt someone but did not have the courage to hold myself accountable, make amends, and bring a healing to the situation and my own selfhood. As a result of the therapeutic work I've done, I now have a deep desire to stay as "clean" as possible in all relationships. When a relationship becomes violating to me, I try to address it. When I have violated someone else, I try to make amends.

As a result of being able to identify my feelings at any particular moment, and the skills that I've learned (and am still learning), I have the ability to stay within Points 1 through 4 in the emotional pain diagram most of the time. Consequently, I have learned how to protect my feelings better, carry much less stress, and feel safer and closer to others. Although I am still learning, I know I have an accurate conception of what emotional health is all about and how to obtain it.

I have carried these same principles and what I have learned from my own life right into my therapeutic approach. Of the clients that I work with, the ones that work the hardest at learning how to properly identify and *own* their own feelings are the ones who progress the farthest towards a place of properly taking care of themselves, of knowing what they want in life, and of avoiding violating others.

Bob's case can be used to expand on these principles. At home, in the hospitals, and in other situations, Bob was not even aware that he often used his catatonic posturing to keep the feelings associated with the rejection of others away from his selfhood. To maximize his method of coping, he went into a denial of his feelings as he entered his catatonic state.

In my office, he would feel an urge to go stand up against the wall. At the wall, his mind would race with thoughts of wondering if he had done the right thing in my presence. But he was so focused on his thoughts, he really had little perception that he was even up against the wall. Only after he felt safe enough could he slow his mind down to feel his fears that were a cover-up of his deeper feelings of the hurt and loneliness he had encountered as a child.

His emotional pain diagram looked like the following:

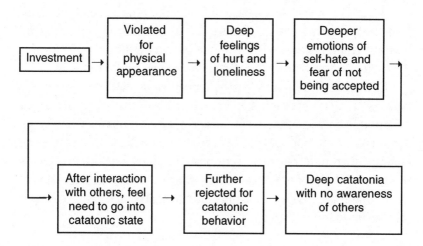

When I began working with Bob, we had to start at where he was: where he needed to protect himself. As he began to trust me, and because I was up against the wall with him, he started to become increasingly aware of his situation and behavior. As we begin to make sense out of his behavior, his awareness started shifting to the area represented by Figure 13.1.

When he finally started to feel the shame of being viewed as ugly, and began to affirm himself, the anger under his shame began to surface. Once he began to feel and share his anger, he could start to feel the hurt and loneliness of his childhood. At that point we were able to begin to heal the pain of his past.

Once he was strong enough to be in touch with the pain of his past, he could begin identifying the pain of the present. When someone looked at him funny, or he felt or suspected a possible violation from others, he now felt strong enough to not start moving back to the right side of the equation into his catatonic coping devices.

Bob's therapeutic process was much more involved than what I could simply present in a few pages, and I did not get as far as I wanted to with him before he ended therapy, but when we were able to do the work outlined above, the healing proceeded.

At first he was barely aware of any of the process, and the more frequently he was put into a hospital, medicated or shocked, the less aware he became. But the healing process raised his awareness, and he was able to begin *reclaiming* his life for himself.

Even though Bob's case may appear to be an extreme one, his healing process represents the same process that everyone must go through to recapture what was lost when violations had to be denied and were not healed. Everyone of us will fill each box in the diagram with different data from our own lives, but the process is the same. The process of becoming aware of one's basic feelings at the moment they begin to manifest is the secret: the path to operating within Points 1 through 4.

Doing What's Right For You

A major step in the road to achieving emotional health is reaching the point where we honor our emotional health and that of others, giving it our highest priority. To do so is to learn how to protect the most vulnerable part of who we are, our investing hearts. At the same time, we must learn how to avoid violating others.

If we neglect our emotional health, we further violate ourselves. In essence, we would be shaming the part of our selfhood that already feels violated by others. When we have been hurt, and we deny the way this makes us feel inside, we discount those feelings. Discounting our own feelings is just as violating as someone else discounting or denying our feelings. Although as a young man I thought I was doing the right thing by just forgetting or enduring my anger, what I was really doing was doubling the impact of the violation, thus doubling my anger.

When a person denies that he has been violated, he creates a more intense anger inside that will either express itself outwardly in a violation of others, or inwardly toward himself. Repressed feelings can ultimately become the source of violence toward others or oneself. Depression, compulsive disorders, and symptoms associated with schizophrenia are often ways of keeping repressed feelings under control.

The ultimate way to take care of ourselves emotionally is to correctly identify our feelings when we feel violated, and to share or address the particular situation when necessary without violating the rights of others. We need to realize that we have both a right and a responsibility to confront others when appropriate, even if the confrontation may result in the other person feeling hurt.

When my psychology professor confronted me about the denial of my anger, I felt hurt and even insulted. But feeling insulted was really my own embarrassment, as I realized that I was out of touch with my own feelings.

Even though his confrontation brought some pain to my life, he was not violating my rights. He had a right to address my anger if I expected him to be in the same room with me. I had a right to leave his presence if I did not want to stay and learn to be honest with my feelings.

Since he chose to be as honest as possible in what he saw, however, he gave me the chance to set me free from myself. Thus, to heal relationships there will often be an element of pain involved. To avoid this pain is to choose to be dishonest and choose to walk the path toward unhealthiness.

Learning how to operate on the left side of our diagram will leave us with the least amount of hurt, loneliness, shame, and anger, guaranteeing us the most freedom from the so-called symptoms of mental illness.

How To Properly Confront

Confronting an issue with a person means giving a clear message of what you are feeling, what you see, and the boundaries you need in order to feel safe. As I present some examples, notice the non-violating power of the confrontational statements and the increased emotional stability and balance that follows them.

A client named Rosa grew up with an overbearing, verbally abusive father. After dealing with these issues in therapy, she had finally came to the point where she didn't want anyone talking to her in a rough way anymore. She wanted to honor the rights of others to express their concerns, but in a manner that did not violate her.

She had a chance to put this decision into practice at work when she was assigned a new supervisor who had a bad temper and wanted to use it to "shape up" the department. The first time he blew up, she went to him afterward and said, "I know you were upset and I could feel your pain, but I must ask you not to yell at me." When he claimed that he wasn't yelling at her, she followed this with, "Then please don't raise your voice at me."

Two weeks later he entered her office, yelling. She turned to him and said, "I am not willing to talk to you when you are yelling. Please lower your voice or leave my office." When he kept yelling, she said, "I have a right not to be yelled at. I am leaving but I am more than willing to talk with you when you're calm." At that point she grabbed her purse and went home for the day. The next day she returned to work as usual. Her supervisor said nothing about her leaving and has never yelled at her again. Even though he never admitted to his violating behavior, Rosa was still able to operate from her own center of power to take care of herself.

Another good example of being confrontational in a positive way can be seen in an experience my wife, Kathy, had when she was helping out on the school playground of our son, Kevin. She became concerned when she noticed that the playground manager was disciplining the children in a very shaming way. When the playground manager corrected the children, she would deliberately embarrass them in front of their peers. My wife went to talk to the principal about it. When she sat down to discuss this issue with the principal, he kept making excuses and changing the subject. Kathy kept bringing him back to the issue by stating, "Sir, I don't feel as if you are hearing me." When he said he had heard her, but continued to disregard what she was trying to say, she changed her statement to "I still don't feel heard and I am not leaving until I feel heard and understood." Finally, he stopped and listened, agreeing with her analysis, and he subsequently changed the school's policy of playground supervision.

A third example involves Kathy and myself. As with all couples, there are times when I ask her to do something and she says "no." If I refuse to take "no" for an answer, and keep on pushing her, she will take a moment to stop, think, and stay connected to her feelings. Instead of disconnecting from her feelings by using the shaming rationalization "I should always do what others want me to," she has the inner strength to stay with what is right for her. Often she will reiterate by saying, "No, I am not willing to do that." Once I hear her clear statement about herself, I have a much better chance to honor her boundaries because I might not have been fully aware of my "pushiness."

Let's take a closer look at these confrontational examples, starting with the last one. When my wife tells me she won't do something, I am usually a little startled at first. At times I will even feel some hurt. It is important to realize, however, that she did not hurt me. I became hurt because I created the expectation that she would always do what I wanted her to. So when she says "No" because the request doesn't feel right to her, I feel some of the same pain that our son feels when he doesn't get a toy.

Whereas Kathy is saying "no" to Kevin mostly for his own good, she is saying "no" to me for her own good. As an adult, she must always have permission to exercise that right.

The hurt that I might feel when she refuses me is small, and I can usually take responsibility for that hurt as long as I am aware of it, while still keeping my own self-esteem intact. It would even be good for me to say at such times "I feel hurt when you say no, but I want to honor your right to do so." Kathy might even go on to say "I feel your hurt, but I need to do this for me."

Again, it is the denial of our feelings that eventually leads to problem areas in a relationship. If the husband, for example, still had a lot of unhealed hurt and anger from his past, he might even become physically abusive if his wife were to say "no" to his wishes. On the other hand, many wives don't give themselves permission to say no, even when their spouses feel comfortable with such statements. They are so busy trying to please and be the perfect mother and wife that they are using the shame and fear of not being perfect to cover up their own needs. Because women in this situation are actually violating themselves, depression, compulsive behaviors, and other emotional problems can and will eventually result.

When my wife says "no" to me, I feel a little hurt at first. Then I feel an inner pride toward her and myself that she can set her necessary boundaries and that I can honor her right to them. As a result there is maximum permission to be honest and to take care of herself with very little violation to others.

In the first two examples, notice the reduction in violence and shaming that takes place when people stand their ground and confront their peers in a healthy manner. If an employee allows her boss to scream at her, she is not honoring her right to be safe and to be treated with respect. If my wife denied that she had the right to be heard by the principal, she not only allowed this violation to continue, but did not correct the shaming practice that was taking place in the school yard.

These individuals have the strength to protect their own selfhood, not by violating others, but by requesting that they be treated with respect, and that the other person make a commitment to listen to them until *they* feel heard.

Notice how the other people in each example kept trying to take this power away from Rosa and my wife. The boss denied that he was yelling at Rosa. The principal tried to avoid listening to my wife. If he had been allowed to only hear what he wanted to hear, then he would have been able to assume that this was the limit of his responsibility. Instead, my wife's insistence that he listen and *understand* brought about a needed change. In the third example, I tried to take my wife's power to protect herself away by trying to push her into doing something that she didn't want to do.

In all three of these situations, to a certain extent, the person's selfhood is being violated. If the person allows the violation to take place, especially when the other person may not even be aware of the violation, the person then violates herself. When Rosa and my wife chose to be honest about their feelings and protect their selfhood, as well as that of others, each situation became much less violating.

Ultimately, to bring about emotional health in our own lives and in the lives of others, we must learn how to properly identify and address violating situations. We must also come to a better understanding of how human violation, violence, self-hate, and emotional disorders are all interrelated.

ISSUES FROM OUR PAST

What keeps us from operating in a sane and emotionally healthy way if we all benefit from this behavior? There are two major reasons. First, most of us were not taught these basic principles as children, just as our parents were not taught them. Second, we are affected by unresolved issues from our past. Alice Miller, a very gifted author and psychotherapist, states "Parents' motives are the same today as they were then (in the time of Nazi Germany); in beating their children, they are struggling to regain the power they once lost to their own parents.[1] For the sake of our own emotional health and that of our children we need to understand what Alice Miller is saying.

If our five-year-old son happens to look out our front window and sees his friends playing, he may become quite excited about going out to play with them. At this point, he has taken his conscious imagination and allowed himself to dream about what it would be like to go outside and have fun. By doing so, he has invested part of himself at that moment in that activity.

If he asks me whether he can go outside, and I say no, because he is just getting over a cold, he feels violated. I, his father, violated his wish to go outside. If he starts to get mad or cry, I might handle the situation by getting mad back at him for his anger, or degrading him for his tears. I have not only violated his wish to go outside, but also his freedom or right to have that wish and the feelings that go with it.

If he knows he has been sick, then he will know that I am being fair in not allowing him to play. But if I also discount his feelings, his right to be excited about life, then I violate and shame that part of him. I take away his right and his power to fully affirm his selfhood.

If I am honest with myself and aware of my own feelings when he becomes angry, I must also admit that his anger sets off my anger associated with not having my own feelings acknowledged when I was young. In this case, when my anger appears, it is saying "If I still have pain about not having my anger acknowledged, then why should I have to acknowledge your right to your anger? I felt powerless as a child in such situations, and now you're making me feel powerless with your crying."

If I do meet his anger with my own, then I am also leaving him with the frustrated need to *reclaim* his right to his feelings later in life. He may later reclaim that power by hurting others, or he may continue to deny this need by shaming himself.

On the other hand, I can choose to affirm his right to his hurt feelings. I can say "Kevin, I hear your anger. You really wanted to go outside. You are mad at your dad for not letting you go. I can see your hurt and your anger, but I want you to stay inside until you feel better."

Such a statement acknowledges his right to the pain I have un-intentionally given him, yet still affirms my right to be the authority in his life. In this manner, I can discipline him and also be with his pain at the same time. When we, as parents and as a society, disci-pline out of anger or the need for control, we further violate the child, leaving him alone with his violated feelings.

The more a person is violated, seeing her rights and power taken away from her, the more she will experience a strong desire to re-claim these rights someday when she is in a position to do so. The person may begin to rebel as a teenager or even earlier. As a par-ent, she might reclaim her power by taking it away from her own children.

When my son begins to cry or becomes angry at me, if I am not connected enough to my own pain and healed enough to understand what is happening to me, he will sense that I am reacting in an inap-propriate way—certainly not in his best interests.

I certainly don't need to be attentive to my son's feelings 100% of the time, but I do need to be able to perceive his pain enough for him to feel heard by me. I must do this without taking the pain of my own past and asking him to be responsible for it. If I am carrying too much pain from my past that was never properly acknowledged or listened to, I will have trouble being there for my son. I will find it difficult to be present with anyone's pain. Since I had to shut off my own pain in those areas, splitting myself off from it, I must split myself off when that kind of pain comes up in others.

Besides being a major issue in child development and in one's relationships, splitting from pain can be a major issue with thera-pists. When a client begins to act out some of her pain with the therapist, often the therapist will not be able to stay with that pain. In such cases, the pain of the client will trigger the subconscious pain of the therapist, who will then begin to feel out of control. If the therapist is not aware that this process is going on, he will be inclined to regain control of his own feelings by attempting to regain control over the client. He may deny or shame the client's feelings or use hospitalization and/or recommending medication to get the client back under control.

On the other hand, the therapist who can sit with his pain and be okay with it as the client begins to get into her pain, is a therapist who can successfully work with "difficult" clients without resorting to medication. In fact, such a therapist will not want to use medication because he knows that helping the client to walk through her pain also helps her toward independence and self empowerment.

SUMMARY

Alice Miller states that parents use violence against their children to regain the power they lost to their own parents; we must all examine our feelings and our behavior toward our children. When our children do something that brings up deep feelings in us, before we blame the child for these feelings, we need to know the true source of those feelings.

This scenario does not take place just between parents and their children, but within our society as a whole. When our son Kevin was having a little trouble sitting still while our family doctor was examining him, the doctor turned to my wife and asked if she ever considered giving him Ritalin. She said to him "For the benefit of whom—him or us?" Looking sheepish, the doctor admitted, "You're right."

I can guarantee that a child who feels loved unconditionally, who is given firm and fair boundaries to live within and is allowed to express and have his feelings heard will not suffer from any major emotional disorder. At times he will experience great emotional pain because life has its treacherous moments, but he will not permanently split off that pain, nor will he be afraid of it. Furthermore, he will know how to correctly identify his feelings and will feel free to reach out to others when necessary.

Most of us were not fortunate enough to learn these principles while growing up. They have only been developed in the last few years as human beings have tried to figure out how to live with one another in a more sane and non-violating way. Just as our parents had to find the courage to survive such times as the Great Depression, World War II, diseases, and great famines, we may need to find the same courage to learn how to live with one another in an open and honest way. We must make this commitment, not just for ourselves, but in order to pass this knowledge and skill on to our children.

PART THREE

A NEW DIRECTION

CHAPTER FOURTEEN

HAS PSYCHIATRY FAILED US?

In this last section I will present a model that, if applied properly can extensively eliminate the problem of emotional disorders. I say "extensively" knowing that mental illness or emotional disorders will never be completely eliminated; nevertheless, I believe that the more this model is implemented, the more we will be able to reduce the incidence, cost, and misery of these conditions. In order to understand how my model can work, it's important to understand how and why psychiatry has generally failed to solve the problem of emotional disorders.

From one perspective, it would appear that biological psychiatry has offered a lot of good to our society. After all, hasn't it helped many individuals who were once almost completely disabled by their illness to live on their own, and even hold down a job with the help of medication? Isn't it true that these individuals, their doctors, and their families would all swear that, without medication, these disturbed men and women would not be able to function?

Obviously there are thousands of individuals whose emotional condition has been stabilized with the help of medication. We now know, however, that these drugs do not stabilize or cure a mental or emotional "disease," but actually stabilize a person's emotional life by disabling it, often permanently. In spite of this, some still claim that these medications represent a solution. If biopsychiatry has reached the point of being able to "successfully" drug and shock people into some semblance of normal function, isn't this a real success...or has psychiatry failed us again?

These issues obviously need to be addressed. I became painfully aware of them in 1992 when I first attended a conference for psychiatric survivors. Generally, individuals who call themselves psychiatric survivors are those who have experienced some form of abuse by psychiatry and are working with others to recover from that abuse, as well as to bring about psychiatric reform. Before the conference, I had never met a so-called "psychiatric survivor." In fact, I had not even heard of the term, or knew that such individuals existed.

I decided to attend the psychiatric survivor's conference out of general curiosity and because I was working on the preliminary stages of this book. Once there, I met and spoke with several of the survivors. Their stories were so disturbing and compelling that I decided to listen to them and record them.

What surprised me was that everyone I interviewed had a very similar history and pattern in their lives. From this pattern I developed the three phases of emotional disorders mentioned in Chapter One. The three phases are as follows:

Phase I: Mild to major abuse or violation in childhood or early adulthood.

Phase II: Signs or symptoms of emotional disorders begin to appear.

Phase III: Psychiatric intervention, i.e., hospitalization and/or medication, resulting in more severe symptoms and the *possibility* of permanent psychological disability.

When speaking of the individuals I met at this conference, I must use the word "possibility" because many of them miraculously made it out of the system. Following are some examples of people who managed to escape the vicious cycle of hospitalization, medication, and other psychiatric approaches.

BIOGRAPHY #1:

Jerry was put into a private boarding school primarily because his parents wanted him to have a good education. Because he was overweight and unathletic, the other students decided to gang up on him and tease him. When he was asleep, they would sneak up with a cigarette and burn his foot. Sometimes they would hold him down and slap his belly until they broke his skin.

As a result of this abuse, Jerry gradually started feeling depressed. His shame of being disliked and his desire to fit in with the other kids made it necessary for him to minimize the abuse in his own mind, but it still had its effect on his overall emotional well-being.

When Jerry was twelve, his mother took him to a psychiatrist who hospitalized him. When the doctors didn't have much success with medication, they started shock treatment, even though it didn't help either. Over the years, Jerry was in and out of fifteen different hospitals. As a result of the antipsychotic drugs that were given to him, today he suffers from a severe case of tardive dyskinesia, a disorder of the basal ganglia of the nervous system causing spasms and twitches. Looking back, he truly believes that the drugs and shock treatments only caused him to become further trapped in his pain.

Jerry cringes now at how the doctors used to decide whether or not he needed further shock. They would give him a newspaper to read, followed by a shot of sodium pentothal to put him asleep during the treatment itself. Afterward, they would ask him about the newspaper headlines. If he could remember them, they figured that he needed additional shock to further deaden his memory.

How did Jerry free himself? He woke up one day, between hospitalizations, and realized that part of the reason he was trapped in institutionalized care was that he was using too much energy blaming others. He began to focus his energy on himself, gradually taking charge of his life, and assuming responsibility for how he felt.

Exercising and developing a proper diet helped him to feel more in charge of his life. Educating himself in the areas of psychiatric law helped empower him even more. Although he had good reasons to blame others, he realized that doing this would never lead to the elimination of his pain.

In addition, while he was becoming aware that he had been harboring anger at his mother for putting him in the boarding school and taking him to the psychiatrist, he was also realizing she might have been quite innocent of any bad intentions. She simply did not know what to do with Jerry's depressive state when she first took him to a psychiatrist.

At the age of thirty-two, Jerry is bright and very active in the survivor movement. He has testified before a House subcommittee on psychiatric reform and has also organized and been involved in many related projects. As an advocate for other patients, when he hears about someone who is being grossly over-medicated, he calls the doctor and exerts pressure (legal if necessary) to reduce the patient's dosage.

Although Jerry still suffers from tardive dyskinesia, he is healthy and happy. He now has a meaning and purpose to his life.

BIOGRAPHY #2:

When Angela, then aged fourteen, was abused by her neighbor, she gradually became depressed. Her concerned parents took her to a psychiatrist, who eventually hospitalized her. When released from the hospital, Angela ran away because she was afraid of the neighbor, who was still trying to sexually abuse her. When she returned, she was placed back into the hospital and drugged. A few years later, she worked herself free of her medication through a local advocacy program. Today she still wonders why no one asked her about the source of her problems and only paid attention to her symptoms.

BIOGRAPHY #3:

When Sally and her husband were having marital problems, she approached her family physician for help. He referred her to a psychiatrist, who put her on Valium. She experienced what is referred to a paradoxical effect of becoming overly agitated, rather than calmer. Her inhibitions were suppressed by the Valium, allowing her anger to freely surface. After Sally attacked her husband and slashed his tires, the psychiatrist told her she had a character disorder. As she became more depressed and suicidal as a result of behavior she couldn't understand or tolerate, she was put on antidepressants. Sally soon began to display psychotic symptoms, which she believes were brought on, at least in part, by the medication. When the psychiatrist put her on anti-psychotic medication, it exacerbated her depression. At one point Sally was taking 10 different prescribed medications.

Even though Sally was down to 75 pounds at one point, she remembers receiving twice the recommended maximum dosage of Stelazine, a powerful anti-psychotic drug. At that point, when she had been in and out of 20 hospitals, her psychiatrist went on an extended vacation. Only then, with the psychiatrist gone, was Sally able to stop all medication. When her doctor returned, the doctor became outraged, verbally abusing Sally and eventually putting her under guardianship.

Sally's guardian, who was a lawyer, started taking long walks with her, letting her talk and simply listening to her. "He cared about me as a person and helped pull me through."

As are many psychiatric survivors, Sally is doing fine today. She has become a close friend of mine, and I consider her a very gentle and sane person. Although she is aware of her pain and still feels the effect of her woundedness, she is currently living a medication-free, productive life.

What shocked me about meeting these individuals was that they represent not just a few isolated cases that fell through the cracks of the system while being diagnosed, but the vast majority of people who have looked to the system for some kind of "help" and been let down by it. Since that first conference, I have come to know many more psychiatric survivors, read some of their biographies, and talked to other patients and parents who have had to live out their lives caring for their emotionally troubled children. Most, if not all, seem to have the same history. The pattern follows the three phases shown in Figure 14.1.

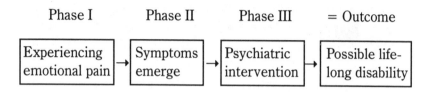

Figure 14.1: The Three-Phase Psychiatric Model

Let's take a look at these three phases in greater detail before we explore the emotional pain model.

PHASE I: MILD TO MAJOR ABUSE

In Phase I, the abuse a person suffers might range from mild to severe. If it is mild, a child may cope by becoming a little too sensitive or compulsive in his efforts to please his parents. Another child might react by developing feelings of inadequacy as she attempts to follow in the steps of an older, more successful sibling.

A gradual accumulation of emotional pain can build up in a child, without the parents' being aware of it. The child is also unaware that he or she is making a daily subconscious choice to feel inferior or less-loved than other siblings.

If a child is the oldest, he may develop a pattern of always being the "responsible" one, and never learn how to care for his own needs. Or, a child may gradually emotionally withdraw a little bit more each day rather than face the negative, angry behavior of an insensitive parent.

As you can see, there are a million different scenarios in which a child growing up can accumulate a lot of unhealed emotional pain. If that child also comes from an abusive family or was severely traumatized in or outside the home, then the violation to his selfhood will be considerably greater. Life today is very stressful, especially for children. Every child, regardless of how hard his parents try to protect him, will be traumatized to some degree.

Phase II: Symptoms of Emotional Disorders

A time will come for everyone when they will enter Phase II and begin to exhibit behaviors or symptoms due to stress and emotional overload, or due to the severe trauma in their lives. Some people may react by beginning to feel depressed; others may try to compensate by controlling others or pushing harder for success.

Recently, I have been counseling several clients who, although they come from good families and would be perceived as living normal lives, nevertheless, have begun to hear voices. Betty, who I introduced in Chapter One, is a good example. Although she has been highly successful and comes from a good, loving family, she is the kind of person who tends to invest her heart into everything she does. When her husband suddenly announced that he wanted a divorce, her whole world came crashing down.

After several months of inconsistent and irresponsible behavior on his part, she started to hear voices. On one occasion, when the children were visiting him and his new girlfriend, she heard the youngest one crying out for her. Since Betty was alone in her house at the time, she knew it was not really her child, but something her mind was doing. She also knew the reason behind the voices—her fear that this "other woman" might steal the love of her children. Already feeling unloved because of the actions of her husband, Betty began to feel overwhelmed by a sense of inner desperation and worthlessness. For the first time in her life, she began to feel helpless, unable to be successful or create a sense of worthiness through her own efforts. In response to all of this stress and pain, her mind came to her rescue, creating the voice of one of her children in need.

Because of the emotional stresses that we must all endure, Phase II symptoms will eventually emerge in our lives. Not everyone will become severely depressed or begin to hear voices. Nevertheless, we should not take certain symptoms and categorize them as indicators of a defective mind. We must all come to realize that emotional pain can push us into Phase II, whatever the symptoms may be.

PHASE III: PSYCHIATRIC INTERVENTION

Phase III is where biopsychiatry can become quite dangerous and seductive. What if Betty had been too afraid to share her voices with me in their earliest stages? They may have intensified as she worked to ignore, avoid, or suppress them, and eventually could have caused serious problems in her life. She was not afraid to talk about her "hallucinations" because she knew my view of emotional illness. On the other hand, if she had worked with someone who didn't believe in the emotional pain model, and had told that person about hearing voices, it is likely that she would have been pressured into being hospitalized and medicated. If the drugs had reduced her symptoms, she would probably have been told, "The drugs are working. Therefore you must be suffering from a chemical imbalance."

Since Betty understood my view of emotional disorders and knew that I would not be alarmed about someone who was starting to hear voices, she took the risk of sharing them with me. Because I did not believe her mind was sick, but that these voices were connected to specific pain issues, she and I were able to make sense out of them, as well as other behaviors that were even more confusing. Since we took care of the problem at an early stage (the beginning of Phase III), correctly identifying her pain, Betty was able to start seeing how she could take charge of it in more appropriate ways. Because we didn't medicate her pain, she was left with a clear mind, and her pain helped lead us to exactly what needed to take place in her healing and recovery process. Because she wasn't on psychiatric drugs, which may have suppressed her symptoms, she didn't become dependent upon drugs for support. Instead, she became temporarily dependent on a therapist to teach her how to recognize her pain and take the necessary specific steps to eventually take charge of her own life in this area.

RENEE

To help clarify these issues let me share the story of Renee as told in her book *Autobiography of a Schizophrenic Girl*. Renee was able to recover from her schizophrenia, and consequently provide some great insights about it in her book. She writes about how she first began to lose touch with reality at the age of five:

I remember very well the day it happened. We were staying in the country and I had gone for a walk alone as I did now and then. Suddenly, as I was passing the school, I heard a German song; the children were having a singing lesson. I stopped to listen, and at that instant a strange feeling came over me, a feeling hard to analyze but akin to something I was to know too well later—a disturbing sense of unreality. It seemed to me that I no longer recognized the school, it had become as large as a barracks; the singing children were prisoners, compelled to sing. It was as though the school and the children's song were set apart from the rest of the world... The song of the children imprisoned in the smooth stone school barracks filled me with such anxiety that I broke into sobs. I ran home to our garden and began to play "to make things seem as they usually were," that is, to return to reality. It was the first appearance of those elements which were always present in later sensations of unreality: illimitable vastness, brilliant light, and the gloss and smoothness of material things. I have no explanation for what happened, or why. But it was during this same period that I learned my father had a mistress and that he made my mother cry. This revelation bowled me over because I had heard my mother say that if my father left her, she would kill herself.[1]

215

Renee's feelings of unreality are actually quite common. Often when clients in therapy start dealing with strong emotional material and the corresponding feelings begin to surface, the protective subconscious will click in and begin to split off those feelings or experiences, resulting in a sense of unreality or going crazy.

For example, in my men's group when a strong emotional topic such as a difficult relationship to one's father comes up, several of the men will share unreal or distorted emotions and perceptions. One man may start to fall asleep, while another will see the room begin to change shape while another man may see the faces of the other men become blurry. It is most important to realize that when overloaded with emotional pain, the mind begins to act "crazy" in the process of splitting off that pain.

In the years to come, Renee described how her unreal feelings and experiences began to increase in frequency. One time while playing jumprope with her friends, Renee yelled out "Stop, Alice, you look like a lion; you frighten me!" The other girls looked at her, saying, "You're silly—Alice, a lion? You don't know what you're talking about."[2] As the game started again, Renee realized that her friend hadn't really looked like a lion, but that this was the only way she knew to describe her perception that her friend was becoming larger and brighter.

Renee also described the fear she experienced during a nightmare that she labelled the "needle in the haystack":

Here is the dream: A barn, brilliantly illuminated by electricity. The walls painted white, smooth—smooth and shining. In the immensity, a needle—fine, pointed, hard, glittering in the light. The needle in the emptiness filled me with excruciating terror. Then a haystack fills up the emptiness and engulfs the needle.[3]

She later wrote that she always associated her unreal perceptions with the dream of the needle.

As Renee began to have more of the same type of experiences, she started to withdraw, keeping close to the fence of the school to "watch the other pupils shouting and running about in the school yard." Explaining further, she says:

> I caught myself in this state only in the yard, never in class. I suffered from it horribly but I did not know how to get free. Play, conversation, reading—nothing seemed able to break the unreal circle that surrounded me.[4]

Renee did try to get help, however. At one point in the book, she described how she once attempted to reach out to her teacher.

> I went to my teacher and said to her, "I am afraid because everyone has a tiny crow's head on his head." She smiled gently at me and answered something I don't remember. But her smile, instead of reassuring me, only increased the anxiety and confusion for I saw her teeth, white and even in the gleam of the light. Remaining all the while like themselves, soon they monopolized my entire vision as if the whole room were nothing but teeth under a remorseless light. Ghastly fear gripped me.[5]

How would you analyze Renee's situation? Would you assume that she suffered from a chemical imbalance, or that she was simply reacting to the intense loneliness and fear that she would feel if her father were to leave her, and her mother were to take her own life? Is that not a very real, intense, and fearful situation for a five-year-old to face?

What might have happened if someone could have sat down with Renee, gained her trust and helped her to verbalize her feelings?

When people are able to verbalize such perceptions and understand the pain and their feelings behind them, they often find that their distorted glimpses of reality begin to make sense, just as Jack's belief that he was half woman finally began to make sense to him.

How many other people, like Renee, have been similarly traumatized as a child; and, because no one helped them to understand their strong feelings, have kept their distortions to themselves? Upon leaving high school, when their world might indeed become too big for them, they might start to hallucinate even more.

We can see that Renee's experiences follow a familiar pattern. Like the people in the other cases discussed, Renee began to feel overwhelmed with an inner sense of desperation in childhood. Renee's desperation quickly built to an intolerable level following a single traumatic moment: when she was suddenly faced with the possibility of her father running off with another woman and her mother killing herself.

Overloaded with desperation, her protective subconscious started working really hard to shield her selfhood. As this part of her mind took over, creating certain illusions, she began to lose a sense of reality. For example, when her teacher did not know how to respond to her and perhaps gave her a phoney "reassuring" smile, it's likely that Renee's protective subconscious told her she could not trust smiles any more. When the teacher used her smile to cover up her own feelings, Renee probably felt betrayed and fearful. As her fear grew, the whole room grew to become nothing but teeth.

Since I have not interviewed Renee, I can not be absolutely assured of my interpretation of her life. What I am sure of, however, is the element of intentionality in her symptoms: As Renee's feelings became too big for her, and as her trust was further violated, the imaginary part of her mind had to come to her rescue.

Renee's emotional condition started in Phase I with an overload of pain and an adjustment to that pain. Her condition worsened in Phase II as she began to fear and reject her mind's attempt to cope in ways that further ignored the pain beneath them. When her symptoms were identified by others, and she was given a label (schizophrenia), hospitalized, and medicated, she entered Phase III. Her symptoms may have been temporarily suppressed by the medication, but her overall condition eventually worsened because her emotional pain was further denied.

HOW IS PSYCHIATRY FAILING US?

When we look at the many cases like Renee's, it becomes clear that biopsychiatry is failing us at three major points:

First: By denying that emotional pain is the root cause of emotional disorders. (Phase I)

Second: By not understanding the true meaning of what it calls symptoms. The person who suffers from the "symptoms" doesn't recognize that his or her pain is causing them, and neither does the psychiatrist called in to help. (Phase II)

Third: By hospitalizing and/or medicating the person with the primary goal of controlling the symptoms, not addressing the cause of the symptoms. (Phase III)

When we understand how psychiatry is failing us, we can take this same scenario and create a solution:

First: By creating proper recognition of and education about the pain all children confront as they are growing up, and helping to heal that pain. (Phase I)

Second: By de-mystifying the major "symptoms" and the context in which they develop, and understanding how to deal with them when they begin to appear; for example, not panicking when someone begins to hear voices. (Phase II)

Third: By having non-drug therapeutic programs available to help suffering individuals properly recognize and heal the pain inside of them. (Phase III)

Figure 14.2 illustrates the main difference between the psychiatric/medical model and the emotional pain model proposed in this book.

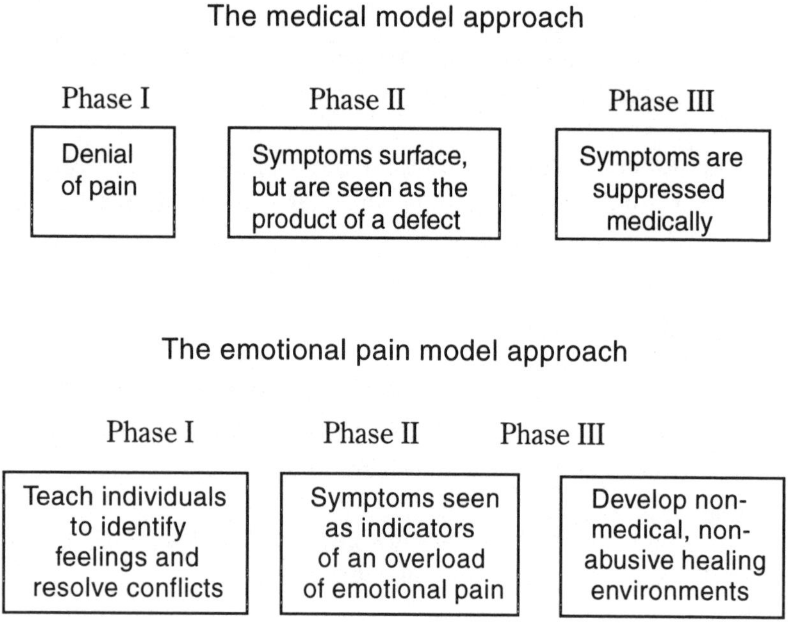

The medical model approach

Phase I	Phase II	Phase III
Denial of pain	Symptoms surface, but are seen as the product of a defect	Symptoms are suppressed medically

The emotional pain model approach

Phase I	Phase II	Phase III
Teach individuals to identify feelings and resolve conflicts	Symptoms seen as indicators of an overload of emotional pain	Develop non-medical, non-abusive healing environments

Figure 14.2: The Three-Phase Model

If you compare and contrast these two models, the end result of each is obvious. The medical model denies the pain and violation in the person's selfhood, waits until a person starts to act a little odd, and then attempts to control the person, primarily through medication. The end result is a drugged person who thinks that he or she has a biological, lifelong illness which requires medication to control.

In the emotional pain model, counselors and parents first make an effort to help children better identify and deal with their emotional pain. When an individual begins to act a little odd or out of-control, he or she is not seen as defective, but just hurting. Once a person's symptoms have been de-mystified, it will be much easier and far less shameful to reach out for help. All of us hurt and act *odd* at times; and we should all have more understanding and compassion for those who are hurting. The end result of this model is a person whose pain has been healed, whose symptoms have been understood, and who will perhaps someday reach out to others with similar problems.

Another advantage to using the emotional pain model is that we will be able to help people take charge of their own choices at a much earlier point in the three-phase process. Thus, as we begin to move away from the medical model and toward a cooperative emotional healing model, we will reduce the need for the dependency on medication, institutional care, and the welfare system.

DEINSTITUTIONALIZATION

I want to address a widespread myth before we move on to explore how we can implement the three phases of treatment centered around the emotional pain model.

Since anti-psychotic medication came into wide use in the late fifties, it has been generally assumed that many patients were successfully treated or stabilized and then released from hospital settings. This process, deinstitutionalization, has lead to the rapid decline in the number of patients in psychiatric hospitals. Deinstitutionalization is now considered one of the shining stars of biopsychiatry.

It is a myth, however, to say that drugs were responsible for emptying the state hospitals. The decline in the inpatient population actually began more than eight years after the introduction of antipsychotic medication—when "mental illness" was first covered under the federal disability programs introduced in 1963. As a result, mental patients could now be sent to old-age homes and board-and-care facilities paid for by their small disability checks. The states were able to empty the hospitals by simply shifting the financial burden from themselves onto the federal programs. The drugs did contribute to this process, but not because they produced some kind of cure. They helped because people are much easier to move into board-and-care facilities in a drugged and passive condition.

Deinstitutionalization is a misleading term because very few patients have truly become free of institutions. Tragically, many of the hospitalized patients were eventually cast out into the streets, and became part of the homeless population. In fact many choose homelessness over the coerciveness of biopsychiatry. As a result, a "revolving door policy" developed, with patients dropping in and out of different hospitals, coping with different living conditions, and taking on one different kind of medication after the another.

TRUE FREEDOM

As I have pointed out in the biographies I have shared, which actually represent the experiences of millions of individuals around the world, psychiatry has failed them as well as us with its medical model. Practitioners have been successful in "stabilizing" many individuals on drugs, but they stabilize by disabling.

Psychiatric drugs can not be seen as a long-term solution, especially with the growing degree of emotional problems and violence we are seeing in our children. It is time for us to begin the necessary shift to an emotional pain model, for it may take a full generation to complete the needed change. After hundreds of years, it is time for us to admit that the biopsychiatric model has failed, and to move on.

CHAPTER FIFTEEN

PHASE I

To effectively solve the problem of emotional disorders, we must start at Phase I, developing the ability to teach our children and ourselves how to correctly identify feelings and resolve conflicts. Learning how to correctly identify feelings must come first, before proper conflict resolution can take place.

In his book titled *Emotional Intelligence*, Daniel Goleman writes about the growing recognition of the importance of feelings and emotions. Quoting from Saloverg and Mayer's basic definition of emotional intelligence, Goleman states that:

> Self-awareness—recognizing a feeling as it happens—is the keystone of emotional intelligence.... People with greater certainty about their feelings are better pilots of their lives, having a surer sense of how they really feel about personal decisions from whom to marry to what job to take.[1]

Let's look a little closer at the significance of feelings in the emotional health process.

FEELINGS-THE SOURCE OF A PERSON'S INNER TRUTH

The emotional pain diagram illustrates why the correct identification of our feelings is critical to our emotional health. Figure 15.1 is an alternate version of the diagram.

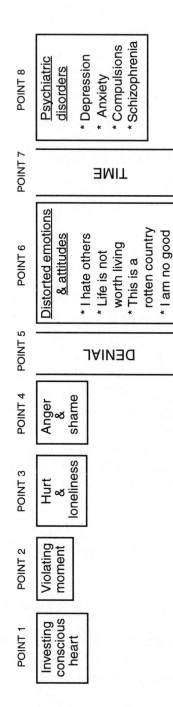

Figure 15.1: The basic emotional pain diagram

224

To understand the significance of correctly identifying our feelings in Phase I, it's helpful to compare this diagram with other psychotherapeutic models. Let's look first at the medical model.

Medical model: The medical model starts at Point 8. Its strategy is to determine a diagnosis from the presenting symptoms, then prescribe medication based upon the belief that some sort of biological defect is causing the problem in the first place. If the symptoms decrease after the person begins taking the medication, the treatment is deemed successful, regardless of the side effects of the medication or its long-term disabling effects.

Cognitive-behavioral model: The cognitive-behavioral approach also starts at Point 8 with the presenting symptoms, but then backs up to Point 6 to examine the distorted thinking that is taking place, and the out-of-control behavior of the person who is suffering. A therapeutic plan is then developed to change either the person's symptoms, distorted thinking, or behavior.

For example, when behaviorism had reached its peak popularity in the 1970s and 1980s, it was quite common to talk in terms of positive and negative reinforcement, especially in reference to children. In this method, instead of drugging the child, clinicians were trying to train the child, as we do animals.

Behaviorism, which grew out of the research done with rats, pigeons, and dogs, showed quite clearly that certain desirable behaviors can be increased and undesirable behaviors decreased by reinforcing the appropriate behaviors. For example, if we wanted to train our dog to get the morning paper for us, we might break the training process into small increments. We might first train him to pick up the paper and give it to us while he is close to us, reinforcing correct behavior with food. Next, we might put the paper further away until we had him trained to bring it to us from a distance.

While a dog might do this act of fetching faithfully every day for years, I am sure that even the most skilled behaviorist could

225

never get his own child to fetch the paper for him with the same obedience as a dog. People are not animals, and are motivated by much more complex emotional systems, needs, and desires.

Even though much of the behaviorist terminology is still floating around, this model has basically failed to work with severely violated human beings. To make it work at all, in fact, psychologists have had to integrate the elements of unconditional love and discipline into the formula. Although the basic model has been changed considerably, psychologists still call it behavioralism because the patients' progress is still measured in terms of his behavior. The model fails, however, when it is primarily used as a means of control. Children soon see through our motives whereas animals don't.

The cognitive approach varies slightly from the behaviorist's approach in that the therapist attempts to control or change the "irrational" thoughts or cognitions in the person instead of his behavior. In Aaron Beck's classic depression triad, the depressed person has a tendency to (1) think negatively about himself, (2) think negatively about his experience and (3) think negatively about his future.[2] Hopefully, changing the way he perceives his life circumstances will lessen his symptoms of depression, anxiety, phobias, and other disorders.

Both the behavioral and cognitive models are helpful, and there is plenty of research to justify their use. Indeed, our world demands that we structure our behavior in a certain way and that we think positively to make it through the challenges of the day. Someone who comes to work late and with a bad attitude will sour the people around him. When I was coming out of my own depression many years ago, I found it helpful to set behavioral goals, as well as thinking positively as much as I could.

Nevertheless, to properly understand my depression and to be free of it, I eventually had to understand how I was identifying my feelings incorrectly and dealing with them ineffectively. Cognitive-behavioral techniques and medication often help only on a temporary basis.

Of course, I am not saying that these models and programs have no value; but they are focusing only on the symptoms and often, the quick fix. When we return to the emotional pain diagram, we can see the reason why. The medical model is only concerned with Point 8, and the cognitive-behavior model focuses only upon Points 6 and 8. What is left out is the hurting person, the healing that may need to take place, and the correct identification and resolution of the violating aspects of the person's life.

This truth is quite obvious. We all know that when we have been deeply hurt emotionally, we lose control over our behavior and our ability to think positively. Our thoughts and behaviors don't just become distorted for no good reason. My depression was the result of my inability to correctly identify *all* my feelings *when* I was feeling them, which would have given me a clear indication of what felt specifically violating to me.

The process of correctly identifying one's feelings has been developed into a very successful therapeutic and healing program called "focusing." In the 1960s Professor Eugene Gendlin and some of his colleagues studied tapes of hundreds of therapy sessions in attempts to determine why psychotherapy seems to help some clients but not others.

As a result of listening to the clients on the tapes, they made a fascinating and important discovery. Not only did they determine the difference between the successful therapy clients and the unsuccessful ones, they could pick out the differences in the first or second session.

What did they find? Quoting from Dr. Ann Weiser Cornell's book *The Power of Focusing,*

> ...the successful therapy clients would *slow down* their talk, become *less articulate,* and begin to *grope for words* to describe something that they were feeling at that moment. If you would listen to the tapes, you would hear something like this: "Hmmm. How would I describe this? It's right *here.* It's...uh...it's...it's not exactly anger...hmmm."[3]

Dr. Cornell is describing the ability of the client to move backwards in the emotional pain diagram to Points 1 through 4. The successful client has the ability to start with the situation, problem, conflict, and corresponding emotions, and then back up to what is taking place in her body on a basic feeling level at the moment. In contrast, Dr. Cornell states, the studies discovered that:

> ...the unsuccessful therapy clients stayed articulate through the whole session! They stayed "up in their heads." They didn't sense in their bodies, and they never directly felt something that at first was hard to describe. No matter how much they analyzed their problems, or explained them, or thought about them, or cried about them, their therapy was ultimately unsuccessful.[4]

Because feelings help make up who we are and give meaning to a particular situation, we can't possibly achieve a proper state of emotional health or a true sense of self-empowerment and self-destiny without the ability to correctly identify our feelings at any particular moment. As we fail to identify our feelings, we end up violating ourselves and/or others.

Ideally, we can start this teaching process at the moment of birth. To help you understand some of the possibilities, let me share with you some of what my wife taught our son about identifying and dealing with his emotions.

TEACHING CHILDREN FEELING AWARENESS

Kathy started teaching our son Kevin how to identity his feelings from the first day she brought him home from the hospital. When she saw that he was happy or smiling, she would tell him he was a happy boy. When he cried, she'd tell him he was sad. When she'd see his body tighten up or stretch out, she'd tell him he was mad. Sometimes she'd say, "I see how red your face is getting. You sure must be mad."

When Kevin was about ten to eleven months old, Kathy started spending more time describing the body reactions that went along with his feelings, and she became more specific. If she saw Kevin tightening up his fists, she would say "I see how you have your fists. You're really mad." By helping him to connect specific feelings to his body, both of them began to understand what he was feeling by correctly interpreting his body language.

When Kevin was just over a year old, he began responding by saying "uh-huh" when Kathy identified one of his feelings. Occasionally, when she'd make a mistake, telling him perhaps that he was sad when he was really mad, he'd correct her. She might say "You're really sad" when he was crying, and he'd say "Un-uh." Then she'd say "You're mad?" and he'd say "uh huh." Before he could even verbalize his feelings, he understood them well enough to tell her whether she had them right or not.

Kathy also tried hard to be very honest with him about her own feelings, even when he was very young. She'd say "Mommy is feeling angry right now," or sad, or happy, teaching him to look at her face and correctly recognize her feelings.

By the time Kevin was two, she began noticing that he would suddenly look a little frightened when he realized she was sad. Kathy would then make a statement such as "Mommy feels sad, but I'm okay." She would say this so that he could learn to trust his perceptions, yet not feel responsible for her feelings. Thus, they could share in each others' feelings without becoming overly enmeshed or dependent upon each other.

At times when she felt irritated or even angry, and knew that those feelings were making it difficult for her to be with Kevin in an appropriate way, she would be extra careful not to make him feel responsible for these feelings. For example, she might say to him "Mom is tired and I am becoming angry at you. It's not your fault, but I need you to listen to me more carefully and do what I am asking you to."

Most parents have been taught that we must use force to get children to do what we want. But by learning how to share our feelings properly, we give the child the opportunity to be empathetic with us.

229

By the age of two, my son could express himself, saying "mad," "sad," and "happy," and could tell both his parents when he experienced these feelings. At about the age of three, he could tell us when he was lonely. By the time Kevin was three and one-half years old, all of us had gained considerable experience operating within Points 1 through 4 of the emotional pain diagram. When one of us violated the other, whether intentionally or not, we had the tools to help us be very truthful about our feelings. As a result there was very little, if any, left-over anger or shame in Kevin to eventually push him past Point 4. Any time he felt angry, we allowed him to freely express those feelings. When his behavior went over the line, and we needed to confront him, he knew that we still loved him as a person; because of this interaction, only a little felt constructive shame surfaced and then quickly was gone.

A TRAUMATIC MOMENT

Since my wife had spent considerable time being present with Kevin's feelings from birth, she could easily tell when something was wrong with him. He was also in a much better place to verbalize his feelings to her or to identify the hurtful situation when something was bothering him.

At one point he started having problems with his pre-school teacher, which we were not aware of at first. The main problem focused around Kevin going to the bathroom, something he was just learning how to do on his own. He would go into the bathroom, then come out with his pants on backward. When the teacher saw this, she would get mad and tell him to go back in and put them on right. Kevin had difficulty with this procedure. When he took them off and put them on again, they would often be backward again. The teacher would tell him that he had them on wrong in front of the entire class and send him back to the bathroom to try again. When this happened, he felt very helpless and shamed.

My wife became aware that there was some sort of problem

when he suddenly didn't want to go to school any more. When she asked him what was wrong, she saw a lot of shame on his face. At this time we realized that he had also started biting his nails. To draw Kevin out, she asked him if anything had happened at school to make him feel bad or sad. He then told her about the incident.

We discovered that the school had been having other complaints about this teacher. I myself had not felt comfortable around her the first time I had met her. After we addressed the issue with the principal, the school decided to replace her.

Unfortunately, this one situation had a considerable effect upon Kevin. For over a year afterward, he would become frustrated if he could not do something perfectly. If he felt that he might fail at a task, often he wouldn't even try. Any time he attempted something difficult, we saw his shame come up. Then we'd see him push it down with his anger; he'd often insist that his way was the right way, even if he was having difficulty with a task. He also reverted to biting his nails again when contemplating trying out a new project.

If we draw the emotional pain diagram for his situation, we can get a clearer picture of how his protective subconscious is beginning to develop behaviors and emotions past Point 4. Figure 15.2 shows that diagram.

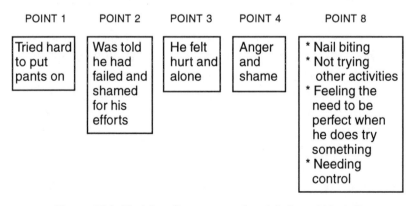

Figure 15.2: Kevin's adjustment to the violation of his self

231

At Point 4, he should and did feel anger resulting from the teacher's violation, but because he had an emotional investment in wanting to please the teacher by putting his pants on right, he felt confused about his feelings after she shamed him. When this happened, his mind suppressed his anger as it also attempted to suppress his shame. In cases such as this, anger might resurface later, misplaced, at peers or parents.

Notice also that, to a lesser degree, Kevin's teacher created the same kind of confusion in him that Charles Manson experienced over and over when he was shamed and disappointed by his loved ones and acquaintances. As Manson reached out, he was constantly shamed and then had to suppress his anger in order to suppress the shame. This is how society creates an out-of-control rage in people. For this reason, it is absolutely vital to help our children correctly identify their feelings at Points 1 through 4, instead of trying to "squash" their symptoms once they have reached Points 6 through 8.

Because Kevin had been taught to identify his feelings of hurt and sadness, his mother had no problem helping him to understand how his feelings were violated. She could say things to him such as "How did you feel?" Did you feel sad (mad, afraid, bad)?" She could then ask him where he was experiencing the feeling in his body, giving her further clues to what he was feeling. Kevin was already skilled at the act of focusing.

My wife and I made sure that Kevin felt safe with his next teacher. We also allowed him the freedom to choose only those projects that he felt he could master. This helped him to redevelop his confidence to the point where he could finally feel strong enough to begin taking on projects or activities at which he might fail. At this point he was also secure enough to admit when he did not know how to do something right, and request assistance. Thus, the healing of this incident required helping Kevin properly identify his feelings, to understand how he had been violated and to provide a safe atmosphere for healing.

It is interesting to notice how Kevin's shaming interaction

with this teacher, an important figure in his life, led to many emotional difficulties. She was using shame to try to control Kevin's behavior, and it was probably a pattern she used in many circumstances with him and the other children. This situation set the stage for the beginning of compulsive behaviors such as nail biting, some signs of early depression such as apathy and not wanting to go to school, and behaviors that could be labeled as learning disabilities such as not being able to complete work. If things had continued in this manner, in a short time Kevin could have very easily become a "diagnosable" candidate for medication.

Since my wife and I were willing to do the feeling work to discover what had taken place, the true source of Kevin's problem could be isolated. Even though Kevin was only three, and had a limited cognitive ability to verbalize the process he was going through, it would still always be remembered at some level of his consciousness.

If Kevin had been medicated, first of all we would have been denying the violating events in his life, and, secondly, we would have been giving him the message that he had to turn over his life to the medication because we, as parents, didn't know how to make his world safe enough for him.

Relating To His Peers and The World Around Him

By the age of four, Kevin could express his feelings quite easily to his friends. Sometimes when Kathy would arrive at the school to pick him up, she'd hear him tell his friends that they were hurting his feelings, and that if they didn't stop it, he was not going to play with them.

Most of Kevin's friends didn't know how to verbalize their feelings. When they were upset about something, they'd just shove, kick, hit, or engage in other behaviors to make their needs known. That didn't matter to Kevin, however. If they didn't respond to his request that they stop hurting him, he would stop playing with them.

For the most part, Kevin knew how to take care of himself emotionally, and could set his boundaries without becoming violent. Once Kathy did hear him say to a kid, "You are making me mad, stop." After warning the kid twice, Kevin said, "Stop or I will hit you." For the most part, however, when he asserted himself only with words, the other children would respond to his request.

Helping Kevin to verbalize his feelings also helps him deal with being frustrated during those times when he doesn't quite know how to let the energy of his feelings out. One of the stories Kathy likes to tell about him took place in a local toy store where Kevin had spotted a toy that he wanted. When she said "no," she saw that it really hurt him. His whole body began to tighten up and he went into a major temper tantrum, kicking and screaming. In spite of the fact that everyone was staring at him, Kathy began talking to him in a calm voice. When she'd say "You wanted that toy?" he'd reply "Uh-huh." Then she'd say "You really feel mad when you can't have that toy," and he would keep agreeing while she kept talking about his feelings. Finally, he stopped for a moment, looked thoughtful, and said, "I sad, Mommy."

This gave Kathy the opening she needed to say to him, "I hear that you're sad." At that point the temper tantrum stopped. She and Kevin had broken through his anger (Point 4) to the hurt (Point 3) underneath. When he was able to verbalize his hurt and know that she heard him, his whole body relaxed.

It's important to correctly understand what our son went though. When he saw the toy, his consciousness, his heart and soul literally reached out and grabbed on to it. He had already possessed it in his mind, feeling the joy of owning it before she could say no.

When she told him he couldn't have it, he felt the pain of that loss. At that point, she could have used her "authority" to make him behave, but she took the time to help him learn how to *walk through his pain*. As she affirmed the sadness beneath his anger, this gave him the strength to go beneath his anger and experience his sadness. Thus, the problem was not one of disobedience, but one of needing someone to help him work through the pain of his disappointment.

When Kevin began to split from his pain, quickly moving to Point 6, Kathy's non-violating firmness and her sincere desire to listen to his hurt allowed him to reverse his emotional course and go back to experiencing his original pain.

In a constantly disappointing, constantly violating world, we need to help our children learn how to walk through their pain. This will give them the necessary strength and tools to cope with violation and pain when we are not around. The more time I spend listening to my son, the more I learn how to listen to him based upon his individuality. When Kevin knows that I honor his individuality and his feelings, he learns to use this technique of verbalization as an outlet for his pain, instead of throwing temper tantrums or withdrawing into his feelings in an unhealthy way.

The development of such skills also takes a lot of the pressure off me. I no longer have to try to be the perfect parent. I can make mistakes, and even hurt his feelings sometimes because we have a way of mending and healing our relationship. Understanding and using Phase I with children from birth gives parents and their children the tools they need to remain emotionally close, even in the midst of conflict.

Applying Phase I To Our Schools

In the last few years there has been a growing emphasis on developing programs to consider the "whole" child, not just the intellectual part. SCORE is one such program.[5] Sharon Marshall Johnson, director and developer of SCORE, divides the developmental needs of the child into four different areas: intellectual, emotional, physical, and spiritual.

Her program, originally a partnership between the University of California at Irvine and the Orange County Department of Education, is now used throughout the United States to help students in high schools become more successful in college or other aspects of life.

Even though such programs will become increasingly valuable in coming years, we must stay focused on an accurate view of what causes emotional and behavioral problems. We must help our children develop the inner strength to correctly identify their feelings, stay connected to them, and move through their pain, building the necessary inner strength to successfully operate in the adult world. One technique that SCORE uses helps illustrate this point.

SCORE utilizes a technique called "building bridges." If a student is upset about something a teacher does or says, the student is taught not to withdraw into a psychic-emotional distance from the teacher, complaining only later to his peers, but to build a bridge back to the teacher. If, for example, the teacher makes what the student perceives as an improper racial statement, the student learns to ask for clarification. This process might take the form of politely asking a question, providing new information, or putting assumptions into words. "What you just said sounded racist to me. Did I hear you correctly?"

As one of the steps toward building this bridge, the student is taught to pay attention to his body and the anger that might be building up in it. This awareness of how the body helps us to correctly identify our feelings is very similar to what we taught Kevin. In this way, instead of withdrawing into his anger, which sets the stage for it to return later as rage or hate for others, the student can build a bridge back to the person who has made him angry. If the student is successful, and the teacher responds in a supportive way, then the student has healed a moment in his life and developed a closer, more honest, trusting bond with the teacher. If the teacher (or adult) doesn't respond in a responsible way, the student will still feel good about himself because he knows he handled his emotions in an appropriate and healthy manner.

By multiplying such experiences over and over, and with other similar lessons, this student can begin to learn how to identify his feelings and to walk through his pain. If he learns how to build bridges correctly, there is much less chance that he will turn his anger onto society, his peers, his co-workers, his wife, or his children in later life.

Last, but Not Least—Adults

We adults also have a responsibility to learn how to better identify our feelings and act appropriately. To do so, however, we must first be able to admit that we block out our feelings and need help to learn to correctly identify them.

The reason we respond to a painful situation by splitting off our feelings is because long ago our trust was broken. We learned that it is safer to hide from those feelings, convincing ourselves that we don't need the help of others. Since it was broken trust that split off those feelings in the first place, however, we need to experience the *felt* love and trust of others if our hidden feelings are ever going to surface.

To stay disconnected from our feelings is to treat ourselves as "non-feeling" objects, and thus to treat others much the same. This does not mean that we are unable to experience intimacy with others in *some* areas. For example, if a man can become emotional over a fine car or an athletic event, he can feel a sense of connection and intimacy with others who are also emotional about those areas. If, however, he is cut off from the sadness he always felt about not being close to his father, then he won't see the sadness in his own children when they don't feel close to him. As much as he tries to love them, they might see his efforts, but they will not feel his compassion when they are *sad* or *lonely*.

Phase I, developing the strength to correctly identify and share our deepest feelings, is the first building block for true emotional health. Let's now take a look at Phases II and III.

CHAPTER SIXTEEN

PHASES II AND III

Once Phase I is in place and children begin learning how to stay connected to their feelings through proper emotional interaction at home and at school, Phases II & III of the emotional model will begin to evolve. If children and young adults know the specific reasons why they become depressed, anxious, hyperactive, or even begin to hear voices, then they will know when and what kind of help they should seek.

Not everyone in society will be able to experience this ideal set of circumstances, in which all children and adults are able to identify and deal with their emotions, and this is where Phases II and III become vital. Let's take a look at how these phases should begin to unfold in the future.

PHASE II

If you remember, it is in Phase II that the symptoms or behaviors begin to emerge due to the unidentified and unhealed violations to the selfhood that took place in Phase I. Someone who has been over-stressed at work for a number of years (Phase I) may likely begin to develop any number of psychological symptoms signifying Phase II. Thus it is in Phase II that either the medical model path or the emotional pain model path is chosen depending on how the symptoms or behaviors emerging in Phase II are viewed.

239

As we have seen, in the medical model, when the "symptoms" of emotional pain begin to surface, the sufferer is told that these symptoms indicate that something is biologically wrong. As the emotionally wounded person accepts this concept, she further divorces herself from the pain below the symptoms and gives over the authority of these wounded parts of her being to an outside authority.

This progression must be understood as part of the diseasing process that can and does often lead to permanent disability and dependency. An example of this result can be seen in the young man named Ken, mentioned earlier, who was depressed and felt like dying. When Ken first shared this information with his mother, she immediately called her family doctor, who referred them to a psychiatrist. During the interview the psychiatrist noticed some behavior that strongly suggested Ken was in the early stages of what he would possibly label as schizophrenia. The doctor wanted to hospitalize him immediately and start him on antipsychotic medication. When Ken refused to go into the hospital, his mother called me.

After spending some time with Ken, I concluded that he was quite suicidal and showed signs of what a psychiatrist could label as hallucinations or schizophrenic behavior. Instead of insisting that Ken was mentally ill and needed to be hospitalized and medicated, however, I helped him to understand that these behaviors represented emotional pain that needed to be understood. After I had given him a couple of examples of the ways I'd manifested my own pain into Phase II behaviors (referring to my past struggle with depression), he began to relax. At that point, and during the following sessions, we could begin to look for the pain that was associated with his behaviors.

If Ken had accepted the psychiatrist's explanation, he would never have focussed his attention on what was going on inside himself, but only on what the psychiatrist was saying. If he had begun taking medication, his cognitive mind would have spent its energy focusing on the relationship between the "symptoms," his pain, and the effects of the medication. His main goal would have become discovering which medication suppressed his symptoms best.

When I asked Ken to focus in on the pain that he had chosen to split off or deny, I was really asking him to begin to take charge of his life and discover the meaning behind his "forced choices." I might have been the authority figure during the process, the trained expert and guide, but the goal of the process was to put Ken back in charge of this aspect of his life.

Working together, Ken and I discovered that he had been a very sensitive child who easily felt bad when another person's feelings were hurt. Even though he had not been abused, this had caused him to emotionally handicap himself at a very early age. Any time he felt his needs might possibly bring pain to others, he shut them off. In essence, these little decisions started killing off his selfhood: He was eliminating choices that were important to him at a very early age. As Ken kept choosing to deny himself, he created what he identified as a "dark spot" deep within. As an adult, he became paralyzed about making certain choices as a result of this huge dark, desperate aspect of his life. This dark and desperate side to him made him feel as if he needed to die.

Ken's "hallucinatory" behavior was hard for us to define because it was just beginning to take form and be used as a way to split from his deeper feelings. To the best of what he and I could determine, it was his creative-spiritual side trying to break through the dark side of him. Since he could not give himself direct conscious permission to make certain choices because he might possibly hurt others, his selfhood was trying to emerge by developing the ability to hallucinate.

Someone who followed the psychoanalytic method might have tried to figure out the symbolic meaning of Ken's dreams and hallucinations. Using the emotional pain model, I tried to lead Ken to his most basic feelings of hurt, loneliness, shame, and anger. These feelings allowed us to know the truth behind the origin of his symptoms. When we began to locate those feelings, the specific way Ken felt when he had to face a painful situation, we knew we were on the right track. Ultimately the truth about what was happening to him came from him.

Ken's case provides a good example of the basic principles of the emotional pain model. He never suffered abuse, he came from a warm and caring family, and he was always quite popular with his peers. He wasn't severely violated by others; in a sense, he began to violate himself as he started making small choices to deny his own needs.

We didn't need to dig deeply into Ken's childhood; we only needed to understand his specific way of dealing with emotional pain. As Ken began to develop this understanding, and found the courage to begin affirming his right to his own life, he started to feel truly in charge of his existence for the first time. In three to four months, Ken had worked through most of his depression, his need to die had diminished greatly, and he had accepted the imaginary-hallucinatory part of his behavior as his way of dealing with his pain. As he gradually accepted this part of him, understanding his deeper pain, the hallucinatory behavior began to diminish.

I was able to put Ken back in charge of the emotional part of his life by (1) de-mystifying the symptoms and behaviors, and (2) working to locate the specific pain behind them. If Ken had been involved in a Phase I educational program as outlined in the previous chapter and had learned the emotional pain view of his symptoms, he and his parents would have been able to address the problem at a much earlier point, and with much less fear and confusion.

When his mother took Ken to the psychiatrist, who gave Ken a preliminary diagnosis of depression with possible psychotic symptoms, everyone suddenly found themselves at the mercy of the labels. Because, from a medical perspective, no one knows what causes these disorders, what do these labels really mean? Everyone, including the psychiatrist, is at the mercy of trying different medications to attempt to decrease the symptoms.

In Ken's case, certain medications might have actually reduced his symptoms by suppressing his pain. Antipsychotic medications that disable or chemically lobotomize part of the brain possibly would have reduced his early hallucinatory behavior. Stimulants such as Prozac might have helped make him feel better and lifted part of his depression. In fact, Ken was already using alcohol to help avoid his feelings.

If he had been given these drugs, however, he might never have learned anything about his own feelings and behavior. With his focus squarely on deciding which medication would reduce the symptoms best, he would most likely not have placed any of his attention on examining his feelings and how he chose to subconsciously deal with his pain. If Ken had accepted that he had a chemical imbalance, what motivation would he have to look past this explanation?

In addition, because his problems were rooted in avoiding hurting the feelings of others, Ken may have found it easier and easier to go along with the psychiatrist in order to please him and his parents. Consequently, it may have been only a matter of time before Ken, along with his parents and the psychiatrist, were all trapped in the medical model and dependent upon medication to control Ken's behavior.

With the emotional pain model, our goal is to begin teaching people Phases I and II. The more that the psychiatric symptoms and labels are de-mystified, the more people will begin working together to identify and heal emotional pain. The more we work together to help identify our feelings, the more we can easily understand our emotional symptoms before they capture too much of our total being.

Thus, there is no mystery to understanding Phase II. As the basic principles of Phase I are taught more and more, helping us to develop a correct view of emotional disorders, understanding and healing the manifestations of pain that arise in Phase II will come naturally.

PHASE III

As the symptoms begin to emerge in Phase II, Phase III represents the kind of help that is sought. In Ken's situation, his condition was properly diagnosed and treated. But what about those who presently have serious emotional disorders? What about those who were severely abused as children and have been in and out of different psychiatric institutions for years? Can provisions be made for these individuals outside of the medical model? The answer is yes: Proponents of the emotional pain model have set up programs and clinics to help people avoid hospitalization, even when they are experiencing extreme symptoms such as hallucinations. Let's look at some examples.

CRISIS HOSTEL

The Crisis Hostel, located in Ithaca, New York, is a place where people who are experiencing an emotional crisis have an alternative to psychiatric hospitalization.[1] The main emphasis at the hostel is to show that even when people are having serious problems, they are capable of and entitled to making their own choices about treatment. The Crisis Hostel uses peer counseling to promote self-healing, enabling people to go to a supportive place for a short period of time to avoid unnecessary or unwanted hospitalizations. The hostel is staffed 24 hours a day by people trained in peer counseling, advocacy, resource access, and crisis intervention. Many of the staff are ex-patients who have "been there," individuals who have gone through the psychiatric medical model system and know how to offer people a different option. People who stay at the Crisis Hostel are grateful for the alternative to mental institutions:

* I really felt like someone would actually listen to me with an open heart and without watching the clock.

* It's hard to get used to the fact that I can come and go as I please and that nothing is locked.

* People here (coordinators) really understand because they have actually been there. It's not like they just learned about "people like us" in books.

* Because of the Hostel I was able to finish my exams at Cornell and no one even knew I was having emotional problems.

* I'm so glad that my children can visit me here instead of some hospital day room. That really freaks them out and makes them worry that I'm sick.

* I haven't stayed at the Hostel yet. Just knowing that I could has kept me out of crisis.[2]

Remember: these are comments from patients who have been labeled mentally ill, who have been through many hospitalizations and medications. I believe we should trust them and their wisdom. Helping individuals to decide what is best for themselves ultimately empowers them to be responsible for their lives.

THE SAN JOAQUIN PSYCHOTHERAPY CENTER

In 1989, psychologist Dr. Kevin McCready was working as Director of Adult Services at a for-profit psychiatric hospital.[3] One day the management decided to put him on a quota system where by he had to admit a certain number of patients each month. He writes, "When they told me I was to be on a quota system, I walked away, got myself a loan, and set up the San Joaquin Psychotherapy Center just outside of Fresno, California."

What is unique about his center is that it is most likely the only full-service center in the United States that does not advocate or rely on any medication, regardless of the severity of the person's problem. What kind of patients do they get? According to McCready, approximately 60 to 70 percent of the individuals they work with have extensive histories of repeated and severe psychiatric treatment, ranging from a few months to 20 years. Many of these individuals have been told that they are "untreatable," and many come to the center taking from six to ten different psychotropic medications. Almost all of them have been told that they have a chemical

245

imbalance and must be on medication for the rest of their lives.

How effective is McCready's program? In response to working with these individuals whom biopsychiatry has failed to help, he states:

> In five years of serving such "untreatable" clients in an unlocked, day treatment facility, without medication, shock, restraint, or seclusion, our facility has a hospital readmission rate of zero. There have been no suicides, no assaults.[4]

According to McCready, success has been consistent; everyone who has stayed in treatment has shown significant improvement—some dramatic. For example, after 20 years of abusive biopsychiatric care, one woman was totally disabled, self-mutilating, suicidal, and homicidal, in spite of the six different drugs she was taking. She is now drug-free and runs her own small business. Another woman, age 25, had been declared "untreatable" after hurling herself through a plate glass window in a locked in-patient ward. She is now drug-free and finishing her undergraduate degree at a state university, where she has maintained a 3.8+ grade-point average.

Because McCready's clinic is only a few hours' drive from my practice, I have personally visited it and quizzed him in depth about his program over the phone. The clinic, currently a 4000 sq-ft facility, is part of a larger office complex. There are a dozen or so buildings in the complex, each with pleasant landscaping and an overall comfortable appearance. This type of setting is readily available and could be duplicated anywhere in the country. The clinic looks like part of the regular, everyday world, instead of a hospital or prison.

Once inside, I was impressed by the feel of the place, which gave the impression of being somewhere between a clinical care facility or hospital and a plush, expensive therapist's office. It doesn't have the "you-are-a-sick-person-needing-to-go-to-a-hospital" atmosphere, nor the "I-am-the-expert-with-all-the-credentials-to-fix-you-up" ambiance. It has more of a community feeling, a place to come to learn about yourself, to be comfortable, and work through some painful emotions. I could see that this setting would feel safe for those who were more emotionally troubled, and for those wanting to get off their medication.

In certain ways, the facility didn't differ much from a full-service psychiatric hospital. There were group rooms, an art room, a sound-proof room to work out strong emotions, as well as individual offices; but there was no room to restrain or tie down the patients, and no locked area. Furthermore, it was obvious that the rooms were being used because the people wanted to be there. They either weren't on medication, or they were trying to minimize and get off their medication, so they weren't staring blankly at the walls.

I am not saying that every patient who enters this facility makes maximum use of what the clinic has to offer, nor does Dr. McCready make this claim. But you can sense a real productivity about the place, compared to the often subtle coerciveness of a hospital, or the plush therapist's office, where you don't dare upset the place.

In the newsletter article that first introduced me to Kevin McCready's facility, he stated that he felt drugs were not good because their main purpose was to restrain behavior, cognitive and emotional, often causing damage and impairment of the person's brain. He also wrote that the person using medication is subject to what he called a "state dependency learning effect." What this term means is that whatever new normal behavior is learned under the influence of the drug is dependent on the continuing use of the drug.

What I was most curious about was how the center was able to help people get off medication, especially those who came to him highly drugged. McCready told me that, under the supervision of a medical doctor, they usually started by slowly dropping the dosage of the more benign drugs. As the medication is slowly reduced, the patient will go through a rough week or two. Because the clinic has no overnight facilities, the patients must provide for their own housing, but the clinic makes sure there is plenty of emotional support available.

When a patient goes through a rough weekend or night, with the staff only available for emergencies, he or she often wants to quickly turn back to the medication. Soon, however, patients begin to realize that, with proper support, they can make it through such rough times. This breaks the toxic cycle of patients believing that drugs represent their only hope for being "normal enough" to receive love or respect. Furthermore, they feel as if they are getting their life back as they let go of the disabling aspect of the medication.

McCready also mentioned that he gets many patients who are violent, so violent that some have been asked to leave hospitals. I knew, before he told me, how his clinic was able to deal with violent patients: because patients are not forced into his facility, forced to take medication, forced to behave in certain ways before they can have equal privileges, most of their violent impulses aren't needed and eventually fade away.

I have known many ex-patients who were suffering emotionally because of the violations in their lives. Already feeling robbed of their dignity, they act out even more when forced to be hospitalized. This behavior was the only way they felt they could be heard, even when it inevitably resulted in their receiving heavy doses of medication and being tied down, often for days at a time.

Once you visit the San Joaquin Psychotherapy Center and sense the warmth and gentleness there, it is easy to see how Dr. McCready can be successful with even the most difficult patients.

NATIONAL EMPOWERMENT CENTER

The National Empowerment Center, located in Lawrence, Massachusetts, is dedicated to promoting recovery, empowerment, hope, and healing to those diagnosed as mentally ill. The center was founded in 1993 by Dan Fisher M.D., Ph.D., Judi Chamberlin, and Patricia Deegan, Ph.D.

At the age of 25, Dan Fisher was diagnosed with schizophrenia and hospitalized several times. Despite these setbacks, he was able to recover, earn a medical degree, and become a psychiatrist. Knowing firsthand what it feels like to be disempowered by psychiatry, he helped start The National Empowerment Center and began creating the *Empowerment Model of Recovery*. In one of his articles, he states:

> For most of us consumers/survivors/ex-patients, our central issues are discrimination, helplessness, and isolation. We need to overcome discrimination to gain access to the areas of policy formation. We need to overcome our powerlessness to consistently participate in the crafting of new policies. We need to keep up our courage, and overcome the isolation and conflicts between ourselves and other disadvantaged groups in society so we can trust each other and work together. These are the elements of social empowerment which are as important as individual empowerment. We need to break the image that people with psychiatric disabilities cannot contribute. That attitude has created more of a barrier to people getting or keeping a job than welfare.[5]

Besides publishing an encouraging and informative newsletter, the National Empowerment Center helps to organize seminars, and build self-help and consumer-run social clubs, as well as low-cost alternative treatment clinics.

In December of 1994, the National Empowerment Center promoted its first "Learning From Us" conference. The goal of the conference was to help mental health professionals learn from ex-patients, many of whom have recovered from their emotional disorders outside of the bio-psychiatric model. The conference was highly successful, as indicated by what one psychiatrist shared.

> I came to this conference as sort of a "spy." I wanted to get the latest scoop on what the consumer movement was up to so I could be ready for the next wave of consumer/survivor advocacy in my state. But that began to change for me here as I learned some new ideas and ways to approach people. I ended up inviting one presenter to repeat his seminar on "Holistic, Low-Cost Alternatives to Coping with Psychiatric Symptoms" at our grand rounds.[6]

249

The truth is, there are many caring psychiatrists like this man who are as locked into the medical model as the patients themselves.

Judi Chamberlin, one of the founders, also directs a research project at the Boston University Center for Psychiatric Rehabilitation. A psychiatric survivor, she is the author of an exceptional book titled *On Our Own*.[7] After being hospitalized several times, she finally found the help she needed in a residential facility similar in philosophy to the Crisis Hostel mentioned earlier. She is a board member of the National Association for Rights Protection and Advocacy (NARPA)[8] and has won several awards for her distinguished service to the disabled. She hopes that some day, along with Dr. Fisher and the rest of the staff at National Empowerment Center, she will be able to run a training institute for mental health providers.

Patricia Deegan, Ph.D., is the Director of Training at National Empowerment Center and is the third founder. Patricia was first hospitalized at the age of seventeen. She rejected the psychiatric label put on her—along with the prophesy that her life would be marginal or functional at best—and went on to earn her Ph.D. in clinical psychology. She has just published a book titled *Coping With Voices: Self-help Strategies for People Who Hear Voices That Are Distressing*.[9]

Besides these two books by Judi Chamberlin and Dr. Pat Deegan, the National Empowerment Center has a rich catalogue of tapes and other information available for those diagnosed with psychiatric disorders. Anyone can join their organization and receive their newsletter.[10]

HEARING VOICES NETWORK

The truth is that there is a world-wide effort to move away from the medical model. Unfortunately the process is slowed considerably due mainly to the influences applied by biopsychiatry, the pharmaceutical companies, and the cooperating research agencies and universities that are funded by the drug companies. One example of an organization moving away from a pure medical solution is the Hearing Voices Network in Europe.[11]

The Hearing Voices Network was formed to help people understand, accept, and deal more effectively with the voices that they hear. The first United Kingdom Hearing Voices Group was formed in 1988. It began as a small planning group originating in Manchester, England, inspired by the pioneering work of Professor Marius Romme, a psychiatrist from Maastricht in the Netherlands.

At first the self-help meetings were small, but the publication of articles in magazines, journals, newspapers, and national media, spread knowledge of Dr. Rommer's work and the meetings. As a result there are now self-help groups established in England, Wales, and Scotland. Professor Marius Romme and Sandra Escher have co-authored a book titled *Accepting Voices*[12] and the Hearing Voices Network puts out an excellent pamphlet titled *The Voice Inside*.[13]

Reading their literature, you will see that their view of hallucinations is very close to the one presented in this book. The support groups are able to help people with their voices by teaching them to accept their voices, to find the meaning to the voices, and to identify patterns which are specific to given situations. *The Voices Inside* states that, "Unless some meaning is attributed to the voices, it is very difficult to begin to organize one's relationship with them in order to reduce the anxiety."[14] Dr. Romme and those hearing the voices have found that discouraging the individual from seeking mastery of the voices tends to yield the least positive results. They also believe that the explanation offered by biological psychiatry is generally not helpful.

Support, acceptance, helping one another, healing, learning about the specific meaning to one's behavior, is the path out of so-called conditions of mental illness. This is becoming more and more self-evident throughout the world as people are given the opportunity and instructed how to properly help themselves.

Soteria House

Unfortunately, there have been programs in the past that have proven themselves more effective than hospitalization and medication, but have not been fully utilized or accepted. Soteria House is one of those programs.

Dr. Loren Mosher is a highly respected and credentialed psychiatrist. For many years he was head of the research on schizophrenia at the NIMH. Growing increasingly dissatisfied with and disillusioned by the medical model, he and various collaborators developed Soteria House, a safe place for individuals undergoing their first "schizophrenic" crisis.

Soteria House was located on a busy residential street and staffed with people who "had sincere interest in listening to the seemingly irrational communications of the patients."[15] Most of the staff had no professional training, but were able to provide adequate help to those in need, illustating that sometimes it's possible to provide care at a relatively low cost by not relying on highly paid professionals.

The staff at Soteria House saw the "disruptive psychotic experience" (i.e., behavior labelled as schizophrenic) as a process for "reintegration and reconstruction," or as the beginning of the healing process. They could flow with the individual, and showed a willingness to be with the individual in his irrational moments. Because of their approach, the program became highly successful.

A series of carefully controlled studies eventually demonstrated the superiority of Soteria House compared to a control group sent to a regular mental hospital. Only eight percent of those at Soteria House received drugs during their initial stay, whereas all hospitalized patients in the control group were medicated with antipsychotic drugs.

According to Mosher, a two-year follow-up showed the experimental group significantly less often receiving medication, using less outpatient care, showing significantly better occupational levels, and being more able to live independently.[16] Mosher also emphasized that patients at Soteria House also gained a much greater sense of self-understanding, self-esteem, and personal empowerment. Instead of being subjected to and taught to accept the brain disabling drugs and isolated hospital conditions, they often emerged from Soteria House feeling more independent, stronger, and better in touch with their feelings and aspirations.[17]

All of us accumulate pain in Phase I and will find times in our lives when our emotional system is pushed to a limit. If we happen to begin losing our sense of reality, or our deeper pain begins to break loose, what program would we do better in? Any of us would feel more comfortable in a warm, residential setting, with someone who is comfortable with such reactions, than in a cold room at a hospital loaded up with mind-crippling drugs.

Mosher and his co-workers were able to achieve such good results in the midst of our present day stigma about mental illness. How much more effective this program would be if we all had a proper view of emotional disorders and, as a larger community, accepted and supported such individuals in their recovery.

Skilled therapists are needed to help people who have entered Phase II to correctly identify and heal their deeper pain, learn to relate to people more effectively, set appropriate boundaries, and so forth. But in the moment of an emotional crisis, Soteria House proved that all any of us need is good, warm, trusting, unconditional understanding and acceptance.

Soteria House had to close its doors because of lack of financial support even when Soteria House was showing better, more cost effective results.

SUMMARY

Places and organizations such as the Crisis Hostel, The San Joaquin Psychotherapy Center, the National Empowerment Center, and The Hearing Voices Network are having a significant impact on individuals who have suffered from their emotional woundedness for years. Many of these individuals have often been terribly isolated or violated in psychiatric hospitals, and have been forced to take medications that may have caused brain damage. It is an interesting irony that, while the proponents of the medical model are set on believing in a "deficit" model to describe those with emotional disorders, the very people they have labeled as incompetent are emerging victorious and living very productive lives, free from the crutches of medication.

If we can come to understand the three different phases of the emotional pain model, first by helping children and adults to correctly identify their feelings and work through violating moments, we will eventually be able to de-mystify the whole notion of mental illness, and to develop more programs of healing and empowerment. Once this understanding is accomplished, we will have come a long way toward solving the problems of those who are emotionally troubled.

CHAPTER SEVENTEEN

KAY JAMISON, ANNA JENNINGS, AND JEFFREY DAHMER

To help bring all these concepts together we will examine three more biographies. Because there is no biological basis for emotional disorders, and because emotional disorders represent how a person has specifically chosen to deal with his or her pain, another person's biography becomes useful in our search to understand our own lives.

KAY JAMISON, M.D.

Dr. Kay Jamison is one of the leading authorities in the area of mania and depression. Besides authoring *Touched with Fire: Manic-Depressive Illness and the Artistic Temperament*, Dr. Jamison coauthored the standard medical text on manic-depressive illness, which was chosen in 1990 as the Most Outstanding Book in Biomedical Sciences by the Association of American Publishers. Her credentials are impressive and well deserved, and she is dedicated both to her work and to finding solutions to the causes behind mania and depression.

In her 1995 autobiography, *An Unquiet Mind*, Dr. Jamison shares how her life gradually slipped beyond her control. For many years she suffered with extreme bouts of mania and depression until finally, through the use of medication, the help of a dedicated friend and some good fortune, she gradually gained control over her illness. Dr. Kay Jamison believes that lithium helped her, perhaps saving her life. In spite of her strong conviction that she could not have recovered without the use of medication, it is my belief that the three-phase model that I have presented in this book would have eliminated much or most of her struggle with mania and depression.

A DIFFERENT VIEW OF MANIA

As we have seen, the psychiatric community believes that mania is caused by a so-called chemical imbalance. In my book *Depression and Mania: Friends or Foes?* I offer an alternative explanation, proposing that mania represents intentional or purposeful behavior. A simple example of how this dynamic works is illustrated by the feelings of a young child who has his heart set on going to Disneyland. Since going there will make him feel good, he invests himself into going, becoming a little manic a day or two before, and especially on the morning of the trip. Upon arriving at Disneyland, if he finds out that he is too small to go on a particular ride he had looked forward to, he will feel violated and perhaps become saddened (depressed) for a short time. Even though no one is intentionally choosing to hurt him, he will still feel bad.

The point of this example is to show that we all go through mini-episodes of manic and depressive behavior as we live out our lives. We may become manic over our wedding, a vacation, or a sporting event, only to feel depressed and let down after the event is over or if things do not go exactly as planned. We go through these mood swings because being alive means investing ourselves, and investing hopes that set us up for disappointments.

The key question we must answer is whether the extreme pathological forms of mania and depression are something different from what we normally experience, perhaps representing a chemical imbalance, or if they are simply exaggerated defenses against a self that has been deeply wounded. In other words, are extreme forms of these emotional swings simply another way that the protective part of the subconscious is working to help a person feel good about himself while hiding from painful feelings?

In 1992 Patty Duke wrote a book about her life entitled *A Brilliant Madness*. At the times when she was diagnosed with mania, she was told that her condition was a biological disease. Yet as she describes her manic episodes, they are full of meaning and purpose. She writes:

> I now interpreted the most trifling incidents as messages from God... Surely I had been selected as the instrument wherewith great reforms shall be effected.[1]

> That's the childlike part of the mania. It's whatever you see you want, that's it, it's yours, with no thought, not the slightest anxiety about what it takes to get it or how you're going to pay for it. It really is like believing that the money's all growing on trees.[2]

> During mania, we own the world, we don't need anybody, we don't need anything. We're going to be millionaires, and we believe it.[3]

Patty Duke experienced a terribly violating childhood and struggled deeply for a sense of meaning in her life. I propose that her mania was her way of finding that meaning. The craving behind her condition was the craving to fill the void and desperation in her life.

I once counseled a woman who, as a child, was severely emotionally neglected by her parents. The only time she felt any consistent validation was at Christmas, when her parents bought her a lot of gifts to make sure all her relatives saw them as good parents. The rest of her extended family was also quite dysfunctional and they showered each other with presents for much the same reason.

This woman survived part of her childhood by dreaming about Christmas. Whenever she fantasized about this season, she felt a superficial warmth that helped her to battle her inner desperation. As an adult, she would become extremely manic and compulsive at Christmas time. Not only did she have to buy everyone a lot of presents, but the holiday had to be celebrated exactly a certain way. Of course, she often suffered a major depression after Christmas.

I believe that the way to understand mania is to see it simply as an extension of normal behavior. When any of us become a little bored, we often take our minds off the reality of the moment and place it on some future enjoyable event. While working, we may dream of getting off work, having a nice meal, or taking a warm bath. We use the imagining part of our mind to escape the painful feelings of the present. In light of this, it makes sense that if a person had blocked out extremely painful feelings, then mania might be a way to both escape and feel good at the same time. Let's see if this explanation fits Dr. Jamison's life.

HER CHILDHOOD

Dr. Jamison does not write much about her early childhood, except to say that she grew up on an Air Force base. Her father was a scientist and a pilot and loved to fly. She and he were both dreamers and loved to stare up into the wide open sky. Her favorite lines from the Air Force song were "Off we go, into the wild blue yonder" and "Climbing high, into the sky." Besides fairly typical difficulties with siblings, Kay feels that her childhood and early adolescence were happy, filled with "warmth, friendship, and confidence."[4]

From the book, the reader gets a strong impression that her father lived a life of vivid imagination, full of fantasies. According to Kay, to him "a snowflake was never just a snowflake, nor a cloud just a cloud. They became events and characters, and part of a lively and oddly ordered universe."[5] Suggesting that he may have had his manic and depressive sides, she writes that when "his moods were at high tide, his infectious enthusiasm would touch everything... like having Mary Poppins for a father."[6]

Because Kay's sister also suffered periodically from depression, and because her father often created his own magical fantasy world, it would be easy to conclude that the severe mood swings that Kay developed in later life were a part of her genetic heritage. I believe, however, that it is more likely that this typical military family, often on the move, with friction between the siblings and a father who lived much of his mental life lost in the skies, was using manic, imaginative behavior to stay away from their deeper pain.

Even though Kay had a warm and happy childhood, her mind could have begun using the imaginary, creative, manic side of her being to stay away from her pain and to try to make her life more meaningful. Kay herself illustrates how she once used her mind to avoid the pain of watching an autopsy on a child. As a nurses' aide, she was allowed to assist in minor surgical procedures and to go on rounds with the medical staff. Describing her reaction while watching the autopsy of a child, she says, "In order to keep from seeing what I was seeing, I reverted back to a more cerebral, curious self, asking question after question, following each answer with yet another question."[7] She later states that her curiosity and temperament took her to other places she was not able to handle emotionally, but that she used that same curious and scientific side of her mind to generate distance.

From here it only takes a short leap of logic to see how she could have used her quick, intelligent, and creative mind to learn how to avoid her feelings. Just as she used the objective, detached part of her mind to protect her from what she saw in the autopsy room and to help her in her quest for scientific knowledge, she could also use it to dissociate from her feelings.

When Kay was fifteen, her father retired from the service and took a job in Southern California. This time was the point at which her life started to fall apart. On her first day at an upper-middle-class high school, she realized that life was going to be "terribly different." When she told her classmates that her father had been an Air Force officer, there was dead silence in the classroom. When she answered "Yes, ma'am" and "No, sir" to her teachers, as she had been taught in her previous schools with other Air Force children, she often heard laughter behind her back.

For a long time Kay felt totally adrift. She missed the military base and felt desperately unhappy about leaving a boyfriend behind.

She also missed her many good friends and all of the tradition and security she had grown up with: "I lost my moorings almost entirely... I was deeply unhappy."[8] She cried a lot, wrote often to her boyfriend, and felt furious with her father for moving them. To make matters worse, she was behind academically in every subject and had trouble establishing herself in athletics.

Kay shared that after he moved the family to California, her father's sparkling-manic side began to decrease, the "blackness of his depressions filling the air more and more." Kay felt unable to help him in any way. "I waited and waited for the return of the laughter and high moods and awesome enthusiasm, but, except for rare appearances, they had given way to anger, despair, and bleak emotional withdrawal...at times his rage and screaming would fill me with terror."[9] Her father also started drinking heavily. Kay's mother, frightened and confused, increasingly escaped from her problems through her work and friends. Kay began to withdraw more and more from her family, relying on her dog, her new boyfriend, and her friends to survive the turmoil of her home life.

It was about this time, while Kay was a senior in high school, that she had her first manic-depressive attack. As she describes it, notice the sense of purposefulness and the drug-like high involved.

> I raced about like a crazed weasel, bubbling with plans and enthusiasms, immersed in sports, and staying up all night, night after night, out with friends, reading everything that wasn't nailed down... The world was filled with pleasure and promise; I felt great. Not just great, I felt really great. I felt I could do anything, that no task was too difficult. My mind seemed clear, fabulously focused, and able to make intuitive mathematical leaps that had up to that point entirely eluded me. Indeed, they eluded me still. At the time, however, not only did everything make perfect sense, but it all began to fit into a marvelous kind of cosmic relatedness.[10]

After the highs, however, the lows would come and her mind would begin to fail her. During these times, her thinking was far from clear and she could not remember what she had read. Nothing made sense and she could not keep up with her classes. When she should have been listening to her teachers, she would find herself staring out the window in a daze.

When her mind speeded up, it was her "best friend." When it slowed down, it felt as if it had "turned" on her. Kay began to dwell more and more on the subject of death. As she continued to experience her lows, her pain became very great. Soon she started drinking alcohol before school in the morning, avoiding her friends, and writing morbid poems. She became convinced that her brain and body were rotting.

Even though Kay says that she tried to disguise her pain to herself and others, she admits, "I knew something was dreadfully wrong but I had no idea what, and I had been brought up to believe that you kept your problems to yourself."[11]

Once out of high school and into college, her struggle with her moods continued. Her college days were a terrible struggle, with violent and dreadful feelings interspersed with a few weeks or months of great highs. These highs had a very seductive side, "filling my brain with a cataract of ideas and more than enough energy to give me at least the illusion of carrying them out."[12] Her highs and lows became more severe, however, especially when she entered the competitive arena of graduate school and eventually sought a teaching position, with the attendant need to be published and recognized as a serious researcher.

In a later passage she writes about how her manic energy felt at this time. Again notice the sense of energy and purposefulness behind her description:

> When you're high it's tremendous. The ideas and feelings are fast and frequent like shooting stars, and you follow them until you find better and brighter ones. Shyness goes, the right words and gestures are suddenly there, the power to captivate others a felt certainty... Sensuality is pervasive and the desire to seduce and be seduced irresistible. Feelings of ease, intensity, power, well-being, financial omnipotence, and euphoria pervade one's marrow.[13]

Early on in her training in her psychiatric residency program, Kay was exposed to a psychoanalytic model that focused on conflicts, dreams and symbols, and their interpretation. Later, she was educated within the paradigm of the medical model. To the best of my knowledge, she was exposed to no feeling-centered therapeutic models during her training. All of her life she had been taught how to stay separated from the basic truth of her emotional life, and her education at the university continued along the same pattern.

MEDICATION

Eventually Kay realized that she had reached a place where she needed help. Things had gotten so bad for her that she realized she now had no choice. Either she must seek help, or lose her job, marriage and likely her life. Writing about how scared to death she felt about her first appointment with a psychiatrist, she says, "For once, I could not begin to think or laugh my way out of a situation."[14]

After giving her an intensive psychiatric examination, the psychiatrist came up with the diagnosis of "manic-depressive illness," telling Kay that she was going to need to be on lithium, probably indefinitely. Over the next several years, she saw him at least once a week—more often when she was suicidal and extremely depressed. Besides stating that she owes her life to her medication, she says that the caring support of the psychiatrist kept her "alive a thousand times over." According to Kay, his goal was to remain tough and convincing when she did not want to stay on her medication.

In sharing why she struggled about taking lithium at first, Kay writes that part of her resistance was due to the drug's horrible side effects:

> I found myself beholden to medication that also caused severe nausea and vomiting many times a month—I often slept on my bathroom floor with a pillow under my head and my warm, woolen St. Andrews gown tucked over me—when, because of changes in

262

salt levels, diet, exercise, or hormones, my lithium level would get too high. I have been violently ill more places than I choose to remember, and quite embarrassingly so in public places, ranging from lecture halls and restaurants to the National Gallery in London... When I got particularly toxic I would start trembling, becoming ataxic and walk into walls, and my speech would become slurred; this resulted not only in several trips to the emergency room, where I would get intravenous drips to deal with the toxicity, but much more mortifying, make me appear as though I were on illicit drugs or had far too much to drink.[15]

She also describes her severe problems with blurred vision and her now impaired concentration, short attention span and poor memory. While taking lithium, she did not "read a serious work of literature or nonfiction, cover to cover, for more than ten years."[16] Kay does state, however, that after a while the majority of her side effects subsided with the use of time-released preparations and the lowering of the dosage.

A Closer Look

Kay's psychiatrist diagnosed her correctly in reference to her symptoms, but he assumed that she was suffering from a physical illness, even though he did not perform one single medical test, such as a blood test or X-ray, to show that a such an illness existed. Once he had put Kay on lithium, her symptoms were reduced. This effect was largely due to lithium's emotion-blunting qualities, which affect non-manics and even animals much the same way. Since the drug seemed to work, her psychiatrist could make the assumption that Kay suffered from a chemical imbalance.

When we look at the other alternatives, however, we can see that it is possible that Kay's mania was her mind's best way of avoiding pain, and feeling good, omnipotent, and powerful about herself. The evidence in her autobiography supports this conclusion. At an early age, as Kay began to develop her unique defenses against pain (Phase I), she found that this process was most easily accomplished by using the creative, imaginative part of her life. When small pains surfaced or she faced even the threat of pain, all she had to do was to speed up her mind, look up into the skies, and dream a little.

Again there is nothing unusual about this process, except that Kay did not learn how to stay connected enough with her pain to take care of herself. She learned instead to take care of her woundedness by becoming manic. When she faced overwhelmingly painful situations in high school and in college, times when her parents were going through their own struggles and were not able to be there for her, she started having major episodes.

Even though Kay's manic episodes had their destructive side, they represented her mind's best attempt to keep the pain away from her selfhood. When she collapsed into her depression, however, she only felt further wounded and shamed. In this manner, a vicious circle developed. The more wounded she became, the more she came to depend on her manic episodes.

Eventually, Kay became so out of control that she was dependent upon a "forced choice." To stop her manic highs, she required a very powerful blunting agent, a "chemical club." Kay's sister disagrees with her use of medication claiming that she had "lithiumized"[17] away her negative feelings. Her sister claims that Kay's personality dried up during this period, and that she was at best a shell of her former self.

Could Kay have been helped in a different way, and could much of her struggle have been eliminated if she had been able to progress through the three-phase model described in this book? I believe so. Kay obviously enjoyed her fantasy world as a young girl because this world was relatively safe and fun. When she began to experience major pain and disappointment, however, neither she nor her parents had the tools to deal with it.

If her parents could have had more feeling-orientated conversations with her when Kay was young, and more when they moved, Kay's life might have gone differently. In place of her family's disintegration, she, her parents, and her siblings could have talked about their pain and supported each other. If Kay had understood the

KAY JAMISON, ANNA JENNINGS, AND JEFFREY DAHMER

emotional-pain view of her disorder, when her manic symptoms began to surface, she would have been able to say, "I am acting a little weird. I must be pushing a lot of pain down, and I need to talk to my parents or my counselor at school." If her counselor had been educated in the same manner, he or she might have noticed Kay's problems and approached them properly. Although taking lithium reduced Kay's symptoms and may have saved her life, she did also try to take her life once by overdosing on lithium. Even if a drug helps for a while, there are no guarantees when someone's real emotional pain goes unhealed. The emotional pain model could have saved Kay's life, eliminating most of her misery, lost time, and part of the money that was spent on her therapy and medication.

ANNA JENNINGS

Even though the medical model and the use of medication appears to be a blessing of the twentieth century, in actuality, it has become a disaster in the lives of millions. Anna is another of those individuals harmed by psychiatric drugs. In an article entitled "On Being Invisible in the Mental Health System," Dr. Ann Jennings writes about her daughter Anna.[18]

Anna was a client of the mental health system for nineteen years, starting at the age of thirteen. During this time, she was moved from one psychiatric facility after another, including hospitals, acute psychiatric wards, psychiatric emergency rooms, crisis residential programs, and locked mental facilities. During those nineteen years, her diagnoses included depression; borderline personality with paranoid and schizotypal features; paranoia; undersocialized conduct disorder, aggressive type; various types of schizophrenia, including hebephrenic and residual; and anorexia, bulimia, and obsessive-compulsive disorder.

In addition to treatment with insulin and electroconvulsive therapy, medication comprised ninety-five percent of Anna's treatment. In 1992, at the age of thirty-two, stretched to her emotional limit, Anna finally took her own life.

Anna's problems began at the age of 2 1/2 when she began to scream and cry uncontrollably. At the time, her parents did not realize that she was being sexually abused by her babysitter. When she was taken to a psychiatrist, he found nothing wrong with her. Later, Anna was also sexually abused by a relative. At first Anna tried to share this abuse with a housekeeper, stating that a man had "played with her when he wasn't supposed to." Unfortunately, the woman refused either to believe her or help her, and the abuse was kept a secret for thirty years.

Looking back, her mother, Ann Jennings, now sees that Anna tried to tell them what was happening to her as a child. She had attempted to communicate her abuse and corresponding feelings with "her rage, her screaming, and her terror," becoming a difficult-to-handle child; and her screaming and crying were frequently punished by spankings and confinement to her room. Although little Anna mentioned a man who "fooled" with her, her mother says that "since sexual abuse did not exist in our minds," no one heard the truth to the child's pain. Later, young Anna began to withdraw within herself, away from other children.

Anna was also subjected to traumas within her family, including alcoholism and divorce. At the age of thirteen, she "broke," and a psychiatrist prescribed an antipsychotic medication called Haldol to "help her sleep." Anna would spend nearly twelve of the next nineteen years in psychiatric hospitals.

In addition to drugs, shock, and insulin therapy, treatments included family therapy; vitamin and nutritional therapy; behavior therapy; and art, music, and dance therapy. Unfortunately, no one attempted to search for early childhood trauma. When, at the age of 22, Anna began to describe the details of her abuse to her mother, she was able to finally listen. Unfortunately, however, most of the damage had already been done. After the abuse she had endured in childhood and from the psychiatric establishment, Anna was so full of shame and worthlessness that she felt the need to abuse herself:

She put cigarettes out on her arms, legs, and genital area; bashed her head with her fists against walls; cut deep scars in herself with torn-up cans; stuck hangers, pencils, and other sharp objects up her vagina; swallowed tacks and pushed pills into her ears; attempted to pull her eyes out; forced herself to vomit; dug her feces out so as to keep food out of her body; stabbed herself in the stomach with a sharp knife; and paid men to rape her.[19]

Even though the professional community ignored her stories of abuse, Ann Jennings shares that many of the mental health professionals (e.g., psychiatric nurses and therapists) she encountered were highly regarded in their disciplines. Many people genuinely cared for Anna, and some grew to love her, but the mental health system continued to reinforce her original trauma. Her perception of herself as "bad," "defective," a "bad seed," or an evil influence on the world was reinforced by a focus on her pathologies, a view of herself as having a diseased brain, heavy reliance on psychotropic drugs and forced control, and the silence surrounding her disclosures of abuse.

Ann Jennings believes that her daughter did not receive the help she needed because, according to the medical model, the source of her pain was "an anomaly—a contradiction" to their thinking. "Her experiences did not match the professional view of mental illness."[20]

Finally, four days after her thirty-second birthday, after another sleepless night, Anna hung herself in her hospital room. She was found by the night staff who were on their way to give her another shot of medication.

Anna lived a horrible, painful life, one that she did not deserve. From the first day of her abuse, until she took her life, she was tormented daily with the pain of her past, the rejection of that pain by the psychiatric community, and the horrible side effects of her medication. She was as tortured by the medical model as she was by her abusers.

After Anna's mother was divorced and had finally heard what her daughter was trying to tell her, Ann Jennings started her own recovery and began to work closely with her daughter. As a result of her daughter's tragic life and death, Ann Jennings has transferred her daughter's case into a doctoral dissertation in psychology. Since then, Dr. Jennings has discovered that there must be thousands of "Annas" lost in the psychiatric system. She has run across studies that state that as many as 81% of hospitalized patients have histories of sexual and/or physical trauma.[21]

What Ann Jennings, myself, and other professionals are saying is that the vast majority of women and men, who have been labeled as mentally ill, forced onto medication and shock treatment, and told that they have a disease, may simply be suffering from the symptoms of emotional pain caused during their childhoods.

Even though Dr. Jennings states that medication can be helpful if used cautiously, with full understanding and consent of the patient, she believes the medication Anna was prescribed continually robbed Anna of her capacity to think and feel, which is essential for recovery. Quoting Dr. Jennings:

> Several years ago, she had been through a crisis period without medication. For days following, she asked for me to hold her. She talked softly about her feelings, crying gently, showing trust through touching and hugs. One day after her newly prescribed meds were beginning to "take effect", she said to me with a flatter voice and her eyes again haunted, "Mom, the feeling of love is going away." As her feelings of rage, grief and terror were suppressed, so were her feelings of love, laughter, caring and intimacy, isolating her again from herself and from others, and preventing the possibility of healing.[22]

Dr. Jennings also made an important point concerning the issue of money:

> An analysis of 17 years of Anna's records shows that she was hospitalized a total of 4,124 days. The total cost of this hospitalization, figured at $640.00 a day, was $2,639,360.00. This figure does not include residential treatment, case management, legal, social service, medical and other costs which are estimated to be

to be over $1,000,000.00, for a total cost of almost $4,000,000.00. Seventeen years of specific trauma based therapy, twice a week at $150.00 a session, would have totaled $265,200.00, and offered her the prospect of recovery.[23]

It is obvious that if the emotional pain model had been the accepted diagnostic procedure, then Anna's abuse would have been identified early, and she would have received the correct help. She would not have suffered through a life so torturous that she felt forced to kill herself.

JEFFREY DAHMER

Serial killing has become a major concern in our society. Can the emotional pain model help prevent such horrendous crimes? In many cases, the answer is yes. When we examine the life of Jeffrey Dahmer, we can see that he just might have been one of those cases.

As you might remember, Jeffrey Dahmer convinced several young men to come up to his apartment, where he drugged them, killed them, dismembered their bodies and then cannibalized them. In all, he took the lives of at least seventeen persons.

After Jeffrey had been arrested, as the court proceedings started, he began to share his story and the events from his childhood that had led him to commit these hideous crimes. During this time and after the final sentence, Jeff's father, Lionel Dahmer, began to feel a deep need to reflect back and put the pieces of his son's story together. He wanted to understand as best he could what went wrong and whether something could have been done to help his son. His thoughts and conclusions have been published in the book, *A Father's Story*.[24]

In looking back, Mr. Dahmer was able to piece together several events, beginning with his son at age four, that very likely represented a growing dark side in his son. Jeff was an extremely shy and introverted child, whether because of his mother's severe emotional mood swings and extreme nervousness, or his own basic personality. The fact that Jeffrey's father spent most of his time outside of the home, committed to his work, probably did not help the situation.

The Dahmer home was quite dysfunctional. His mother's nervous disorder was so severe that she took as many as twenty-six pills a day. At times her husband would find her wandering around in a lost, semi-catatonic state. Once he found her five blocks from their home lying in a field of grass, wrapped only in her nightgown.

Because Mr. Dahmer knew that his wife had grown up with a violent, extremely explosive alcoholic father, he figured that much of her emotional condition was due to abuse in her childhood; and because he loved her, he committed himself all the more. Yet his way of committing himself, working longer and harder hours and avoiding conflict, was completely ineffective.

It is important to note that, even though they had serious problems themselves, both parents still tried to raise Jeff in the best way they knew how. In spite of these good intentions, as Mr. Dahmer remembered his son's past, he began to remember little evidences of Jeff's "darker side." There were unusual episodes of anger and an early fascination with the bones of dead animals, along with an unhealthy interest in gutted fish. Reflecting back, however, Mr. Dahmer says, "I only saw a quiet little boy because I was rushing past my son too quickly... I wasn't there to see him sink into himself."[25]

As Jeff grew older, he became more withdrawn, not enjoying physical or competitive games. He grew more inward, often sitting quietly for long periods of time. During these times, his father remembers feeling quite helpless. A shy child himself, Mr. Dahmer writes, "I simply didn't know how things worked with other people."[26] But where the father suffered from shyness, Jeff experienced near total isolation.

Jeff's isolation and fear of people would eventually drive him toward the terrible acts that he committed. Feeling uncomfortable yet desperately in need of human contact and touch, Jeff began to act out these needs by waiting in the bushes with a baseball bat for a jogger to come along, hoping to knock the person unconscious so he could "lie down with him." Later, his fear of people and need for control and touch would only be satisfied when he lay with a dead body. Only then could he relax and feel the comfort of another human being.

We can get a sense of the craving developing in Jeff and the corresponding set of forced choices that became part of his behavior. Just as any of us might feel a slight need to touch or be close to the dead body of a loved one to recapture the warmth from that person, Jeff had only one way to feel love or warmth: the person had to be dead and in his total control.

When Mr. Dahmer reflected back on Jeff's childhood, he realized that he had tried to help his son as best he knew how to at the time. He had worked hard to be a provider, and was always there to help in whatever way he could when Jeff began to get into trouble, first with his drinking. He stayed in his marriage mostly for his son's sake. With all the ways he attempted to help his son, however, he believes now that he never really "connected" with Jeff's innermost self and his pain.

Mr. Dahmer also admits that he himself had a dark side that is fascinated with fire and making bombs. As a young boy, he almost burned a neighbor's garage down. After a stern lecture from his father, he realized that he had gone astray and ultimately channelled his interests in chemistry, bombs, and fire into a doctoral degree in chemistry.

Mr. Dahmer got control of his dark energy by directing it in an externally productive way. For this reason, when his son started having problems, the only way he knew how to help him was to "do things," such as trying to find Jeffrey a job. Yet while Mr. Dahmer was trying to help his son, in his mind he felt "separated" from him. He did not know how to connect on a feeling level.

> I began to realize that there were areas of my son's mind, tendencies and perversities which I had held within myself all my life... His sexual perversive generating acts were beyond my understanding,

271

and far beyond my capability. Nevertheless, I could see their distant origins in myself.[27]

What if Mr. Dahmer had been able to have a conversation like the following with his son?

Dad: When I was young I had a real fear of people. I just didn't know how to fit in. I didn't know how to make friends or feel comfortable around people. Do you ever feel that way?

Jeff: Yeah, I guess so, Dad.

Dad: Does it make you feel strange and worthless like it did me?

Jeff: Yeah, a lot. I just want to be by myself yet my loneliness often overwhelms me.

Dad: I can hear your pain. Does it make you mad at people at times?

Jeff: Sure! Sometimes I feel like I want to hurt someone.

Dad: I used to have those thoughts also.

Jeff: Really? When?

Dad: Lots of times, but especially when bullies at school would attack me or make fun of me.

Jeff: They did that to you also?

Dad: Yep. Bullies like to pick on shy people.

Jeff: What did you do?

Dad: I now realize that I took my anger and used it to dream about making bombs to hurt people. Such dreams gave me a good feeling inside, a sense of power. Do you ever have such hidden desires?

Jeff: Yes. In fact I have been thinking about hiding behind bushes at the park with a baseball bat and...

I admit this conversation sounds a little contrived, but my son Kevin at age five is starting to have these kinds of conversations with his parents. I also know of other parents who have similar conversations with their children. But if such a conversation sounds contrived, maybe that's an indication of our society's lack of ability to communicate on such a level. Conversations like these are not easy to have, but are much more probable when the proper training for such a conversation begins in childhood.

In fact, Jeff did try to reach out to his father at least once. As a teenager he told his father that he repeatedly dreamed of murdering people, usually after attacks from bullies. Mr. Dahmer tried to help, but did not know how to reach back to this part of his son. If the two of them could have really learned to communicate on a feeling level, it is hard to see how Jeffrey's "dark side" could gotten so out of hand that he needed to kill people.

People who end up becoming mass murderers live with their dark secrets for years. Along with these secrets is a desperation to be known and to have the pain beneath these desires be acknowledged. When their cries are not heard, more of their pain is turned to rage, giving them more justification for their acts. Both Manson and Dahmer reached out, maybe more times then we or even they know.

The more a person's pain is denied, the more evil desires become their main way of dealing with the pain, much the same way a person diagnosed as a schizophrenic uses her voices, the diagnosed manic his mania, the crooked politician or minister his thirst for power, and the diagnosed alcoholic her alcohol.

Because Jeffrey Dahmer wasn't able to identify and talk about his dark side and his inner desperation, he was unable to heal in this area and his darkness continued to grow and develop greater and greater power over him. Once he had killed his first person, he was forced to keep his dark side a total secret.

SUMMARY

I hope by now that you realize the enormously disastrous effect the medical model is having on the lives of millions of individuals and their loved ones. This issue is not just one of a few people becoming addicted to prescription medication or a few others suffering from the side effects of these medications.

The medical model totally robs individuals of their life, harming those around them in the process. Kay Jamison may have her life together and be doing quite well on low dosages of her medication, but she is one of the lucky ones. She still needed plenty of support to get to her present point, and she had a great career to fall back on. Anna Jennings, however, suffered a daily hell worse than many of the most abused prisoners of war. Her life and what we can learn from it must not be forgotten.

There are also too many Jeffrey Dahmers, Charles Mansons, and others in whom it has taken years to develop such a compulsive evil mind. The medical model will never be able to bring the necessary solution to the growing problem of violence. By the development of the emotional pain model, however, and the implementation of corresponding programs, we can give individuals such as Dahmer a real chance to reach out for help at earlier stages. If we can accept the darkness in each of us, and the fact that each of us is capable of out-of-control behavior, then the Dahmers and the Mansons who do try to reach out will have a real chance. Given real opportunities to reach out for help, regardless of their craving to hurt others or themselves, such individuals can acquire tools and the necessary healing that will help them to be more accountable for their behavior.

Under our present society, with all of its collective denial, and the psychiatric system's belief that there is a medical reason for problem behavior, people in need can only keep on trying, all on their own, to maintain or control their impulses, until they gradually lose their ability to freely choose.

CHAPTER EIGHTEEN

UNDERSTANDING "MENTAL ILLNESS"—A GIFT TO US ALL

I believe that most of us have a desire to be healers of pain, both physical and emotional. We dislike the pain we must often endure and we hate to see others suffer. There are, of course, those individuals who desire and need to inflict pain on others; but I believe that, behind this behavior, is the need to remove or justify the pain that was originally inflicted upon them. For example, one man in therapy with me who had been sexually abused as a child felt a compulsive need to abuse children, even though, fortunately, he had not as yet acted upon it.

When I asked if he knew the reason behind this compulsive need, he said it gave him a sense of *control* and *dignity*, the same sense of control and dignity that had been taken away from him as a child. To deal with his pain, his subconscious mind had produced a need to control and hurt children. Taking away their dignity helped him to feel better for a while. Even though he had not yet acted upon his fantasies, they gave him a sense of relief from his deeper pain.

Each of us, in our own way, lives in a state of inner desperation, trying to deal with the pain in our lives. Unfortunately, as researchers and doctors have attempted to solve the issues of the pain and suffering of others, some abusive and mind-crippling remedies have emerged, especially in the field of psychiatry.

While doing research for this book, I ran across an interesting bit of information. Ugo Cerletti is considered the father of electro-convulsive shock therapy, but he was not the first person to use electricity as a therapy for emotional problems. John Wesley, the founder of the Methodist Church, was probably the first to formally use it in this manner. On November 9, 1756, he recorded, "Having procured an apparatus on purpose, I ordered several persons to be electrified...some of whom found an immediate, some a gradual cure."[1]

As history tells it, John Wesley was a caring man, dedicated to the physical health of people as well as their spiritual welfare. He wanted to be a healer of pain, but he made the same mistake that has been made throughout the history of psychiatry. The faulty reasoning goes, "If the treatment has an effect on the symptoms, the treatment must be related to the causes, or is directly affecting the cause." In commenting on the "wonders" of electricity, he stated: "Yet all this Time it is striking at the Root of the Disease, which in a while it totally removes."[2]

What John Wesley did not realize is that the shock treatment was working because the electrical current paralyzed or disabled the brain, thus helping to block out the emotional pain that was causing the symptoms. The treatment was, therefore, not related to the cause at all.

The field of psychiatry has had its share of caring individuals much like John Wesley, those who have attempted to find the most effective way of eliminating human pain and the corresponding symp-toms of madness. Eventually, however, psychiatrists *must* admit that all their remedies from the old practices of bloodletting, forced seclusion and dropping individuals into cold water, to the more mod-ern techniques of surgical lobotomy, insulin shock therapy, electro shock therapy and medication all do the same thing: they disable the patient. In some cases people may feel that the "disabled" per-son is easier to be around than in his "mad" state; but a disabling process has, nevertheless, taken place.

I understand there will be individuals who will disagree with this notion, saying, "I have never felt better. I could not survive without my drugs." Fortunately, for those who are feeling slightly depressed and only need to take medication for a short period of time to get a slight emotional pick-up, drugs may not have long-term devastating effects. With the more emotionally confused or troubled, however, the disabling effects can be permanent.

MAKING THESE CONCEPTS STICK

I have thought long and hard about how to conclude this book so that the main concepts I've presented would become a permanent part of how you think about emotional disorders. Our society has become so conditioned by the disease model that such a switch in perspective is often difficult, even for professionals. To help solidify these points, I will share with you another biography of a person diagnosed as schizophrenic.

Joan was an only child born into a very abusive family. Her mother often suffered from long bouts of psychotic rages. During these times, which often lasted for days, Joan's mother would constantly talk to herself, talk to others who were not present and explode with anger at a moment's notice. During some days, when she was not violent, she would spend hours sitting in a chair. Then she would suddenly snap back into her rage, talking and screaming at fictitious characters.

During pregnancy and shortly after Joan's birth, her mother became physically sick with the flu. This sickness seemed to make Joan's mother crazier and more paranoid, as if she feared not being seen as a "good mother."

During the time of her mother's out-of-control rages, Joan's father would start drinking and then leave home for a few days. This pattern, which probably existed prior to Joan's birth, resulted in her being left alone with her mother.

When Joan began approaching puberty, her mother started acting even more bizarre, especially regarding her fear of her daughter's future romantic and sexual involvement with men. She began to dress Joan in younger-looking clothes, refused to let her wear any makeup and denied her anything that would have made her feel like a young adult. She also began to lock Joan in her room for the whole weekend.

Being confined like this was actually not that much of a problem for Joan since she had spent a good part of her childhood in her room, often playing for hours under the bed to hide from her mother. Creative and bright, she entertained herself with the fictitious friends she had begun to create as a child.

In junior high, Joan remembers starting to hear voices, especially at school. At times the voices told her that she was no good or ugly, mimicking the words of her mother. At other times they were voices of her fictitious friends who lived under her bed with her. All through high school she kept the voices to herself, but once out of school, she shared them with her minister who was already concerned about her shyness and her inappropriate mode of dress. He sent her to see a marriage and family therapist, who then referred Joan to a psychiatrist. During the very first session the psychiatrist told her, "You need to face up to the fact that you will always be sick and need medication."

His comment hit her hard. She accepted his medication, promised to take it, walked out the door, threw the medication into the trash and told herself that she would never share her "voices" or any other part of her inner life with anyone ever again.

Several years later, she married. After her second child, a girl, was born, the voices began to overwhelm her and she felt as if she were beginning to lose control. Fearing that she might turn out like her mother, Joan decided to risk seeking psychological help again.

She interviewed twelve therapists before she found one that felt right to her. This therapist, Rosemary, made two promises to Joan: never to ask her to use drugs and never to forcibly hospitalize her. Rosemary herself had a special understanding of what it meant to be abused because she herself had been abused by a neighbor as a child and had successfully worked through her inner madness. Out of her own journey for healing and wholeness, she had become a very gifted therapist.

When Joan started her recovery, she did not know how difficult such a path could become. With the help of Rosemary, she learned how her subconscious had created the voices, along with other behaviors such as food addictions and a need to cut herself to help control her inner pain. As Joan began to feel safe with Rosemary, who was willing to commit up to ten hours a week to be with her, most of it for free, the intensity of her pain started to surface.

Often when the pain was at its highest intensity, Joan felt as if she might be swallowed up by the voices and her need to cut herself. At every one of these craziest moments, however, Rosemary never weakened in her commitment to Joan. Because she had experienced the same therapeutic process, she knew how to hang right in there. As she did, Joan was able to start shifting more and more trust over to Rosemary. Soon when Joan's pain began to emerge, instead of the voices getting louder and the need to cut herself increasing, she was able to use her trust to experience the unconditional love of Rosemary. As this trust developed, and as a healing gradually began to take place, the voices and the cutting began to lose their power. As more and more of her emotional pain was healed, Joan needed her defenses less and less.

A few years later, and after many hours of very hard work, Joan emerged victorious. Today she has also become an excellent therapist. Joan has to be vigilant, however. If she is not taking good care of herself emotionally, setting appropriate boundaries with others, there are still times when she will begin to faintly hear her voices again. Yet these voices do not scare her. They have become her key to taking better care of herself, the same as *felt* stress may be for any of us "normals."

Although Joan's case may be seen as extreme, basically it is not that far away from what most individuals experience: the difference is only in the degree. When a couple fights, leaving each other wounded, each person may spend hours upon hours in his or her own head having one imagined dialogue after another with the significant other. Then, if they can get together, feel each other's pain and care for each other, their minds will stop needing to create "voices."

Alcoholics, or anyone caught up in an addiction, will need to hold on tightly to a sponsor and friends as support against being overwhelmed by the pain they feel in the first stages of their recovery. As they struggle in these early stages, they will, like Joan, gradually transfer their need to pursue their addiction over to the unconditional love of others, and eventually to their own self-love. Individuals like Joan can best be helped by a therapist who recognizes that their struggles and behaviors are caused by emotional pain; and that, while extreme, these behaviors are the same kind of behaviors experienced by lovers who have quarreled or other ordinary people experiencing difficult emotions.

Two Paths

There are two different paths a person may take in attempting to recover from an emotional disorder: The psychiatric medical path, which often leads to permanent disability, and the emotional recovery path.

Joan's success story is unusual, but it can become anyone's success story. Her life has been duplicated by many psychiatric survivors who have also successfully emerged from their condition. The emotional healing process involves two vital ingredients: (1) a strong determination on the part of the person to pay any price and walk the necessary road to recovery; and (2) at least one committed, trustworthy and perhaps skilled person to walk along side of the person.

Joan's story also exposes the two different paths quite well. It would be very easy to look at her family and conclude that a genetic predisposition caused her condition; but telling Joan this and then suggesting that medication would help could only weaken her fight to understand and heal herself. Fortunately, Joan did not weaken, but grew stronger fighting off such heresy.

It is often hard to understand the significance of these two paths and the need for absolute clarity about the choices involved. Just last night I saw a TV talk show on obsessive and compulsive behavior. The show's expert, who I believe was a psychologist, was suggesting that a biochemical problem might be involved in people suffering from obsessive/compulsive behavior. Meanwhile, the other guests who were clients of the psychologist were making comments such as "I become compulsive when the feelings in my stomach become too painful or big."

These clients were caught between two different sets of truths. On one hand, they were being told by an expert that they had a biological problem; but on the other hand, their own inner reality was telling them something different. Often an emotionally troubled person's destiny depends on which truth he or she chooses to believe in.

It takes a tremendous amount of courage for someone like Joan to walk out of her illness. Likewise, it takes a tremendous amount of courage to walk out of alcoholism and other addictions, or to walk through the problems of a troubled marriage.

One of the people in my men's support group has a severe sexual addiction. His behavior only involves himself, through activities such as masturbation, pornography and phone sex, but it has begun to severely affect his daily life. At times Aaron's out-of-control addictive and compulsive needs become so strong that he must leave work for half a day to find places to act out his behavior.

Aaron, single and in his early thirties, grew up with a controlling, guilt-producing mother, and with no father. To gain some control over his addictions and to work on the pain beneath them, he made the decision to stay separated from his family, including his mother, his sister and his grandmother.

After he had finally achieved seventy days of abstinence from his addictive behavior, Aaron's sister called and left a very degrading message on his answering machine. He chose not to call her back, fearing that this would aggravate the situation. He also decided to continue maintaining a distance from his family so that he could keep working on his issues. In spite of these resolutions, the distress and shame he felt from this message took its toll on him. Three days later he acted out his sexual addiction by spending several hours with pornographic material.

Thinking back to the process that led him to break his abstinence, he remembers how his mind drifted off after hearing the negative message from his sister, and how he began to feel bad and have negative thoughts about himself. He also remembers feeling that somehow he was failing his family. In the men's group, we helped him to get in touch with the pain and anger underneath his need to act out. He was then able to see how the sequence of events had unfolded.

After understanding the sequence that led to his acting out, with the support of the group, Aaron began to feel his own power come back. He called his sister that evening and expressed his feelings to her. The next week in group, he told us that he had realized that, when violated, he can not continue to simply suppress his feelings because the end product is destroying his life with his addictions.

Another man in the group was a severe alcoholic. Although he comes from an alcoholic family, he does not blame his condition on his genes. He says, "I drank to fill the deep void in me." Because of the severity of his disorder, and because he takes a non-medical view of his addiction, he too knows that he must stay on top of every situation lest he slip back into his self-destructive behavior.

These two men, along with Joan, all come from families with emotional disorders going back many generations. But they all know the *truth* about their disorders, whether they have been diagnosed as schizophrenic, obsessive—compulsive, depressed, or alcoholic. They all know that there is a direct connection between the unresolved pain they attempt to suppress and their so-called "mental disease."

Furthermore, every man sitting in my men's group, and anyone who knows Joan personally, is aware that there is a direct feeling-to-disorder connection in the strange behaviors under-lying emotional woundedness. As Aaron successfully deals with the feelings beneath his sexual addiction and his other symptoms, we can see the life and strength come right back into his mind and body.

In order for these individuals to be fully in charge of their lives and on a path toward a true healing, they must be willing to be responsible for every moment of their lives. To be fully responsible, they must be able to fully connect with their feelings. None of them would *ever* think about giving over this special inner awareness to the disabling effects of medication.

As a result of their insistence on clarity, these three individuals I have talked about in this chapter are three of the most sincere, honest and trusting people you can find. They know how to be honest with themselves, and they know the sickness that results from not being honest. They are committed to the highest degree of truth between individuals. Out of their own commitment to self-honesty, they bring great clarity into the lives of the people around them.

A Gift To Us All

Individuals like Joan, the men in my group, and other psychiatric survivors who have walked out of their conditions, bring a great gift to us all: At the heart of truly understanding emotional disorders is the key to our own emotional salvation and the emotional salvation of our society.

To see schizophrenia and other emotional disorders as diseases to be drugged is to hide from our own pain, as well as the pain of the afflicted. To see mental illness as a disease is both to fail to see the pain in our society, and fail to learn how to move forward in a more cooperative, non-violating way. To see the pain behind the behavior of people diagnosed as schizophrenic, and to make the commitment to help such individuals is to *heal a potential healer*.

Perhaps Joan could have been stabilized on drugs, put on disability, and then cared for by the state for the rest of her life. Instead, she found a therapist who had undergone the same courageous journey of discovery that she needed to take. The therapist was first able to walk through her own pain; then she was able to walk with Joan through hers. Now Joan is helping others to seek the healing necessary for their own wholeness.

I have used many examples of diagnosed schizophrenics in order to help each of us to better connect with our pain and the madness it can bring. I see no fundamental biological difference between Joan's hearing voices, the mental distortions of a racist, a lover's jealousy thoughts, the intensity of a religious fanatic or the behavior of a married couple unable to correctly identify and share their own pain. If there is a difference, then it is only that the labeled schizophrenic who hears voices might be using a much kinder, non-violating way of dealing with her inner pain.

This is the gift that the diagnosed schizophrenic, the recovered alcoholic, the depressed person or the recovered sex addict can bring to us. The more we see and understand their pain, the more we will be able to see our own pain and become unafraid to reach out.

The client I mentioned earlier who felt a compulsive need to abuse children found the courage to reach out. He has become one fewer potential child abuser. With more stories like his, perhaps other potential child abusers will find the courage to come forward. With more stories like Joan's, Ken's and Betty's, maybe more individuals who are just beginning to hear voices will lose their fear of getting proper help. Perhaps as we all come to see the normal intentions behind those with the most pronounced behavior, we will quit "diagnosing" individuals who are simply struggling with their lives at any particular moment.

As more people come forward to share their pain, you and I may feel more encouraged to risk sharing our own pain. To call an emotionally troubled person "diseased" and to block his pain with drugs is to lose the gift of seeing our own pain and being touched by the love of others.

Hemingway, who took his life because of his depression and the effects of shock treatment, perhaps said it best:

The world breaks everyone, and afterwards many are strong at the broken places.[3]

As human beings, we have a responsibility to each other, and we can't let the medical model circumvent that responsibility lest we lose the glue that holds our society together: the healing of each other's wounded hearts.

Appendix A

How To Choose A Therapist

Choosing a therapist can be a difficult process. For some people, it's one of the most important choices they make. This outline might help you in the process; it is geared toward the basic tenets in this book. Read the outline and adjust it to your needs.

In you are in need for a psychotherapist who believes in the basic tenets of this book, please refer to Appendix B.

Step One: First Contact

Call ten to fifteen therapists acquired from personal recommendations and/or your local telephone book. Use the telephone interview to reduce your list down to three to five. Ask the following questions as you interview the therapists over the telephone. Be considerate of their time. If you are prepared, each interview should take from ten to fifteen minutes. Ask simple questions and let them do the talking.

1. What type of therapy do you do?
It is important to know if they work with people on a feeling level. The therapist can certainly use a multitude of therapeutic approaches, but you want to know if the person can be there for you on a deep feeling level when necessary. If it isn't clear about how they do therapy, ask them to give you an example of a case or an area. Try to get a picture of what it's like to be in therapy with this person. For example, if someone were to ask me how I work with depressed patients, I might say something like the following.

> When someone is depressed, I try to help him or her locate the original pain that they had to suppress. If we can correctly identify

287

this pain or the issues causing the pain, then knowing the source of the pain will lead us to the best solutions. In some individuals, the solution might be learning how to say "no" or setting proper boundaries. With others it might be dealing with the shame of past events. With some, there may be deep hurt and anger pertaining to certain issues that must be dealt with. Knowing the specifics of the pain, I will be able to help each person find his own particular path out.

As you listen to the therapist talk about his or her approach, see whether it makes sense to you and whether you feel safe with that approach. If you choose a particular therapist and his approach doesn't work, you will still have made a step forward in your quest for proper help, and you can always start your search again.

2. How long have you been a therapist and where have you worked?

The type of license (clinical psychologist, licensed clinical social worker, marriage and family counselor, etc.) and/or the length of time that someone has been doing therapy doesn't indicate how good the therapist is. But it is important to get an idea of how long they have been doing therapy and the extent of training and experiences that they have had. Ask them if they have been in therapy, and how that experience was for them. It is significant that the therapist has and is willing to continue to deal with his or her own issues.

If you feel you have a lot of pain inside of you, you might want to see whether the therapist has done some hospital work and what kind. Some therapists hospitalize patients too quickly and you want to be aware of this if possible. Other therapists in their hospital work have experienced stressful situations with patients, and as result, feel more comfortable with patients struggling with their deeper pain. Choose a therapist who can deal with your pain, help you work through it, and not push for hospitalization unless it's for extreme emergencies or truly therapeutic reasons.

3. Do you have a specialty, and if so why did you choose it?

Again, you are trying to get an idea of their experience, training, and the areas they feel most confident in. One of the areas I specialize in is depression, partially because I went through a major bout of depression and have a personal feeling for it. Therapists who have been sexually abused as children and have successfully worked through their pain often are better equipped to bring greater sensitivity and clarity to your own pain. Those therapists who have not worked through their pain might show a definite insensitivity to your pain.

These issues are very difficult to ascertain in a short telephone conversation but, collectively, these questions will give you an overall feeling about the therapist.

4. What are your fees?

Ask them about the following areas

a) What do they charge?

b) What insurance do they accept?

c) Do they work on a sliding scale, especially if you must see them for more than one hour per week?

5. Can I share some of my issues with you?

If you feel comfortable at this point, give the therapist a little of your background and specific issues. Ask the therapist how he or she pictures your therapy proceeding.

STEP TWO: PERSONAL INTERVIEW

After interviewing the therapists and taking notes as appropriate, pick three to five that you feel most comfortable with and connected to. Call them back and set up an interview. Upon entering the office, get in touch with how the office feels to you. During the interview, ask the following questions. You might ask these questions over the telephone if that feels more comfortable to you.

1. What are your views on the chemical imbalance model and the use of medication?

If they truly believe in the chemical imbalance model, they might be inclined to want you on medication if the therapy or your emotions become too intense. It is important to choose a therapist who does not see medication as the answer or cure and who will work with you if you are presently on medication and want off. If you and the therapist agree to use medication on a short-term basis to get you through a rough emotional time, that should ultimately be your choice and the choice should make sense to you.

2. At what point do you refer patients to hospitals?

In most states therapists are obligated by law to hospitalize a patient if the situation is life-threatening to the patient or others. But some therapists use this law to eagerly hospitalize out of their own fears, or for financial gain.

Most individuals in pain occasionally have thoughts of suicide. Such thoughts do not make a person suicidal. You will want a therapist who can tell the difference, is not afraid of strong emotional pain, and will only use a hospital as a last resort.

If you are suicidal, you will want a therapist who will develop a contract with you, who will promise to be reachable by phone so you can call anytime you want to take your life, providing you are sincere about such a commitment.

3. What are your views on people who hear voices, injure themselves (self-mutilate), or have a lot of emotional pain?

If any of these issues or behaviors are relevant to you, you may want a therapist who does not panic, but sees those behaviors as your best way at controlling or blocking out your feelings. Once again, you don't want a therapist that jumps to conclusions about whether you are suicidal, psychotic, or in need of medication and hospitalization. You want a therapist who affirms your way of taking care of yourself and your woundedness, and will help you walk through the corresponding pain and get to a point where self-destructive behaviors are no longer necessary.

Forced hospitalization should be a last result and your therapist should be willing to stay in daily contact with you and be an advocate for you in such a situation. Ask the therapist under what conditions she or he hospitalizes people.

4. Have you ever personally dealt with or walked through strong feelings?

To help with the above questions, inquire more about how the therapist may have been traumatized and how she has worked through her feelings. If she has worked through issues similar to yours, she may have an extra sensitivity and clarity in those areas. But, remember the therapist is entitled to his or her own privacy.

5. At what point do you end therapy?

This may be a difficult question to concisely answer and I struggle with it when a patient asks me this question. But as I try to answer it or explain why it is difficult to answer especially in the first session, the patient still ends up with a better understanding of me and my approach.

6. What is your position on emergency support calls?

Get an idea of how the therapist will respond to emergency support calls. A therapist definitely needs his own space and boundaries away from his work, but you also want to know he is available when necessary.

7. What kind of cases do you feel uncomfortable with?

You may already have a good feeling for this question, but it might be worth asking it again for more clarity. At this time you can share more about your issues and get a better feeling for the therapist's level of confidence in this area.

Step Three: Choosing the therapist

After interviewing the different therapists, find a quiet spot and review each one. How honest and open did each one seem to you? Which ones could you trust the most? How safe did you feel; how calm inside did you feel in the therapist's office?

After choosing one, you can start, and if something doesn't feel right, try to bring up the issue with the therapist. If you don't feel comfortable enough, you have other options already available.

Most importantly, remember: this is your life and you have a right to the kind of treatment and therapist that feels most appropriate for you.

Appendix B

REFERRAL TO A PSYCHOTHERAPIST

Appendix C contains a position statement and response card that interested therapists can fill out. Kevco Information and Network Services (KINS) is building a referral list of like-minded therapists who want to help people without drugging or hospitalizing them. The position statement basically asks therapists their position on such issues as what causes mental illness, the use of medication, and their views on hospitalizing patients.

Therapists who fill out the position statement will be put on a referral list. If you want to have the names of therapists in your area, photocopy the request card on the next page and send it in with a self-addressed, stamped envelope. KINS will hopefully be able to send you back some referral sources in your area. We will also be compiling a mailing list in hopes of sending you future information. If you don't want your name on this list, please let us know by marking the appropriate box. The referral service will be available after January 1, 1997.

Please Note: KINS has no personal knowledge about any particular therapist, except that he or she has signed the position statement. We are looking for therapists who do not believe in or are currently struggling with the validity of the medical model; who can do therapeutic work on a feeling level; who do not believe medication corrects a chemical imbalance, but works by disabling the mind; and who are committed to minimizing any psychiatric violation in your life. In using this referral service, it becomes your responsibility to properly interview the therapist and make sure he or she is licensed as a psychotherapist in your state, has current malpractice insurance, is compatible with any religious beliefs that may be important to you, and meets any other vital criteria that are pertinent to you.

REQUESTS FOR REFERRALS FOR PSYCHOTHERAPY
(Photocopy and submit)

I am interested in any referrals you can supply me in my area. Enclosed is a <u>self-addressed stamped envelope</u>. In requesting a referral, I will take full responsibility in the selection of the therapist, knowing that this referral service is not screening therapists but only attempting to network between therapists and potential patients.

In requesting referrals, please include your telephone <u>area code</u> because that is how the lists are organized. If you are close to another area code, you may submit a second area code.

Please print the following information:

Name: _____

Address: _____

_____

_____

_____

Telephone area codes: (_____) (_____)

 Please do not include my name for future mailings or information.

Appendix C

PSYCHOTHERAPIST REFERRAL FORM

Dear therapist:

In an attempt to better meet the needs of those who desire counseling, and to create a network, Kevco Information and Network Service (KINS) is compiling a referral list to be used as a resource for future patients. We are looking for therapists who (1) do not believe in the medical model or are currently struggling with its validity, (2) do not use medication as a part of their main therapeutic plan, unless for short-term conditions with cooperation from the patient, (3) are very conservative about hospitalizing patients, (4) work well with traumatized clients, (5) who can do therapy on a feeling level when appropriate, and (6) have worked on their own issues on a feeling level.

In compiling a referral list KINS does not want to be in the business of choosing or screening therapists. KINS also does not want to interfere with how you believe therapy should be conducted for a particular patient. In addition, having your name on the list does not hold you responsible to any of the above tenets. We only want to help facilitate the first step in connecting the right therapist to the right patient. If you are in basic agreement with the above six tenets, then we would like your name on our list. Please photocopy the following referral card, filling in the necessary information and mailing it to KINS at the following address.

KINS
2639 North Grand Ave., Suite 265
Santa Ana, CA 92705

KINS' REFERRAL AND NETWORK SERVICE

In requesting my name to be included on KINS' referral list, I am not to be held responsible for any of the KINS' position statement tenets. I am only making a statement that I am in basic agreement with the six tenets listed in <u>Broken Brains</u> (1996, p.295), and that I am properly licensed and insured in my state as a psychotherapist.

Please print the following information:

Name/Title: _____

Address: _____

_____

_____

_____

Phone: (___)_____

Specialties (Maximum of three; include religious specialty if pertinent)

(1) _____
(2) _____
(3) _____

Date: _____ Signature: _____

Appendix D

RESOURCES

RESOURCES QUOTED IN BOOK:

1. Crisis Hostel, 206 South Geneva Street, Ithaca, New York, 14850, Telephone: (607) 272-3724. See page 244 of text.

2. Hearing Voices Network, c/o Creative Support, Fourways House, 16 Tariff Street, Manchester, England M1 2EP. See page 250 of text.

3. National Association for Rights Protection and Advocacy, 587 Marshall Avenue, St. Paul, MN, 55102. See page 250 of text.

4. National Empowerment Center, 20 Ballard Road, Lawrence, Massachusetts, 01843. See page 248 of text.

5. San Joaquin Psychotherapy Center, 3114 Willow Avenue, Clovis, CA 93612, Telephone: (209) 292-7572. See page 245 of text.

6. SCORE, 30100 Town Center Drive, Suite 379, Laguna Niguel, CA, 92677. See page 235 of text.

ADDITIONAL RESOURCES:

1. Children First!, Center for the Study of Psychiatry, 4628 Chestnut Street, Bethesda, MD, 20814.
Children First! is the only national program that focuses on the dangers of biopsychiatric interventions into the lives of children and youth while supporting more caring alternatives.

2. Dendron, David Oaks publisher, P.O. Box 11284, Eugene, OR, 97440, Telephone: (503) 341-0100.

An excellent newsletter offering articles on psychiatric oppression, human rights, and self-help alternatives.

3. The Prozac Survivors Support Group Inc., 3080 Peach Avenue, No. 104, Clovis, CA, 93612.

This organization brings together hundreds of victims of the adverse effects of Prozac and other SSRI drugs such as Zoloft and Paxil.

4. TURN, Tranquilizer Users Recovery Network, 228 'B' South Cedros Avenue, Solana Beach, CA, 92075, Telephone: (619) 793-9606.

TURN is a network of people devoted to helping those who are dependent on benzodiazepine tranquilizers such as Xanax, Valium, Ativan, Klonopin, etc. Call or write for additional material.

ADDITIONAL READING

1. *Challenging the Therapeutic State: Critical Perspectives on Psychiatry and the Mental Health System* by David Cohen, ed. (Vol. 11, nos. 3 and 4, 1990, of the Journal of Mind and Behavior).

Contains many important articles on psychiatric reform.

2. *How To Become A Schizophrenic* by John Modrow (Apollyon Press, Everett, WA, 1992).

John Modrow, a psychiatric survivor himself, meticulously challenges all the major research that claims schizophrenia is a biological disorder.

3. *In the Name of Psychiatry: The Social Functions of Psychiatry* by Ronald Leifer (Science House, New York, 1969).

Excellent theoretical criticism of psychiatry in general.

4. *Not in Our Genes* by R. C. Lewontin, Steven Rose and Leon Kamin (Pantheon, New York, 1984).

Challenges and rebukes the genetic basis of psychiatric disorders.

5. *On Our Own: Patient-Controlled Alternatives to the Mental Health System* by Judi Chamberlin (Mind, 1988).
Very informative concerning the psychiatry survivor movement.

6. *The Myth of the Hyperactive Child and Other Means of Child Control* by Peter Schrag and Diane Divoky (Pantheon Books, New York, 1975).
A classic revealing the myth behind the research to support the diagnosis of hyperativity or attention deficit disorder.

7. *Talking Back To Prozac* by Peter R. Breggin, M.D. and Ginger Ross Breggin (St. Martin's Press, New York, 1994).
This book is very easy to read and understand. It explains the fallacy behind the chemical imbalance theory, how drugs are approved and focuses on the controversy behind Prozac.

8. *The Limits of Biological Treatments for Psychological Distress: Comparisons with Psychotherapy and Placebo* by Fisher, Seymour, Greenberg, eds. (Lawrence Erlbaum Associates, Hillsdale, NJ, 1989)
Informative, scientific critiques of the alleged efficacy of antidepressants, minor tranquilizers, neuroleptics and Ritalin.

9. *Too Much Anger, Too Many Tears: A Personal Triumph Over Psychiatry* by Janet and Paul Gotkin (Harper Perennial, 1992).
A classic biography by a psychiatric survivor and her husband.

10. *Toxic Psychiatry* by Peter R. Breggin, M.D. (St. Martin's Press, New York, 1991).
This book not only examines the toxic properties associated with psychiatric medication, but also presents an indepth look at the lack of evidence to support the medical model.

References and Notes

Chapter One

1. Barney, Ken, Limitations of the Critique of the Medical Model, *The Journal of Mind and Behavior*, Vol. 15, No. 1, 1994, p.22.

2. Breggin, Peter R., *Toxic Psychiatry*, St. Martin's Press, New York, 1991, p.143.

3. Cohen, David, *The Journal of Mind and Behavior*, Vol. 15, No. 1, 1994, Preface.

4. Kemker, Susan, Psychiatric Education: Learning By Assumption, in Ross, Colin, A. and Pam, Alvin, *Pseudoscience In Biological Psychiatry*, John Wiley & Sons, Inc., New York, 1995, p.241.

5. Ross, Colin, A., Errors Of Logic In Biological Psychiatry, in Ross, Colin, A. and Pam, Alvin, *Pseudoscience In Biological Psychiatry*, John Wiley & Sons, Inc., New York, 1995, p.85.

6. Ibid., p.116.

Chapter Two

1. Franciscus Mercurius van Helmont in a book published in Amsterdam in 1692, describes the ducking technique used by his father Jean Baptiste van Helmont. Franciscus Mercurius van Helmont's description was summarized in Richard Hunter and Ida Macalpine, eds., *Three Hundred Years of Psychiatry (1535-1860)*, Oxford University Press, London, 1963, pp.254-257.

2. Ibid.

3. Rush, Benjamin, "Letter to John Redman Coxe," September 5, 1810, in *Classics of American Psychiatry*, Warren H. Green, Inc., St. Louis, Missouri, 1975, p.18.

4. David Herman and Jim Green, The Female Malady, *Madness: A Study Guide*, 1991.

5. Kraepelin, Emil, *One Hundred Years of Psychiatry*, Citadel, New York, 1917, p.60.

6. Ibid., p.86.

7. Emil Kraepelin, describing (in her presence) a patient with "katatonic excitement" to a class of medical students, *Lectures on Clinical Psychiatry*,

1904, pp.82-83, 3rd English edition, revised and edited by Thomas Johnstone, 1913.

8. Manfred Sakel, discussing insulin coma treatment, cited in Marie Beynon Ray, *Doctors of the Mind: The Story of Psychiatry*, 1942, p.250.

9. Kennedy, Cyril J. C. and Anchel, David, Regressive Electric-shock in Schizophrenics Refractory to Other Shock Therapies, *Psychiatric Quarterly*, 1948, Vol. 22, pp.317-320.

10. Sargant, William, *Battle for the Mind: A Physiology of Conversion and Brain Washing*, Penguin Books, Baltimore, 1957, p.71.

11. Freeman, Walter, West Virginia Lobotomy Project: A Sequel, *Journal of the American Medical Association*, September 29, 1962, pp.1134-1135.

12. Hotchner, A. E., *Papa Hemingway: A Personal Memoir*, Bantam Books, New York, 1967, p.308.

CHAPTER THREE

1. Harvard Medical School Health Publications Group, *The Harvard Medical Health Letter*, Boston, Massachusetts, Vol. 11, No. 10, April 1995, p.3.

2. Ibid., May 1995, p.1.

3. *Review in Psychiatry*, American Psychiatric Press, Washington, DC, Vol. 13, 1994.

4. Kaplan, Harold I., Sadock, Benjamin, J., *Synopsis of Psychiatry*, Williams & Wilkins, Balitimore, 6th ed., 1991, p.645.

5. American Psychiatric Association, *Tardive dyskinesia: a report of the American Psychiatric Association Task Force on Late Neurological Effects of Antipsychotic Drugs*, American Psychiatric Press, Washington, DC, 1980, p.45.

6. Gualtieri, C. Thomas, *Archives of General Psychiatry*, April 1986.

7. Keefe, Richard S. E. and Harvey, Philip D, *Understanding Schizophrenia*. The Free Press, New York, 1994, p.107.

8. Ibid., p.107.

9. Ross, Colin, A., Errors Of Logic In Biological Psychiatry, in Ross, Colin, A. and Pam, Alvin, *Pseudoscience In Biological Psychiatry*, John Wiley & Sons, Inc., New York, 1995, p.108.

10. Breggin, Peter R., *Toxic Psychiatry*, St. Martin's Press, New York, 1991, p.67.

11. Tow, P. Macdonald, *Personality Changes Following Frontal Leucotomy; A Clinical and Experimental Study of the Functions of the Frontal Lobes in*

Man, Oxford University Press, London, 1955.

12. Rylander, Gosta, *Personality Changes After Operations On The Frontal Lobes; A Clinical Study of 32 Cases*, Oxford University Press, London, 1939.

13. Delay and Deniker, *Congre's des Medecins Alie'nistes et Neurologistes de France*, (Quoted in Breggin, Peter, R., *Toxic Psychiatry*, St. Martin's Press, New York, 1991, p.54).

14. Breggin, Peter R., *Toxic Psychiatry*, St. Martin's Press, New York, 1991, p.56.

15. Sterling, Peter, Psychiatry's Drug Addiction, *New Republic*, March 3, 1979.

16. Lehmann, H. E., Therapeutic Results With Chlorpromazine (Largactil) in Psychiatric Conditions, *The Canadian Medical Association Journal*, Toronto, Canada, Vol. 72, No. 2, January 15, 1955, pp.91-99.

17. Klerman, Gerald, in Alberto DiMascio and Richard Shader's *Clinical Handbook of Psychopharmacology*, Science House, New York, 1970, p.51.

18. Breggin, Peter R., *Toxic Psychiatry*, St. Martin's Press, New York, 1991, p.22.

19. Pam, Alvin, Biological Psychiatry: Science Or Pseudoscience?, in Ross, Colin, A. and Pam, Alvin, *Pseudoscience In Biological Psychiatry*, John Wiley & Sons, Inc., New York, 1995, p.41.

20. Breggin, Peter R., *Toxic Psychiatry*, St. Martin's Press, New York, 1991.

21. This information made available through the Freedom of Information Act and cited in Breggin, Peter R. and Breggin, Ginger Ross, *Talking Back To Prozac*, St. Martin's Press, New York, 1994, p.66.

22. Breggin, Peter R. and Breggin, Ginger Ross, *Talking Back To Prozac*, St. Martin's Press, New York, 1994, pp.146,149.

23. Ibid., p.67.

24. Talk given by Peter Breggin at the 1994 NARPA conference, November, 1994, San Diego, California.

25. Breggin, Peter R. and Breggin, Ginger, Ross, *Talking Back To Prozac*, St. Martin's Press, New York, 1994, p.66.

26. Tracy, Ann Blake, *Prozac: Panacea Or Pandora?*, Cassia Publications, West Jordan, Utah, 1991, p.265

27. Tracy, Ann Blake, *The Prozac Pandora*, Mundo Placido, Inc., Salt Lake City, Utah, 1991.

28. Grahame-Smith, D.G., and Aronson, J. K., *Oxford Textbook of Clinical Pharmacology and Drug Therapy*, Oxford University Press, Oxford, 1992, p.141.

29. Fieve, Ronald M.D., *Moodswing*, Bantam Books, New York, 1989, p.11.

30. Ibid., p.12.

31. Cade, John, F. S., Lithium Salts in the Treatment of Psychotic Excitement, *The Medical Journal of Australia*, Vol II, No. 10, September, 3, 1949, p.350.

32. Judd, Lewis L., Effect of Lithium on Mood, Cognition, and Personality Function in Normal Subjects, *Archives of General Psychiatry*, Vol. 36, July 20, 1979, p.864.

33. Annitto, W., Prien, R., and Gershon, S., The Lithium Ion: Is It Specific for Mania?, *Mania: An Evolving Concept*, Spectrum Publications, New York, 1980, p.127.

34. Prien, R.F., Mc Caffey, E.M., and Klett, C.J., Relationship Between Serum Lithium Level and Clinical Response in Acute Mania Treated with Lithium, *British Journal of Psychiatry*, 1972, 120, p. 413.

35. Annitto, William, Prien, Robert, and Gershon, Samuel, The Lithium Ion: Is It Specific for Mania?, *Mania: An Evolving Concept*, Spectrum Publications, New York, 1980, p.129.

36. Interview with Ron Leifer, in Farber, Seth, *Madness, Heresy, and the Rumor of Angels*, Open Court Publishing Company, Peru, Illinois, 1993, p.177.

37. Palladino, Lucy Jo, Times Books, New York, In press

38. Palladino, Lucy Jo, Ph.D., Phone conversation on March, 3, 1996.

39. Harvard Medical School Health Publications Group, *Harvard Mental Health Letter*, Boston, Massachusetts, February, 1996, p.6.

40. Grahame-Smith, D.C., and Aronson, J. K., *Oxford Textbook of Clinical Pharmacology and Drug Therapy*, Oxford University Press, Oxford, 1992, p.141.

41. *Treatments of Psychiatric Disorders*, American Psychiatric Association, Washington, DC, 1989, p.374.

42. Fisher, Seymour and Greenberg, Roger P., *The Limits of Biological Treatments for Psychological Distress*, Lawrence Erlbaum Associates, Hillsdale, New Jersey, 1989, p.311.

43. Goleman, D., New Light on How Stress Erodes Health," *The New York Times*, December 15, 1992, p.C1.

44. Lewontin, R.C., Rose, Steven, and Kamin, Leon J. *Not In Our Genes*, Pantheon Books, New York, 1984, p.181.

CHAPTER FOUR

1. Ross, Colin, A. and Pam, Alvin, *Pseudoscience In Biological Psychiatry*, John Wiley and Sons, Inc., New York, 1995, p.87.

2. Lewontin, R.C., Rose, Steven and Kamin, Leon J, *Not In Our Genes*, Random House, New York, 1984, p.115.

3. R. T. Smith, A Comparison of Socio-environmental Factors in Monozygotic and Dizygotic Twins: Testing an Assumption, in *Methods and Goals in Human Behavior Genetics*, ed. S. G. Vandenberg, Academic Press, New York, 1965.

4. Lewontin, R.C., Rose, Steven and Kamin, Leon J, *Not In Our Genes*, Random House, New York, 1984, p.116.

5. Torrey, E. Fuller, Bowler, Ann E., Taylor, Edward H. and Gottesman, Irving I., *Schizophrenia and Manic-Depressive Disorder*, Basic Books, New York, 1994, p.10.

6. Ibid., p.11.

7. Ibid., p.11.

8. Boyle, Mary, *Schizophrenia-A Scientific Delusion?* Routledge, London, 1990, p.131.

9. Torrey, E. Fuller, Bowler, Ann E., Taylor, Edward H., and Gottesman, Irving I., *Schizophrenia and Manic-Depressive Disorder*, Basic Books, New York, 1994, p.12.

10. Lewontin, R.C., Rose, Steven and Kamin, Leon J, *Not In Our Genes*, Random House, New York, 1984, p.218.

11. Ibid., p.220.

12. Jackson, D., A Critique of the Literature on the Genetics of Schizophrenia, in D. Jackson (Ed.), *The Etiology of Schizophrenia*, Basic Books, New York, 1960, pp.37-87.

13. Boyle, Mary, *Schizophrenia-A Scientific Delusion?* Routledge, London, 1990.

14. Kringlen, E., Twins-Still Our Best Method, *Schizophrenia Bulletin*, 1976, p.430.

15. Boyle, Mary, *Schizophrenia-A Scientific Delusion?*, Routledge, London, p.124.

16. Ibid., p.137.

17. Ibid., pp.124-125.

18. Torrey, Bowler, and Gottesman state that the three most accurate twin studies are Tiernari, Kringlen, and Fischer. Torrey, E. Fuller, Bowler, Ann E., Taylor, Edward H., and Gottesman, Irving I., *Schizophrenia and*

Manic-Depressive Disorder, Basic Books, New York, 1994, p.12.

19. Gottlesman, I.I. and Shields, J, A Critical Review of Recent Adoption, Twin and Family Studies of Schizophrenia: Behavioral Genetics Perspectives, *Schizophrenia Bulletin*, Vol. 2, 1976, pp.360-398.

20. Kety, S.S., Rosenthal, D., Wender, P.H., Schulsinger, F., and Jacobsen, B., Mental illness in the Biological and Adoptive Families of Adopted Individuals Who Have Become Schizophrenic. A Preliminary Report Based on Psychiatric Interviews, In R. Fieve, D. Rosenthal and H. Brill (eds) *Genetic Research in Psychiatry*, Johns Hopkins University Press, London, 1975.

21. Lewontin, R.C., Rose, Steven and Kamin, Leon J, *Not In Our Genes*, Random House, New York, 1984, p.222.

22. Ibid., p.223.

23. Breggin, Peter R., *Toxic Psychiatry*, St. Martin's Press, New York, 1991, p.97.

24. Lewontin, R.C., Rose, Steven and Kamin, Leon J, *Not In Our Genes*, Random House, New York, 1984.

25. Breggin, Peter R., *Toxic Psychiatry*, St. Martin's Press, New York, 1991, p.98.

26. Ibid., p.98.

27. Wender, Paul, *Medical World News*, 17 May, 1976, p.23.

28. Wender, P. and Klein, D., The Promise of Biological Psychiatry, *Psychology Today*, February, 1981.

29. Keefe, Richard S. E. and Harvey, Philip D, *Understanding Schizophrenia*, The Free Press, New York, 1994, p.83.

30. Ross, Colin, A. and Pam, Alvin, *Pseudoscience In Biological Psychiatry*, John Wiley & Sons, Inc., New York, 1995, p.50.

31. Wiener, Harry, The Genetics of Preposterous Conditions, in Ross, Colin, A. and Pam, Alvin, *Pseudoscience In Biological Psychiatry*, John Wiley & Sons, Inc., New York, 1995, p.200.

CHAPTER FIVE

1. Egeland, J., Gerhard, D., Pauls, D., Sussex, J., Kidd, K., Allen, C., Hostetter, A., and Housman, D., Bipolar Affective Disorders Linked to DNA Markers in Chromosome 11," *Nature*, Vol. 325, 1987, pp.783-787.

2. Sherrington, R., Brynjolfsson, J., Petursson, H., Potter, M., Duddleston, K., Barraclough, B., Wasmuth, J., Dobbs, M., and Gurling, H., Localization of a Susceptibility Locus for Schizophrenia on Chromosome 5,

Nature, Vol. 336, 1988, pp.164-167.

3. National Alliance for the Mentally Ill, *Advocate*, Arlington, Virginia, March/April, 1995.

4. Wingerson, Lois, *Mapping Our Genes*, Penguin Books, New York, 1990, p.129.

5. Egeland, J., Gerhard, D., Pauls, D., Sussex, J., Kidd, K., Allen, C., Hostetter, A., and Housman, D., Bipolar Affective Disorders Linked to DNA Markers in Chromosome 11, *Nature*, Vol. 325, February, 1987, pp.783-787.

6. Ibid., pp.805-808.

7. Wingerson, Lois, *Mapping Our Genes*, Penguin Books, New York, 1990, p.140.

8. Harsanyi, Zsolt and Hutton, Richard, *Genetic Prohecy: Beyond The Double Helix*, Rawson, Wade Publishers, New York, 1981, p.194.

9. Ibid., p.194.

CHAPTER SIX

1. Johnson, E.C., Crow, T.J., Frith, C.D., et al (1976) Cerebral Ventricular Size and Cognitive Impairment in Chronic Schizophrenia, *Lancet*, ii, pp.924-926.

2. Chua, S.E. and McKenna, P.J., Schizophrenia--A Brain Disease?, *British Journal of Psychiatry*, Vol. 166, 1995, pp.563-582.

3. Torrey, E. Fuller, Bowler, Ann E., Taylor, Edward H., and Gottesman, Irving I., *Schizophrenia and Manic-Depressive Disorder*, Basic Books, New York, 1994, p.103.

4. Keefe, Richard S. E. and Harvey, Philip D, *Understanding Schizophrenia*, The Free Press, New York, 1994, p.125.

5. Harvard Medical School Health Publications Group, *Harvard Mental Health Letter*, Vol. 11, #12, June 1995.

6. Chua, S.E. and McKenna, P.J., Schizophrenia--A Brain Disease?, *British Journal of Psychiatry*, Vol. 166, 1995, p.564.

7. Van Horn, J.D. and McManus, I.C., Ventricular Enlargement in Schizophrenia: A Meta-analysis of Studies of the Ventricle:Brain Ratio (VBR), *British Journal of Psychiatry*, Vol. 160, 1992, pp.687-697.

8. Smith, G.N. and Iacono, W.G., Lateral Ventricular Size in Schizophrenia and Choice of Control Group, *Lancet*, i, 1986, P.1450.

9. Van Horn, J.D. and McManus, I.C., Ventricular Enlargement in Schizophrenia: A Meta-analysis of Studies of the Ventricle: Brain Ratio (VBR), *British Journal of Psychiatry*, Vol. 160, 1992, pp.687-697.

10. Smith, G.N. and Iacono, W.G.,Lateral Ventricular Size in Schizophrenia and Choice of Control Group, *Lancet*, i, 1986, p.1450.

11. Jones, P.B., Harvey, I., Lewis, S.W., et al, Cerebral Ventricle Dimensions as Risk Factors for Schizophrenia and Affective Psychosis, *Psychological Medicine*, Vol. 24, 1994, pp.995-1011.

12. Suddath, R. L., Christison, G. W., Torrey, E. F., Casanova, M. F., and Weinberger, D. R., Anatomical Abnormalities in the Brains of Monozygotic Twins Discordant for Schizophrenia, *New England Journal of Medicine*, Vol. 322, 1990, p.793.

13. Breggin, Peter R., M.D., *Toxic Psychiatry*, St. Martin's Press, New York, 1991, pp.113,114.

14. Goodwin, Frederick K., Improved Treatment for Depression and Bipolar Disorders, Continuing Medical Education talk given in Atlanta, Georgia, December 1-3, 1995.

15. Kaplan, Harold I., and Sadock, Benjamin J., *Synopsis of Psychiatry*, Williams & Wilkins, Baltimore, Sixth Ed., 1991.

16. Goodwin, Frederick, K., Improved Treatment for Depression and Bipolar Disorders, Continuing Medical Education talk given in Atlanta, Georgia, December 1-3, 1995.

17. *The Biology of Mental Disorders*, Congress of the United States, Office of Technology Assessment, U.S. Government Printing Office, Washington, DC, September, 1992, p.128

18. Chua, S.E. and McKenna, P.L., Schizophrenia--A Brain Disease?, *British Journal of Psychiatry* Vol. 166, 1995, p.572.

19. Ibid. p.578

20. Ibid. p.578

21. Liddle, P.F., Friston, K.J., Frith, C.D. et al, Patterns of Cerebral Blood Flow in Schizophrenia, *British Journal of Psychiatry*, Vol. 160, 1992, pp.179-186.

L   22. Frith, C.D., Friston, K.J., Herold, S. et al, Regional Brain Activity in Chronic Schizophrenic Patients During the Performance of a Verbal Fluency Task: Evidence for a Failure of Inhibition in Left Superior Temporal Cortex, *British Journal of Psychiatry*, Vol. 161, 1995.

23. Chua, S.E. and McKenna, P.L. (1995) Schizophrenia--A Brain Disease? *British Journal of Psychiatry*, Vol. 166, p.579.

24. Baughman, Fred A., Jr., correspondence by letter, April 4, 1996.

25. Chua, S.C. and McKenna, P.L., Schizophrenia--A Brain Disease?, *British Journal of Psychiatry*, Vol. 166, 1995, p.563.

26. Baughman, Fred A., Jr., correspondence by letter, April 23, 1996.

CHAPTER SEVEN

1. *Abnormal Psychology: Current Perspectives*, Random House, New York, 1977, p.10.

2. Ibid., p.16.

3. Breggin, Peter R., *Toxic Psychiatry*, St. Martin's Press, New York, 1991, p.4.

4. Ibid., p.4.

5. Ibid., p.5.

6. Ibid., p.6.

7. Ibid., p.6.

8. Ibid., p.8.

9. *Counterpoint*, Facing Goliath: An Interview with Peter Breggin, East Topsham, Vermont, Spring, 1995, p.4.

10. Ibid., p.4.

11. Masson, Jeffrey Moussaieff, talk given at National Association for Rights Protection and Advocacy, Kansas City, Missouri, 1992.

12. Sulloway, Frank J., *Freud, Biologist of the Mind: Beyond the Psychoanalytic Legend*, Basic Books, New York, 1979, p.142.

13. Ibid., p.145.

14. Ibid., p.140.

15. Masson, Jeffrey Moussaieff, *The Assault on Truth*, Farrar, Straus and Giroux, New York, 1984.

16. Ibid., p.61.

17. Ibid., p.68.

18. Ibid., p.68.

19. Ibid., p.71.

20. Ibid., p.72.

21. Ibid., p.99.

22. Ibid., p.99.

23. Ibid., p.101.

24. Ibid., p.102.

CHAPTER ELEVEN

1. Nuel Emmons, *Manson In His Own Words*, Grove Press, New York, p.27.

2. Ibid., p.27.

3. Ibid., p.35.

4. Ibid., p.36.
5. Ibid., p.45.
6. Ibid., p.51.
7. Ibid., p.53.

CHAPTER TWELVE

1. Nuel Emmons, *Manson In His Own Words*, Grove Press, New York, p.35.

CHAPTER THIRTEEN

1. Miller, Alice, *For Your Own Good*, Noonday Press, New York, 1990, p.16.

CHAPTER FOURTEEN

1. Renee,*Autobiography of a Schizophrenic Girl*, Grune & Stratton, New York, 1951, p.21,22.
2. Ibid. p.23.
3. Ibid., p.24.
4. Ibid., p.24.
5. Ibid., p.26.

CHAPTER FIFTEEN

1. Goleman, Danied,*Emotional Intelligence*, Bantam Books, New York, 1995, p.47.
2. Beck, Aaron T., Rush A. John, Shaw, Brian F. and Emery, Gary, *Cognitive Therapy of Depression*, Guilford Press, New York, 1979, p.11.
3. Cornell, Ann Weiser Ph.D., *Power of Focusing*, New Harbinger Publications, Oakland, California, 1996, p.4.
4. Ibid., p.5.
5. See Appendix D.

CHAPTER SIXTEEN

1. See Appendix D.
2. Crisis Hostel: Alternative to Psychiatric Hospitalization,*NEC News-*

letter, The National Empowerment Center, Lawrence, Massachusetts, Spring, Summer 1995, p.4.

3. See Appendix D.

4. McCready, Kevin, Ph.D., What Heals Human Beings? Technology or Humanity--There is a Choice!, *The Rights Tenet,* National Association for Rights, Protection and Advocacy, Summer 1995, p.3.

5. Fisher, Dan, The Empowerment Model of Recovery, *National Empowerment Newsletter,* The National Empowerment Center, Winter 1994-1995, p.5.

6. Deegan, Pat, Learning From Us, *National Empowerment Newsletter,* The National Empowerment Center, Winter 1994-1995, p.14.

7. Chamberlin, Judi, *On Our Own,* Mind, London, 1977.

8. See Appendix D.

9. Deegan, Pat, *Coping With Voices,* National Empowerment Center, Lawrence, Massachusetts, 1996.

10. See Appendix D.

11. See Appendix D.

12. Romme, Marius and Escher, Sandra, *Accepting Voices,* Mind Publications, Granta House, 15-19 Broadway, London E5.

13. Baker, Paul, *The Voice Inside,* Hearing Voices Network, Manchester, England,

14. Ibid., p.2.

15. Breggin, Peter, *Toxic Psychiatry,* St. Martin's Press, New York, 1991, p.384.

16. Ibid., p.385.

17. Ibid., p.386.

CHAPTER SEVENTEEN

1. Duke, Patty and Hochman, Gloria, *A Brilliant Madness,* Bantam Books, 1992, p.17.

2. Ibid., p.24.

3. Ibid., p.188.

4. Jamison, Kay Redford, *An Unquiet Mind,* Alfred D. Knopf, New York, 1995, p.12.

5. Ibid., p.15.

6. Ibid., p.17.

7. Ibid., p.22.

8. Ibid., p.31.

9. Ibid., p.34.

10. Ibid., p.36.

11. Ibid., p.39.

12. Ibid., p.47.

13. Ibid., p.67.

14. Ibid., p.87.

15. Ibid., pp.93-94.

16. Ibid., p.95.

17. Ibid., p.99.

18. Jennings, Ann, *Journal of Mental Health Administration*, Vol. 21:4, Fall 1994, pp.374-387.

19. Jennings, Ann, Anna's Story: The Effects of Sexual Abuse, the System's Failure to Respond and the Emergence of a New, Trauma-Based Paradigm, *National Empowerment Newsletter*, National Empowerment Center, Lawrence, Massachusetts, Winter 1994-1995, p.9.

20. Ibid., p.10.

21. Blaska, Betty, Two More Views on SB 220: Include PTSD, *Emerging Force*, PREVAIL, Madison, Wisconsin, July-August, 1995, p.19.

22. Jennings, Ann, *Journal of Mental Health Administration*, Vol. 21:4, Fall 1994, pp.374-387.

23. Blaska, Betty, Two More Views on SB 220: Include PTSD, *Emerging Force*, PREVAIL, Madison, Wisconsin, July-August, 1995, p.19.

24. Dahmer, Lionel, *A Father's Story*,

25. Ibid., p.60.

26. Ibid., p.65.

27. Ibid., p.66.

CHAPTER EIGHTEEN

1. Hunter, Richard and Macalpine, Ida, *Three Hundred Years of Psychiatry (1535-1860)*, Oxford University Press, London, 1963, p.420.

2. Ibid., p.422.

3. Hemingway, Ernest, *A Farewell to Arms*, Ch. 34, 1929.

INDEX

313

Keefe, Richard, 90
Kemker, Susan, 3
Kety, Seymour, 63
Klerman, Gerald, 40
Kraepelin, Emil, 22,23
Kringlen, E., 59

L

LeBlanc, Betty, 78
Laborit, Henri, 26
Lehmann, Heinz, 39
Leifer, Ron, 48
Lewontin, R.C., 64,65
Liddle, P.F., 96
Lithium
 discussion of, 46-48
 effects on general population, 47
 John Cade discovered, 27,47
 Kay Jamison, 256,262-265
 mania, 27,33,47
Lobotomy, 23,24,37,276
 Breggin, 106
 effects of neuroleptics, 36,37,39,40
Logarithm of the odds (LOD),
 76,79,81,82,83

M

Magnetic resonance imaging (MRI),
 88
Mania
 Kay Jamison, 255-273
 lithium, 27,48
 neuroleptics, 48
 purposeful view, 256
 search for gene, 79
Manson, Charles, 172,173,184,231
 childhood, 160-165
Masson, Jeffrey, 112-114,116
McCready, Kevin, 245-248
McKenna ,P.S., 89,95,96,98
McKusick, Victor, 85

McManus, 90
Moniz, Egas, 37
Mosher, Loren, 65,252,253
N

National Alliance for the Mentally Ill
 (NAMI), 71,107
National Association for Rights,
 Protection and Advocacy, (NARPA),
 250
National Institute of Mental Health
 (NIMH), 2,51,63,80,93
Neuroleptic, 32,47,104
 brain damage, 91,92
 compared to lithium, 47,48
 discussion of, 33-42
Neurotransmitter
 dopamine, 34,39,50
 explanation of, 27,28,34,41
 serotonin, 42

O

Oedipal phase, 108
Omenn, G.S., 51

P

Pairwise statistical method, 56,57,61
Pam, Alvin, 3,40,66
Parkinson's disease, 25,26,28
Pinel, Philippe, 101,102,107,108,115
Positron emission tomography
 (PET), 94,101
Prien, R.F., 47
Proband statistical method, 56,57
Protective subconscious, 154,168
 actively searching, 177
 always on guard, 153
 anxiety, 155
 choosing guilt over anger, 178
 choosing hand washing, 153
 denying child's pain, 169

315